ANTICIPATING
AND APPRECIATING
YOUR CHRISTIAN LIFE

THE 3-DIMES THEORY FULFILLED

BY WESLEY "WES" WADDLE

Anticipating and Appreciating Your Christian Life

Trilogy Christian Publishers

A Wholly Owned Subsidary of Trinity Broadcasting Network

2442 Michelle Drive

Tustin, CA 92780

For information, address Trilogy Christian Publishing

Rights Department, 2442 Michelle Drive, Tustin, Ca 92780.

Trilogy Christian Publishing/ TBN and colophon are trademarks of Trinity Broadcasting Network.

For information about special discounts for bulk purchases, please contact Trilogy Christian Publishing.

10 9 8 7 6 5 4 3 2 1

Library of Congress Cataloging-in-Publication Data is available.

ISBN 979-8-89333-044-1

ISBN 979-8-89333-045-8 (ebook)

AUTHOR DISCLAIMER

This book is not intended to provide financial, legal, or spiritual advice. If such advice is needed, please seek competent counsel. Remember Proverbs 11:14 (KJV), "Where no counsel is, the people fall: But in the multitude of counsellors there is safety."

DEDICATION

To my beautiful wife, Mary.
You have been an inspiration to me since the day we met.

TABLE OF CONTENTS

Introduction 11

Chart Your Life 15

Desire 17

    The Anticipation of Desire 17

    The Acceptance of Desire.. 23

    The Authoring of Desire 27

    The Activation of Desire 33

    The Appreciation of Desire 37

Dedication... 41

    The Anticipation of Dedication 41

    The Acceptance of Dedication 45

    The Authoring of Dedication.. 49

    The Activation of Dedication 53

    The Appreciation of Dedication................................... 55

Determination 59

    The Anticipation of Determination............................... 59

    The Acceptance of Determination............................... 65

    The Authoring of Determination 69

    The Activation of Determination 73

    The Appreciation of Determination.............................. 79

Decisions (Your Bonus "D").. 83

Inspiration 87
   The Anticipation of Inspiration 87
   The Acceptance of Inspiration..95
   The Authoring of Inspiration 99
   The Activation of Inspiration 103
   The Appreciation of Inspiration 107
Intent 111
   The Anticipation of Intent 111
   The Acceptance of Intent..115
   The Authoring of Intent 119
   The Activation of Intent 125
   The Appreciation of Intent 129
Imagination 133
   The Anticipation of Imagination 133
   The Acceptance of Imagination 137
   The Authoring of Imagination 141
   The Activation of Imagination 145
   The Appreciation of Imagination 149
Integrity (Your Bonus "I") 153
Motivation..159
   The Anticipation of Motivation 159
   The Acceptance of Motivation 163
   The Authoring of Motivation 167
   The Activation of Motivation 171
   The Appreciation of Motivation 175
Momentum 179
   The Anticipation of Momentum 179
   The Acceptance of Momentum 183
   The Authoring of Momentum 187
   The Activation of Momentum 191
   The Appreciation of Momentum 195

Mentorship 199

   The Anticipation of Mentorship 199

   The Acceptance of Mentorship 205

   The Authoring of Mentorship 209

   The Activation of Mentorship 213

   The Appreciation of Mentorship 217

Mindset (Your Bonus "M") 221

Enthusiasm 225

   The Anticipation of Enthusiasm 225

   The Acceptance of Enthusiasm 229

   The Authoring of Enthusiasm 233

   The Activation of Enthusiasm 239

   The Appreciation of Enthusiasm 243

Enlightenment 249

   The Anticipation of Enlightenment 249

   The Acceptance of Enlightenment 253

   The Authoring of Enlightenment 257

   The Activation of Enlightenment 261

   The Appreciation of Enlightenment 267

Empowerment 271

   The Anticipation of Empowerment 271

   The Acceptance of Empowerment 275

   The Authoring of Empowerment 281

   The Activation of Empowerment 285

   The Appreciation of Empowerment 289

Errors (Your Bonus "E") 295

Safety 301

   The Anticipation of Safety 301

   The Acceptance of Safety 305

   The Authoring of Safety 309

   The Activation of Safety 313

   The Appreciation of Safety 319

Separation 325

    The Anticipation of Separation 325

    The Acceptance of Separation 329

    The Authoring of Separation 333

    The Activation of Separation 337

    The Appreciation of Separation 341

Synergy 345

    The Anticipation of Synergy 345

    The Acceptance of Synergy 351

    The Authoring of Synergy 355

    The Activation of Synergy 359

    The Appreciation of Synergy 363

Self (Your Bonus "S") 367

Conclusion 375

Postscript 377

About the Author 379

INTRODUCTION

When I wrote my first book, *Overqualified/Underqualified*, I included "The DIMES Theory" as a brief supplement in the book. That outline only included the words that started with D-I-M-E-S: "desire," "inspiration," "motivation," "enthusiasm," and "success." After hearing success from teaching that concept, I decided to expand the outline to create "The 3-DIMES Theory." That is the basis for this book. As I was creating this book, I had a nice talk with the publisher, which would allow me to add the scriptures to the manuscript, which would help clarify some of the topics and be beneficial to the readers who want to use the Scriptures as their basis for making decisions. All Scripture references quoted in this book are taken from the King James Version of the Bible.

This book is written in such a manner that these concepts will never go out of style. You may want to read this for pleasure to determine how you can use these for yourself, your children, and your grandchildren. If you are involved in any type of book club or church environment, you may want to have the entire group discuss a different concept on a weekly basis for many weeks. This may inspire and motivate your church! This book will discuss synergy and the "multitude of counselors" to encourage wise ideas and assist one another.

As I was writing the index to the book, I realized that the graph of the index (which doesn't show any scripture) can be used as a teaching tool in every school (elementary, junior high, and high school). This graph can also be used in every college and university so that a greater percentage of students will graduate. This graph contains eighty different boxes that you can use to determine what it might be that is holding you back from success. If you are not at the point of success in your life that you want, you can decide which of those eighty boxes you need to overcome in order to reach your goal.

If you are involved in a Christian school, this book could be a semester project for every student. Use the entire book with the Scriptures, as it will help your students. Perhaps you are a teacher who is a believer; you can teach the ideas from this book and be beneficial to your students. If others ask you about the book, then you can use the Scriptures and tell them about your faith.

If you are a coach, you will want to use this graph and these concepts to help your team achieve a winning season. If you are not having a winning season, look over the graph and find out what element your team is missing. It may be the inspiration. If that is the missing element, find something that you anticipate will put your team in the right spirit so that when they hit the playing field or the basketball court, they will be unstoppable. You can use that same idea with any part of this outline.

At the end of each lesson, you will see the words, "How will this lesson help me?" There are topics underneath this question, which include "personal," "marriage and family," "church," and "community." Some readers will want to concentrate on what will help them personally. Some readers will want to concentrate on marriage and family. Some readers will be more concerned with their church activities or their community and how these concepts can help build a better business or a better future. You can decide what works best for you. In the near future, you may want to hold a one-day seminar for your church, business, or school. Some readers may want to hold a "revival" meeting.

This book should help every reader to complete any type of project. For instance, many students will anticipate a desire to go to college or technical school. They later accept the fact that they want to go to college. They may even author or write down ideas that will help them go to college so they can activate their plan and start taking college classes. The first "D" stands for desire. The third "D" stands for "determination," which means "de-termination" or "not terminating," which means never stopping. So they anticipate determination. However, for various reasons, they may not activate that determination. If so, there is the possibility of quitting before they have success.

This book was written with extra space for you to write ideas and notes to be used throughout various stages of your life. This book may help you, your friends, your relatives, and your work colleagues to create the lives of their dreams.

You have been given the power to change lives. This book should help!

CHART YOUR LIFE

REACHING YOUR DESIRED OUTCOME
WHICH ELEMENT IS MISSING?

	Anticipation	Acceptance	Authoring	Activation	Appreciation
Desire					
Dedication					
Determination					
Decisions (Bonus)					
Inspiration					
Intent					
Imagination					
Integrity (Bonus)					
Motivation					
Momentum					
Mentorship					
Mindset (Bonus)					

Enthusiasm					
Enlightenment					
Empowerment					
Errors (Bonus)					
Safety					
Separation					
Synergy					
Self (Bonus)					
*Self-Image					
*Self-Esteem					
*Self-Worth					
*Self-Forgiveness					
*Self-Awareness					
*Self-Acceptance					

DESIRE
THE ANTICIPATION OF DESIRE

Have you ever gone to your refrigerator and opened it in order to find out what looked good to eat? Have you ever been to a restaurant (even a fast-food restaurant), looked at a menu, and tried to decide what looked good? Then, after you decided, did you change your mind? This could have happened because you were on a particular diet, or possibly it was a special occasion, and you decided to treat yourself to something special.

Are you hungry yet? As you begin reading this book, think about all of the restaurants you have been to over your lifetime. What sounds good to you? If you had extra money, where would you go to eat later today? Do you like a good steak dinner? Are you in the mood for Italian food or Spanish food? Think about the dessert at each restaurant.

From where did this desire originate? If you studied Spanish as I did in high school, you know that the prefix "de" means "from" or "of." The word "sire" means "father." Therefore, the word "desire" literally means "of the father" or "from the father." What does this mean for you? Who is your father? Some of your desires will come from your biological father inherited through your genetic makeup. My father loved to eat ice cream every night at 8:00 p.m. I used to love visiting my father in the evenings. Now, I often have a desire for ice cream around 8:00 p.m. It brings back memories of my father.

Maybe your desires are coming from a "father figure" (stepfather, adopted father, elderly friend, etc.) whom you admire. Maybe your father figure plays a musical instrument. You may love to sit, listen, and learn to play like he does. Maybe your father figure flies airplanes, and you desire to learn about flying with him. Maybe you watched your father or mother cook great meals. Now, you may be desiring to go to the kitchen and create something appetizing.

Take a minute or two and dream about "the anticipation of desire." We all have desires. The question for this lesson is, *"What do you think you will want to desire in the future?"*

You get the idea. You see the advantage of "the anticipation of desire." Before you actually have a desire, you have "the desire for desire." Your mind and your body want to have a desire for something. Mankind inherently desires to want. That is one of the greatest blessings that God has given us. We all want to be happy. What is it that you desire that will fulfill that happiness? When asked, "How much money does it take to make a man happy?" the famous John D. Rockefeller answered, "Just one more dollar." If you had "one more dollar," then what would you want next? What do you anticipate your next desire might be?

Your desires (meaning "of the father") will be caused by the one whom you love and admire. Think about this verse for a minute…

Psalm 37:4, *"Delight thyself also in the* LORD: *and he shall give thee the desires of thine heart."*

You will notice that this verse, Psalm 37:4, does not mention that your desires will be fulfilled. However, Matthew 5:6 mentions fulfillment.

Matthew 5:6, *"Blessed are they which do hunger and thirst after righteousness: for they shall be filled."*

As we go through this book together, we will discuss how you can attain your desires. Maybe your desire is unique to you, and you do not want to discuss it with any person that you currently know because they may be critical of your aspirations. Maybe your desire is to be involved with a great church or in a great ministry where you can learn about what the Lord wants for your life. Maybe your desire is a happy marriage, but you are not sure all that is required to make that happen. Perhaps your church wants to get more involved in your community so that each member can have a fulfilled life. Each of these topics will be discussed throughout this book.

In each lesson of this book, you will have the opportunity to write down your ideas and take notes so that you can refer back to them on a regular basis.

This will keep you headed toward your idea of success. Whether your idea is regarding your health, your career and wealth, or your spiritual condition, you will be guided to make beneficial decisions so that you can safely move toward your destination.

Having the "aspiration of desire" will require you to dream about what you think you will want to desire in the future. You will want to write down things that you want right now. This is important because it will help you decide what you want after you receive the fulfillment of that desire. For instance, if your current desire is to have $10,000 in the bank, what will be your next desire? Would you want a $10,000 vacation? Would that be your next desire? Would your next desire be $20,000 in the bank, then $30,000 in the bank? Then, would your next desire be a new car or $40,000 in the bank?

Do you see how important it is to anticipate what you will desire in the future? Understanding that question and understanding your answer will determine your future. That is a basic thought that will help to guide you as you read through this book.

You may want to ask yourself what you might want for your next birthday. What will you want for Christmas? Do you want presents for yourself or is your goal to give more presents away than what you receive? If you get everything that you want, then what will you want next?

Proverbs 27:20, *"The eyes of man are never satisfied."*

I enjoy having a goal. What goal do you have? You may have a goal of becoming a college graduate. Ask yourself, "Is that a goal or a desire?" If it is only a goal, then what are you planning to do with your college degree? If it is a desire, you probably have a plan about how that degree will help you with your next goal or desire.

As you continue to read this book, you will be asked to write down your dreams, goals, and desires. What do you want to accomplish? After you accomplish that objective, what's next? Who would you like to meet? Why? Where would you like to travel? What would you like to do while you are there? Some of us will have twenty to twenty-five ideas to think about. Others may have close to seventy-five items on their "bucket list" (what we want to do while we are alive). Work on that project in some manner every day. It will change your life. Why will it change your life? You have now been able to anticipate your desires.

One of the greatest lessons I have learned throughout my life is this truth…

Proverbs 13:20, *"He that walketh with wise men shall be wise: but a companion of fools shall be destroyed."*

It is often said that you will be the average of your five to ten closest friends! Your goals will be similar. Your health will be similar. Your wealth will be similar. Even your desire to speak about ideas from the Bible will be similar. Your spirituality is affected by your friends. Your desires are influenced (not necessarily created) by your friends.

Before you take the next step in life, look around. Think about the word "circumspect." The prefix "circum" means around. We use the word "circumnavigate" to travel around something. The term "spect" means to "inspect" or see clearly. As you make your plans, *"see then that ye walk circumspectly, not as fools, but as wise"* (Ephesians 5:15).

How will this lesson help me?

Personal—This lesson will help you learn about yourself so that you can understand what you want now and what you will want in the future. This is a good lesson as you plan to go to college, plan for your career, and plan your life. You will want to take some time (maybe a few hours or a few days) to ponder how you will live your life.

Marriage and family—This will be an important lesson as you plan your marriage. Before you get married, think about what you would do if you had $10,000 in your bank account. Ask your fiancé or who you are dating what they would do if they had $10,000 in the bank. Do your goals align with one another? Maybe you have children and you want to go on vacation, but you also want to save for the children's college fund. Now is the time to anticipate what you will want in the future so that disagreements do not arise in the future.

Church—This is important in any church. Often the church is prepared for the next three to four months as a planning budget and their activities for the coming year. Maybe you are anticipating raising your attendance or changing the direction of the church. What is your plan after that time? Whether you are a Sunday school teacher or involved with church leadership, make plans of what you will do after you accomplish and fulfill your next desire.

Community—As community leaders, we always need to plan ahead. Look at your six-month goal. Look at your annual budget. Look at your five-year outlook. Think about where your community is located and the advantages of being there, then think about how you can benefit your community for the next generation. If your community could get another church, another park, or another parade, what would be its next goal or desire?

THE ACCEPTANCE OF DESIRE

As I was writing about "the anticipation of desire," my wife contacted me and asked me what I wanted for dinner. In essence, she was asking me what I would desire in the near future. I made a decision. Now, it is time to accept what I asked for.

John 16:24, *"Hitherto have ye asked nothing in my name: ask, and ye shall receive, that your joy may be full."*

"Ask, and you shall receive." But what if I change my mind and decide that I really want something else?

James 4:2, *"Ye lust, and have not: ye kill, and desire to have, and cannot obtain: ye fight and war, yet ye have not, because ye ask not."*

"You have not because you ask not." Now that you have been able (in some manner) to determine what God wants for you, you must be comfortable with your decision. One great rule in life is "Never second-guess God!" Leaders make decisions.

You can have, do, or be (pretty much) whatever you want in life. A great concept that you will want to remember is this:

You can do anything that you want to do, but you cannot do everything!

There simply isn't enough time in this life to do everything because every time you accomplish a goal, there will be something else that you want to accomplish. Don't be dismayed…keep accomplishing your goals.

Every time you have "the acceptance of your desire" and you are comfortable with your decision, you will find yourself working on your project often. (I recommend working on your project on a regular basis.) For example:

If you are trying to build a Sunday school class and a new ministry in your church, you will want to make a call or visit. Schedule this. Is it important? Is it urgent?

If you want to learn to buy real estate, you will want to read about real estate daily in your spare time. This is especially valuable just before you go to bed at night. This will have your mind thinking about the acceptance of your desire as you fall asleep. "Ask, and ye shall receive."

If you want to learn to fly airplanes, I highly recommend reading the Federal Aviation Regulations. It is free on the Internet, and you will learn a great deal about flying. This will save you a great deal without the larger expense of the aircraft.

Colossians 3:2, *"Set your affection on things above, not on things on the earth."*

If you are in high school and your goal is to be on the winning basketball team, you will want to work on your free throws daily. In your spare time, think and dream of making perfect half-court shots. This should help you.

Proverbs 23:7, *"For as he thinketh in his heart, so is he."*

Accept your desires. Decide what you want. This is like choosing the subject that you want to be your major in college. Accept the fact that your college has decided what classes you will need in order to be proficient in your course of study, your curriculum, and your syllabi. Once you accept your desire, the world aligns to help you achieve your desires.

When you make the decision to go to a particular church, accept your choice. A church is not only a place where you go every Sunday; it is more like a family with which you belong. When you make your decision to believe the teachings that you have learned in your church, accept your desires.

Second Timothy 1:7, *"For God hath not given us the spirit of fear; but of power, and of love, and of a sound mind."*

Once you accept your desire and you are comfortable with your decisions, you are on your way to achieving what you desire.

How will this lesson help me?

Personal—As you finished the last exercise of anticipating your desires, you thought about many different avenues of your life. You decided what was important. Did you pray about each aspect? Did you decide who you will take with you on your journey to a successful life? If you are sure that is the direction you are supposed to move, then make it happen! Together, you and God can move mountains.

James 1:8, *"A double minded man is unstable in all his ways."*

Matthew 17:20, *"And Jesus said unto them, Because of your unbelief: for verily I say unto you, If ye have faith as a grain of mustard seed, ye shall say unto this mountain, Remove hence to yonder place; and it shall remove; and nothing shall be impossible unto you."*

Marriage and family—This lesson may help many marriages. The previous lesson on anticipating your desire will help you to make the decision about whom to marry and what decisions to make after your marriage. This lesson is asking you to confirm and agree with your past decision. This lesson may keep your marriage together in a very loving manner for many years to come.

Numbers 30:2, *"If a man vow a vow unto the LORD, or swear an oath to bind his soul with a bond; he shall not break his word, he shall do according to all that proceedeth out of his mouth."*

Colossians 3:19, *"Husbands, love your wives, and be not bitter against them."*

Church—Your church has many different people who have great minds and different ideas. The leadership and governing board of your church may have different ideas that will be beneficial to your church and your community. Once a decision is made, be sure that it is agreed upon as necessary for your church to move forward. Keep harmony among the people of your church so that you can move forward with sweet fellowship. While you're going through this transition for this project, be sure to keep your fundamental duties in place no matter what season or time that this change occurs.

Second Timothy 4:2, *"Preach the word; be instant in season, out of season; reprove, rebuke, exhort with all long suffering and doctrine."*

Community—If you are involved with any community activity personally or as a church, you will want to make sure that every document is in order. This is important when we work with government officials or other nonprofit organizations so that each entity knows and understands what is going to be required for the completion of the project. If your church is involved in a parade, documentation will be required. As you accept the desires within your community, be sure to follow all the rules and regulations as prescribed. This will keep your reputation as a good report (and a good rapport) in the community.

Proverbs 22:29, *"Seest thou a man diligent in his business? he shall stand before kings; he shall not stand before mean men."*

THE AUTHORING OF DESIRE

You will achieve a certain level of success as an individual and a leader. By picking up this book, you have proven to yourself that you have a desire for success. By being able to read the words of this book, you have proven to yourself that you have the ability to reason and analyze what you desire. You are already successful. Keep the momentum moving forward. Make this a fun trip! This is *your* successful life. Visualize it well!

As you begin to author (scrip) your desire, you will need to consider the different levels of desire. Every great teacher discussing goals and desires will remind you that you need to write down what you want. I realize that you may think that some small desires may not need to be written. Well, maybe they do. If the question is "What do you want for dinner?" you may find it in your kitchen. What if it is not there? Admit it… How many of us will immediately start a grocery list? Yes. We write it down. Then, we go to the grocery store and buy whatever we really desire. We go to the store with a list of five items and come home with a cart full. You author your desire with a list, then activate your list with a cart. Am I right?

Let's discuss the levels of desire. Similar to the grocery example above, let's discuss your life. In every aspect of life, you will have levels of desire. Many times, these desires will be determined by your time, money, and health. That may be your initial desire: to gain health by exercising and eating correctly. You will gain money through smart investing, which will allow you time to exercise and enjoy life.

Since there are levels of desire, you will need to rate your own desires. I have studied several goal-setting and assessment ideas. There are short-term goals, mid-range goals, long-term goals, and life-long goals. (Use the Eisenhower cross or the list that you created.) When you complete this chapter on desires, I highly recommend that you write your goals and desires. In my book *Overqualified/Underqualified*, I call this a "Life-Planning Session." This is not a one-time activity. Your desires may change every year. Many families move to different locations; therefore, their needs and desires change. Many college students change majors. That's okay!

Challenge yourself! Ask yourself these questions…

"Who am I?" You know your name, but what greatness lies within you?

"Where am I?" You know your location, but where are you in your studies, your job, your goals, and your desires?

"Where am I going?" What are your aspirations? What can you visualize for yourself? Where can you see yourself going?

"Why am I going there?" This may be the biggest question of all. A professor of mine once said, "If your 'why' is strong enough, nothing can stop you!"

Set aside one hour this week and write down your answers to these questions:

Where do I want to go? What do I want to be? Who do I want to meet? What do I want to create?

Next, prioritize these (number them) as to their level of importance to you.

Next, list them in either your "short-term goal," "mid-range goal," "long-term goal," or "lifetime goal."

Now, it is time to "author" your desire. What does an author do? Let's think back to when you were in elementary school and your teacher asked you to write a book report or other type of report to test your language ability. You were required to think about how you would present this information to others. We all remember those days. If you have not made your list yet, now is the time to make that list. Some of you will use the Eisenhower cross.

EISENHOWER MATRIX

IMPORTANT- URGENT	IMPORTANT – LESS URGENT
DO THESE FIRST	**PLAN AND SCHEDULE THESE**
PRIORITIZE THESE WITH DEADLINES	

LESS IMPORTANT - URGENT	LESS IMPORTANT – LESS URGENT
DELEGATE THESE (IF POSSIBLE)	**DELETE THESE (IF POSSIBLE)**

ASK YOURSELF…

- Did your marriage and family move from very important to less important?
- Did your prayer life move from very important to less important?
- When will your prayer life move from not urgent to very urgent?
- When does studying for final exams move from not urgent to very urgent?

YOU HAVE THE POWER TO CHOOSE EVERY DAY!

Some readers will make a list. Each reader should take the time to decide what is most important to you, such as where you will spend your lifetime here on earth. However, the most important decision we will make will be the choice of where we spend eternity. Please keep eternity in mind in all of your decisions. You will want to be sure that when your life on earth ends and you stand before your Heavenly Father, He will be able to look at you and say, "Well done!" As you author your life, remember these words.

First Corinthians 14:33, *"For God is not the author of confusion, but of peace, as in all churches of the saints."*

You are both the author and the audience. You are presenting to yourself the idea of this desire. You have to write the script, but you will soon be the "platform speaker" (presenter) to your audience. You have to sell your audience (the many parts of you) on the idea that this desire is what they want to buy.

Okay… Admit it! We have all been there at one time or another. You know. At that time when you are alone in your room and you pace the floor presenting this idea or desire to the audience. The only audience is you. Sometimes, however, you will do this in a crowded room. You may be talking with others, but you will still be building your story (authoring) your ideas.

This is where your success will be influenced. You will author such a compelling manuscript that you will be the first to buy into the concept. If your desires are for greatness and "success," you will visualize it with such passion that the reader (the inner you) will want to follow your lead and adhere to your leadership. You are in command of your thoughts.

Micah 6:8, *"He hath shewed thee, O man, what is good; and what doth the LORD require of thee, but to do justly, and to love mercy, and to walk humbly with thy God?"*

How will this lesson help me?

Personal—By authoring your desires and writing them down, you have the opportunity to review your progress on a regular basis. Sometimes, it is good to write everything down, put it away for one week, pray about it, and then have a joint meeting with your wise advisors who know you well. This will bring clarity and build trust, as the same advisors may be your mentors in the future.

Proverbs 13:20, *"He that walketh with wise men shall be wise: but a companion of fools shall be destroyed."*

Marriage and family—As you write down the desires that you and your family want to see happen in the near future, this will also help you to plan your budget and prepare for vacation and your work schedule. This will also help you plan for college or that new car. Think about some short-term goals and some long-term goals. Plan for children if that is your goal. Take some time and consider where you will be living and if you will be buying a house. You may want to spend some time praying about this with your family. God can work miracles. Plan accordingly!

Church—By authoring your desires of your church, you will be able to present those plans to the congregation and members of your church. You will also be able to use this manuscript to take to people in your community. Others who are in the community and see a vision of what your church is doing will probably want to join and become members of your church because you have an active membership.

Community—Community leaders such as the mayor or city council may want to work with you if you decide to have a homeless ministry or a rescue mission that will benefit the community as a whole. Jesus Christ did not only teach in the synagogues. He often spoke in the community. He went to where the people needed Him and where the Holy Spirit led Him. We should do likewise.

Matthew 19:2, *"And great multitudes followed him; and he healed them there."*

THE ACTIVATION OF DESIRE

By activating your desire, you are creating "mental momentum." You are mentally making it happen. The words "anticipation" and "acceptance" are more of a mental activity. The word "activation" is more of an action verb. In order to accomplish your desire, you will need to take some type of mental (not necessarily physical) action. Your spirit must move toward your desires. (We will discuss inspiration later in this book.) This will be an exciting time of your life. This is *your* desire. This is what you have decided that you truly want to activate and accomplish. Enjoy it!

Nothing happens until something moves. This sounds like a simple statement, and yet it is so profound that we almost miss it while reading our Bible. God taught a very important lesson in Genesis 1:2.

Genesis 1:2, *"And the earth was without form, and void; and darkness was upon the face of the deep. And the Spirit of God moved upon the face of the waters."*

In the same manner, as your desires are "without form," so was the world. Yet, the Spirit of God (the Holy Spirit) moved. Nothing can move until thought occurs. Because you are creating your thoughts and your desires, your spirit will begin to move toward your dreams and desires. If God is your Heavenly Father and He has given you your desires, then you can follow His example. He will walk you through the process until His desires are fulfilled through you.

Ephesians 2:10, *"For we are his workmanship, created in Christ Jesus unto good works, which God hath before ordained that we should walk in them."*

As you were preparing for this exercise and you authored your desires, you were both the author and the audience. You presented to yourself the idea of this desire. You wrote the script, and you will soon be the "platform speaker" (presenter) to your audience. You have to sell your audience (the many parts of you) on the idea that this desire is what they want to buy. Once you do this, you can activate that desire.

This is where your success will be influenced. You have authored such a compelling manuscript that you will be the first to buy into the concept. If your desires are for greatness and "success," you will visualize it with such passion that the reader (the "inner" you) will want to follow your lead and adhere to your leadership. If you and God are likeminded, then you can let God take command.

Let's think of this idea in a more personable manner. The reason I use the word "personable" is that it's more descriptive of this situation. We are discussing this as you would discuss a friendly conversation with your dad. God is your Father. You are in God's family. Because you are so close to your Dad, you and your Dad have the same desires. Your Dad can speak and open every door so that your desires will be fulfilled. If there is an issue along the way, call your Dad and let your Dad know what the problem is. He will make a "spirit call" (instead of a phone call) and contact the right people so that the doors will be open on His desires (which are now your desires), and they will be fulfilled in a timely manner!

How will this lesson help me?

Personal—When you activate your desires because they are also God's desires, nothing can hold you back. Your Father is stronger than anybody else's Father. Your Father can help you do whatever He wants. That is why He has allowed you to talk with Him personally anytime you want. If there's a problem, simply pick up the "spirit phone" through prayer, and He will tell you how to solve the problem. We have a great God! Always remember, as Jesus said:

Luke 22:42, *"Saying, Father, if thou be willing, remove this cup from me: nevertheless not my will, but thine, be done."*

Marriage and family—You have a family that needs to know your Heavenly Father. Your family can be your best prayer partners. If you are married, be sure your spouse knows your Heavenly Father. If they do not listen to you, ask your Heavenly Father to introduce you to someone who may be able to help you to introduce them to Him.

John 16:24, *"Hitherto have ye asked nothing in my name: ask, and ye shall receive, that your joy may be full."*

If you share the same Heavenly Father, then if there is ever an issue, you two can talk to your Father and ask for His wisdom and restore sweet fellowship with one another. Keep your marriage sweet!

Church—Through prayer, your church will be able to activate the desires so that the Holy Spirit of God can help unify the church members. By activating the desires and using one spirit, each member will be edified and grow personally and as a church.

First Corinthians 6:17, *"But he that is joined unto the Lord is one spirit."*

Ephesians 2:18, *"For through him we both have access by one Spirit unto the Father."*

Community—As the members of your church begin to activate God's desires by using each member in your church, the community will recognize that something is happening. Your community will not understand it immediately. They will simply know that something is different. They will look at the members of your church as being peculiar, but they will see great things happening.

Titus 2:14, *"Who gave himself for us, that he might redeem us from all iniquity, and purify unto himself a peculiar people, zealous of good works."*

THE APPRECIATION OF DESIRE

Since you started reading this book, many ideas have gone through your mind. You probably prayed about many different scenarios in life. You have thought about your past, future, and present situation. You have written down ideas about where you want to go, who you want to meet, things you want to do, and how the Lord will be with you throughout your journey.

Hebrews 13:5, *"Let your conversation be without covetousness; and be content with such things as ye have: for he hath said, I will never leave thee, nor forsake thee."*

You are an amazing person! Your God is an amazing God! Your church and your Christian brothers and sisters will travel with you through your journey. As you have thought about your desires, you have reflected on different people. You have thought about your heroes. You have thought about those whom you admire. You have thought about biblical heroes. Now, it is time to appreciate what you desire.

Psalm 100:4, *"Enter into his gates with thanksgiving, and into his courts with praise: be thankful unto him, and bless his name."*

Take some time right now to take a deep breath or take a walk. Perhaps grab your favorite beverage, sit quietly, and appreciate what you really desire. Now is the time to appreciate who you are, who your Heavenly Father is, and the love that Jesus Christ has given you. Your greatest desire, of course, is to go to heaven when you pass away. One of the goals of this book is to have every reader of this book meet me in heaven so that we can discuss how this book has helped you through your earthly life and we can celebrate on golden streets in just a few years.

When you think about your heavenly desires, remember this…

John 3:15–17:

That whosoever believeth in him should not perish, but have eternal life. For God so loved the world, that he gave his only begotten Son, that whosoever believeth in him should not perish, but have everlasting life. For God sent not his Son into the world to condemn the world; but that the world through him might be saved.

When you think about your earthly desires, remember this…

Psalm 37:3–5, *"Trust in the LORD, and do good; so shalt thou dwell in the land, and verily thou shalt be fed. Delight thyself also in the LORD: and he shall give thee the desires of thine heart. Commit thy way unto the LORD; trust also in him; and he shall bring it to pass."*

Now, sit back, enjoy, and appreciate your desires!

How will this lesson help me?

Personal—One of the most important life lessons is to enjoy your life and appreciate what you desire. By establishing what you desire, you also establish your present and future relationship with your Heavenly Father. This should make you so happy that you want to rejoice, smile, and sing!

Philippians 4:4–5, *"Rejoice in the Lord always: and again I say, Rejoice. Let your moderation be known unto all men. The Lord is at hand."*

First Thessalonians 5:18, *"In every thing give thanks: for this is the will of God in Christ Jesus concerning you."*

Marriage and family—If you are preparing to get married, then you have some idea of the kind of person you would like to spend your life with. Be thankful that God is leading you in the right direction. God may be leading you to a particular college or career where that person will meet you. Don't force the issue. Remember the words of Jesus Christ, "Not my will, but thine, be done" (Luke 22:42)!

Perhaps you and your family will eat together. If so, you will often discuss your desires. Some desires are personal to you. Be sure to discuss those matters with your Heavenly Father before you sleep. Pray for your family and be thankful for them.

Colossians 1:3, *"We give thanks to God and the Father of our Lord Jesus Christ, praying always for you."*

Church—Your church will have certain desires as a group about what they would like to accomplish in the near future. Also, each member of your church has individual desires. It does not matter your age or which Sunday school class or activity you attend at church; help the other members to appreciate what they desire because those desires may have come from the Lord and will help that person to become everything that the Lord wants him or her to be.

Psalm 30:4, *"Sing unto the LORD, O ye saints of his, and give thanks at the remembrance of his holiness."*

Community—Every community has certain desires. Members of your church are part of the community. If there is ever a crisis in your community, your community will appreciate the fact that your church is willing and able to pray for them. Your community will also appreciate your desire to promote a safe and honorable society. Maybe you want to build a municipal park or start a parade in your community. Appreciate your desire, as it will give you the opportunity to be of service to your God in your community. Be sure to pray for your community.

First Thessalonians 1:2, *"We give thanks to God always for you all, making mention of you in our prayers."*

THIS PAGE HAS BEEN LEFT BLANK SO THAT YOU CAN MAKE
NOTES ABOUT DESIRE

DEDICATION
THE ANTICIPATION OF DEDICATION

The first lesson of this book was about your desires. If the Lord has given those desires to you, your life will change forever. Some of the decisions that you have made will seemingly be short-lived, yet the repercussions of your action and the consequences will be with you forever.

Maybe you may have just signed up for that big goal. You did not know the Lord was going to lay that burden or that exciting opportunity as a desire in front of you today. But now you are ready to begin. Now is the time that you will want to anticipate the amount of dedication that will be needed in order for you (with the Lord's help) to complete that project. Do not try to do it alone. Your Heavenly Father has put this on your agenda so that He can be with you as you move forward.

Ephesians 5:15, *"See then that ye walk circumspectly, not as fools, but as wise."*

Did you sign up to run a race? A number of years ago, I signed up to complete a triathlon. I did not have a goal to "compete" in a triathlon. My goal was only to "complete" the race and not be the last person to cross the finish line. As I signed my name as a participant, I was anticipating the dedication that would be needed to complete the swim, then complete the long bike ride, and then run the 5K to the finish line. Oh! I didn't mention I did not know how to swim! That's right! I was forty-seven years old, and I had never learned to "dog paddle" more than a few feet. So I went to swim lessons and learned enough that I ended up swimming the entire course using a "backstroke" so I could control my breathing. When I signed up for the race, I immediately had to anticipate the dedication that would be needed to survive this event. I was dedicated because failure was not an option. One of the first thoughts that came to my mind was, *Lord, help me!*

My brother served over twenty years in the United States Marine Corps. As he signed up for the Corps, he was anticipating the dedication that would be needed for such a career. I remembered his words, "Marine Corp all the way." I honor those men and women who were able-bodied enough to serve their country in military forces. You must anticipate the dedication needed for success. In a similar manner, we are soldiers of Jesus Christ.

Second Timothy 2:1–3:

Thou therefore, my son, be strong in the grace that is in Christ Jesus. And the things that thou hast heard of me among many witnesses, the same commit thou to faithful men, who shall be able to teach others also. Thou therefore endure hardness, as a good soldier of Jesus Christ.

As you start your journey to success while reading each section of this book, you will begin to anticipate the different levels of dedication that will be needed. In my true story of the triathlon, I knew it would take extra dedication for the swim portion of the event. My mind was on the "fun run" at the end of the race. I have completed two half-marathons. Running was easy for me. The bike ride was not too difficult; however, I did not anticipate that my legs would be so weak after the bike that I could barely walk. However, I had anticipated the dedication that would be needed to complete the run.

Now that you are on your journey to success, you may want to consider the different aspects of the anticipation of your dedication. Your success will probably not be just the hundred-yard dash. Your end goal may be a one-mile run. It takes dedication to complete that goal. Maybe your goal is like a 5K (3.1 miles). That can be hard work! For most of us, our complete journey to success is more like a triathlon. There are many parts. After you finish the first part (like the swim of a triathlon), you will be exhausted. Anticipate it! You may want to quit. But you are dedicated, so you dry yourself off and jump onto your bike. Now, you're moving and the wind is cooling you off, but you are getting tired and thirsty. Finally, you complete the bike race. You will be more tired, but your competitors will be passing you. You will muster the energy to start the running portion of your event. The great thing for you is that you anticipated this dedication when you signed up for this race. Then, the race becomes a "fun run." You are now dedicated to seeing that finish line where you will have a boost of energy and pass your competition.

Galatians 6:9, *"And let us not be weary in well doing: for in due season we shall reap, if we faint not."*

What has the Lord put on your agenda in the coming days? Perhaps you are in high school, and you want to be more active in the youth department at church, but you have a history test coming up that you need to study for. On top of that, you have an algebra test on the principles of logarithms next week. You walk into your English class, and the teacher assigns a term paper. Can you now anticipate the determination that will be required of you in order to do what the Lord wants you to do in the youth department at church and still do well in school? If so, anticipate the dedication that will be required. The Lord is with you. Believe that you and the Lord can do it together.

Second Timothy 1:7, *"For God hath not given us the spirit of fear; but of power, and of love, and of a sound mind."*

If you anticipate the dedication, then the finish line of success will be closer than you had planned.

How will this lesson help me?

Personal—If you are in high school and you want to do well in school and do well on a winning sports team, you must dedicate time and be able to focus on whatever project needs your attention. If you take the time now to anticipate that dedication, you should do well!

Throughout your career, you will cross the path of many adult learners. Some want to go to college. Some want to advance their career. Others want to learn to fly airplanes. Often, these individuals will plan for the financial part of their success but not consider the dedication needed to complete the tasks.

Ecclesiastes 9:10, *"Whatsoever thy hand findeth to do, do it with thy might; for there is no work, nor device, nor knowledge, nor wisdom, in the grave, whither thou goest."*

Marriage and family—Taking the time to anticipate the amount of dedication it will take in order to complete any task will help you as you go through difficult times. Maybe you are planning for a marriage or family, your spouse will want your time, your children will want your time, your church will want your time, *and* you still have personal goals and dreams. Your family may have you running in different directions. Be patient.

Hebrews 12:1, *"Wherefore seeing we also are compassed about with so great a cloud of witnesses, let us lay aside every weight, and the sin which doth so easily beset us, and let us run with patience the race that is set before us."*

Ephesians 5:25, *"Husbands, love your wives, even as Christ also loved the church, and gave himself for it."*

Church—Is your church planning a building project? As you read this, some churches plan to build a new building. This takes a great deal of dedication. Some churches will be planning on building their attendance. This takes the same amount of dedication with a different focus. If some of your members are not anticipating the amount of dedication that will be required, your attendance may drop for a while until the project is completed. If everyone has the same vision, success is imminent.

Proverbs 29:18, *"Where there is no vision, the people perish: but he that keepeth the law, happy is he."*

Community—As you just read Proverbs 29:18 (above), it mentions a very important concept between churches and their communities. *"He that keepeth the law, happy is he."* As you become dedicated to your project, be sure to invite and, as needed, involve community leaders. It is common for churches to believe that they are not under the authority of the local or federal government.

Hebrews 13:17, *"Obey them that have the rule over you, and submit yourselves: for they watch for your souls, as they that must give account, that they may do it with joy, and not with grief: for that is unprofitable for you."*

Matthew 10:16, *"Behold, I send you forth as sheep in the midst of wolves: be ye therefore wise as serpents, and harmless as doves."*

Mark 12:17, *"And Jesus answering said unto them, Render to Caesar the things that are Caesar's, and to God the things that are God's. And they marvelled at him."*

Anticipating and Appreciating Your Christian Life

THE ACCEPTANCE OF DEDICATION

An amazing paradigm shift takes place when you reach this stage of your success. The speed of your success will be accelerated by your mental acceptance of your dedication. Let's review our discussion on the anticipation of dedication.

We discussed all of your high school assignments, but what about joining the high school sports team? Your coach will encourage you as you have accepted the position on the team. You have accepted the challenge to be dedicated to the team's success. Your time will be dedicated to the team. Your mental capacity will be dedicated to the team. Your money (or your parents' money) will probably be dedicated to the team's success through fundraisers and other activities. You have accepted the challenge, and you are focused on success. Are you able to accept the dedication?

If you are thinking about challenging yourself to complete a triathlon, you have anticipated the dedication needed. Now, you must accept the dedication that it takes for all three events: the swim, the bicycle ride, and the run. That is a triple dedication. It takes work. It is not easy! It is a challenge. Each portion takes dedication. You have accepted that challenge. The mental shift is actually a paradigm shift as it changes how you view your world. You have accepted the dedication to be a better swimmer. You have accepted the challenge to be faster on the bicycle. You have accepted the dedication to be a faster and stronger runner. You sleep with the idea of that dedication. You eat and drink with that reality.

This happens in the basic training in the military. You enter into the military with the acceptance that your dedication will protect your homeland. You accept that dedication in every activity. Your military leadership will be able to encourage you as you accept the dedication that it will take to succeed in your mission, great or small. There are systems in place for your benefit.

Perhaps you are a single adult with young children. You want to get married. Can you accept the added dedication that will be required for a new spouse, your children, your career, and your service to the Lord? As we read in Ephesians 5:15, *"See then that ye walk circumspectly, not as fools, but as wise"*; the word "circumspectly" means to look around and look from different angles.

This same acceptance of dedication is important in business. Many small business owners look at their spreadsheets and the number of their sales to indicate the local economy. More successful entrepreneurs will "crunch the numbers" during the late nights and early mornings to figure out how to make their businesses and the lives of their employees flourish in any economic condition.

Where are you on your acceptance of dedication level? Whether you are a salesperson, a personnel officer, or a "C-level" executive, accept the dedication that will be required to help your business to be successful. Train your team members in your department and throughout your company to work together. The success of your team and your business will be determined by the success and dedication of each individual.

One final thought here—make this "acceptance of dedication" an honor and something you can be proud of. Whether building your church or expanding your family, the acceptance of dedication will be very similar. If you are building a high school sports team, a military mission, a business event, or your personal triathlon, this will change from a burden to a revered challenge simply by shifting your mindset. Your success is closer than you think!

How will this lesson help me?

Personal—On a personal basis, accepting the amount of dedication will help your mind to be prepared for any obstacle that is placed in your path to success. As you accept the amount of dedication needed for success, be sure to allow the Lord to lead you.

Psalm 119:105, *"Thy word is a lamp unto my feet, and a light unto my path."*

Marriage and family—Getting married may be easy. Being part of a great family takes dedication. A family takes time, energy, and money. As you grow older, whether you are in high school or have a great career, family unity will become more precious to you. Being able to speak with your parents, your children, and your siblings will take dedication that you can start at any age. Help your family to be successful. Teach your children. Help your siblings. Husbands, love your wives. Dedicate yourself to having a great family environment.

Philippians 2:2, *"Fulfil ye my joy, that ye be likeminded, having the same love, being of one accord, of one mind."*

Church—Once your church has accepted the amount of dedication that will be required to complete your large project, you will see teamwork develop. You will also see camaraderie and fellowship as your members work together and eat together.

Second Corinthians 4:1, *"Therefore seeing we have this ministry, as we have received mercy, we faint not."*

Community—When you accept the dedication that will be required for any project, large or small, you will be noticed by the community. People talk! You will be surprised at how many people will want you to succeed. People love success! Show them how the Lord can use you and your members as good neighbors.

Matthew 22:36–39:

Master, which is the great commandment in the law? Jesus said unto him, Thou shalt love the Lord thy God with all thy heart, and with all thy soul, and with all thy mind. This is the first and great commandment. And the second is like unto it, Thou shalt love thy neighbour as thyself.

THE AUTHORING OF DEDICATION

This is where your mindset regarding your dedication becomes a reality. You have accepted the dedication. Now, it is time to complete the process in your spirit and on paper. Remember, authoring means that you will physically "script" (in writing) your plan and ideas for the dedication.

Many leaders will recommend that the reader use a mentor to guide and teach you and your people. You can choose whether you need to use a mentor, consultant, or instructor. Each of these will help you to learn whatever you lack in wisdom and knowledge. When you are in school, you are assigned to a classroom where a teacher wants to help you to be successful. When you finish high school, you can choose your college or technical education. As you author and activate your dedication, you will have the ability to dedicate yourself to the subject matter at hand. There are many great institutions of higher learning. Take some time now and write down some ideas about what it will take to be dedicated to that particular institution.

Proverbs 9:10, *"The fear of the Lord is the beginning of wisdom: and the knowledge of the holy is understanding."*

This is a key point to your success. You will recognize your dedication to your success by your dedication and desire to study what is needed to be successful. This is a great time to form a mastermind group. Maybe have a few (three to five) friends get together. Ask each other this question, "What intrigues you?" You can openly express what is so interesting to you that you will always be interested in learning more. This will give you personal guidance on what subject you would want to dedicate your life to.

Proverbs 13:20, *"He that walketh with wise men shall be wise."*

If you are on an athletic team, think about the dedication it will take to have your team win the championship. If you are the coach, take the time to write down some ideas that will help your team bond together and get a vision of holding the championship trophy. Take this dedication from the authoring (writing it) to the activation phase.

If you are in a small business, ask yourself about your personal dedication to growth. Do you want to grow? Do you want to stay small? By staying small, you may have more time with your family and have opportunities at your church. Would opening a second location be a good idea? What about expanding to another city? Do your employees have the same mindset? A business is only as good as its employees. Do the employees show up to work on time? Are they dedicated to helping the business to have a successful day? Is the dedication of the assistant manager and leadership team the same as the vision of the owner?

If you are about to enlist in the military or planning to embark on a new career, take some time as you finish reading this lesson to write down all the dedication you envision will be needed. This will be a handy reminder of what you and the Lord have planned. This should be done before you activate your dedication. We will discuss that in the next segment.

How will this lesson help me?

Personal—Take out a sheet of paper or use the blank page that follows this and write down why you are dedicated and will dedicate your future success to what the Lord has put in front of you. You can call this a "prescription" (something you write before it happens). Just like a doctor writes a note to a pharmacy before you arrive, he will prescribe. You and God have decided to "pre-scribe" the amount of dedication you need. As you write this down, you will want to use this to help your church and your community.

Mark 2:17, *"When Jesus heard it, he saith unto them, They that are whole have no need of the physician, but they that are sick: I came not to call the righteous, but sinners to repentance."*

Marriage and family—What are you and your family dedicated to? As you look around your house, you will typically see pictures or posters with ideas, words, or phrases that will indicate a certain amount of dedication. An old proverb says, "A picture is worth a thousand words." Each thing that is hanging on your wall indicates a certain amount of dedication, which your family sees will help unite the family. If your family wants to be dedicated to something new, change what you see daily in your house. It will help to change the focus, but it will take a change of heart in order to solidify the dedication.

Proverbs 23:7, *"For as he thinketh in his heart, so is he: Eat and drink, saith he to thee; but his heart is not with thee."*

Church—By writing down your amount of dedication and encouraging your church to do likewise, you will help others to reach their goal. Some members of your church may be preparing to go to college. By authoring your dedication, you will help them as they see your amount of dedication. Some members of your church may have just heard that they have a life-altering medical condition. By authoring your dedication, you can help them to be dedicated to serving the Lord as they go through their trial while they are still on earth.

Community—You may not see it now, but as you write the amount of dedication that you have, you will be affecting others in your community. You will meet others who are going through trials. You can use the lessons that you have written for yourself using scripture that you will be able to quote to them and encourage them along the way.

Luke 10:29–37:

But he, willing to justify himself, said unto Jesus, And who is my neighbour? And Jesus answering said, A certain man went down from Jerusalem to Jericho, and fell among thieves, which stripped him of his raiment, and wounded him, and departed, leaving him half dead. And by chance there came down a certain priest that way: and when he saw him, he passed by on the other side. And likewise a Levite, when he was at the place, came and looked on him, and passed by on the other side. But a certain Samaritan, as he journeyed, came where he was: and when he saw him, he had compassion on him, And went to him, and bound up his wounds, pouring in oil and wine, and set him on his own beast, and brought him to an inn, and took care of him. And on the morrow when he departed, he took out two pence, and gave them to the host, and said unto him, Take care of him; and whatsoever thou spendest more, when I come again, I will repay thee. Which now of these three, thinkest thou, was neighbour unto him that fell among the thieves? And he said, He that shewed mercy on him. Then said Jesus unto him, Go, and do thou likewise.

Anticipating and Appreciating Your Christian Life

THE ACTIVATION OF DEDICATION

You have accepted the dedication. You have even authored and written about your dedication. Now, it is time to complete the process. This is the activation of dedication. One of the great lessons that Jesus Christ taught about the dedication to what you believe is the lesson regarding the second greatest commandment.

Matthew 22:38–39, *"This is the first and great commandment. And the second is like unto it, Thou shalt love thy neighbour as thyself."*

Luke 10:36–37, *"Which now of these three, thinkest thou, was neighbour unto him that fell among the thieves? And he said, He that shewed mercy on him. Then said Jesus unto him, Go, and do thou likewise."*

Activating your dedication means that you will take action to which you are dedicated.

If you are on an athletic team, think about the dedication it will take to have your team win the championship. If you are the coach, in the last segment you took the time to write down some ideas that will help your team to bond together and get a vision of holding the championship trophy. Take this dedication from the authoring (writing it) to the activation phase.

How will this lesson help me?

Personal—Activating your dedication to your spouse and loved ones on a regular basis will keep their importance in front of you. Sometimes your friends or outside activities will seem more urgent or important than your family. Be sure to keep your priorities in proper order.

Marriage and family—Earlier in this book, you wrote down your desires regarding your family. In this chapter you were asked to write down what activities would help you to be dedicated to the fulfillment of those desires. Now the fun begins! Go do some of the activities that will help to bond that dedication. Go have a family picnic. Go pray together! Go out on that date with your spouse that you have been putting off because other activities got in the way.

Think about activities that you can do with your parents, your brothers and sisters, your children, and your grandchildren. Maybe invite a cousin or two. Make special memories and take lots of pictures because you are dedicated to keeping the family bond for many years to come.

Church—Activating your dedication to your church will give you perfect attendance. If you are a Sunday school teacher or in charge of some ministry, this same dedication will build your class or ministry. Your students and congregation will appreciate your dedication and faithfulness.

Lamentations 3:23, "*They are new every morning: great is thy faithfulness.*"

Matthew 25:21, "*His lord said unto him, Well done, thou good and faithful servant: thou hast been faithful over a few things, I will make thee ruler over many things: enter thou into the joy of thy lord.*"

Community—When you activate your dedication to your purpose, your neighbors may notice! If it is a community project that you're working on for the good of others, you may become known all over your city or town. The word "activating" means there will be activity. Members of your community can see activity because you will purchase items in the community, you will go to lunch in the community, and you will talk to others in the community about your activities. Your activation of dedication will be recognized throughout your community.

Just a note here… This is how some aspiring politicians become elected. They activate their dedication to the betterment of their community. This is important to remember because maybe the Lord would want you to be that type of leader in your community. This is not a recommendation but an observation.

THE APPRECIATION OF DEDICATION

This is where you will soon be experiencing success. This is where your real "vision" begins. What is the appreciation of dedication all about? Many of the consequences and results of dedication are often the fulfillment of your dreams. If you are a sophomore in high school and considered an equal to the seniors due to your dedication to practicing your skills, you understand! If you are the outstanding rookie in your profession who is more successful than the veterans in your field, you understand! If you are a "C-level" executive who has helped many of your coworkers and your company to be successful, you understand. Each of you is now being honored and rewarded with nice recognition or a nice pension.

You are experiencing your appreciation for your dedication. This is personal to you! This starts with your personal appreciation of your personal dedication as you begin your success or your retirement. There are a number of other great people whose lives you have touched. These friends and coworkers also appreciate your dedication, as you have impacted their lives in a good way.

Many people through the years have appreciated the opportunity of watching your dedication. Maybe you have climbed the educational ladder and earned a doctorate degree. Maybe you have won a medal in a sporting event. Maybe you are the president or vice president of your company. Maybe you have become an officer in your club, your corporation, your church, or perhaps a military officer. Sit back! Allow yourself to smile! Appreciate the dedication it took to get you to what the Lord has allowed you to accomplish. You may be a young person or a senior citizen, but others admire your dedication.

If you are a military veteran who has dedicated your life to protecting your country, your country appreciates your dedication. If you are a successful sports professional, those who wish to emulate your success appreciate your dedication. The world admires your dedication.

Every success starts with dedication. This dedication does not have to last forever in order for you to be a success. Some people are wealthy within a few years. Some careers last twenty years. Other careers last longer because the amount of dedication creates a desire to continue. Every diploma, degree, certification, and pay increase results from some type of dedication. Appreciate it!

How will this lesson help me?

Personal—Appreciating your personal dedication is one of the keys to happiness. As you appreciate the effort that you have made in the past and have watched how it has helped others, you can then look back and enjoy the memories. Not all of the memories will be smiles! Some of the memories will be blood, sweat, and tears. Each of these activities has helped you to share greatness as you and the Lord have walked together through life.

Luke 24:13–16:

And, behold, two of them went that same day to a village called Emmaus, which was from Jerusalem about threescore furlongs. And they talked together of all these things which had happened. And it came to pass, that, while they communed together and reasoned, Jesus himself drew near, and went with them. But their eyes were holden that they should not know him.

Marriage and family—Your family will appreciate your dedication to your family activities and your family values. When you have the choice of taking care of your spouse or something at work, be sure that your spouse is your number one priority. As your children are growing, be sure to take care of them. They grow up fast! If you are involved with an important activity in church, but you have a family member who is ill, be sure to keep the right priorities.

If you are a teenager, it is sometimes easy to want to neglect your family and be dedicated to activities at school and church. Be sure to make wise decisions and honor your parents. Never sacrifice family relationships for temporary friendships.

Church—Your church congregation, members, and visitors will appreciate the dedication that you have had to your church for many years to come. Your church can remain a vital part of the community through good times and hard times. You may not understand the influence that your church is having today until the children who attend your church become adults. Memories are powerful! They will influence the lives of your community and the world as the future generations make decisions that will affect other future generations.

Community—Your church may not be the only church in your community, but it can be the most dedicated church in your area. If your people and visitors feel that they are loved, appreciated, and enthused, they will also become dedicated to the future of your church. They will want it to succeed! For example, a banker may visit your church and be influenced. That banker may not attend your church regularly, but if you ever need a banker, that personal connection can be beneficial. Likewise, if the banker needs you as a Christian influence, you may be vital in changing the future of your community by your loving testimony.

Matthew 7:24, *"Therefore whosoever heareth these sayings of mine, and doeth them, I will liken him unto a wise man, which built his house upon a rock."*

Matthew 10:16, *"Behold, I send you forth as sheep in the midst of wolves: be ye therefore wise as serpents, and harmless as doves."*

THIS PAGE HAS BEEN LEFT BLANK SO THAT YOU CAN MAKE NOTES ABOUT DEDICATION

Anticipating and Appreciating Your Christian Life

DETERMINATION
THE ANTICIPATION OF DETERMINATION

The anticipation of determination may be one of the most important lessons in this book. Many of us start a project, such as learning a musical instrument, going to college, or taking on a new career, and plan to focus on that activity until we are successful. However, it has been proven that many people will not complete their projects. After doing a great deal of research, I have realized that most college freshmen do not graduate. Many great authors have never completed writing their books. There are many great fortunes that have been lost due to terminating or stopping just short of success. This is a complete change of mindset for many people. Think about this as you read through this section. How do you anticipate the idea within yourself that you will need to "de-terminate"? Many of us will now view the word "terminal" with a different visual effect.

The words "terminal" and "terminate" mean that there is an ending. That is a simple idea. But, if we take that idea further and consider the idea of "de-ter-mination," we realize that there is no ending. Even if we complete a project, such as a college degree, there is no termination before the "finish line." That is why we sometimes refer to graduation as a "commencement" or a new start. Even when you think you are about to finish, you are actually just starting.

I realized that same concept one day when I was studying to teach a class. I have the privilege of being an instructor in the areas of real estate, mortgage, and aviation. One day, as I was studying for a lesson, I realized that every time I learn another subject well enough to teach it, an entirely new field of study will open up to me, and I realize how little the mind can grasp in this lifetime. Learning never stops!

That is one reason why we all should honor our doctors at any level. They are actually your teachers and instructors who have so much more knowledge than they can explain to you while you are in their office. Yet, they still will take the time and effort to study long hours if there is something new in their profession that they need to learn in order to determine what might be ailing you.

Maybe you are a coach at your school or college. You understand this concept as you motivate your team. Maybe you are a member of the sports team, and you are encouraging your teammates. As you are warming up, you can hear your coach encouraging you to "de-terminate." Don't stop until it is time to stop. Are you "determined" to run across that goal line and win that game? Are you determined to shoot the winning basket? Don't stop short of your goal line. You only receive points if you cross the line.

Maybe you have decided to run your first 5K run (3.1 miles). You can visualize the finish line. But you anticipate that you will be determined not to stop until you reach that finish line. In every area of racing, we have a finish line. That finish line is just your commencement. If you are on the sports team, your anticipation of determination will keep you awake at night. It will have you practicing when your friends are relaxing. It will have you studying when your friends are sleeping.

A great phrase to describe determination is "I can't quit!" There is something inside of you at the beginning of the endeavor that will not allow you to end. Graduation is just a commencement or a new start. A finish line to you on that 5K or that marathon is just practice as you are anticipating being faster on your next race.

Can you feel it? Can you feel the anticipation of the determination that is needed to accomplish your goal? Success is inside of you. Feel it! Visualize it! Don't stop!

Perhaps you are thinking about getting married. It is likely that the marriage vows will have a "de-termination clause" as a minister quotes the words "till death do you part" or "as long as you both shall live." Are you prepared for such a commitment?

Ecclesiastes 5:5, *"Better is it that thou shouldest not vow, than that thou shouldest vow and not pay."*

Perhaps you are preparing to go to college. Congratulations! This is a big step in life. Before writing my first book about education, I researched colleges and universities and looked at the size of the senior class as compared to the size of the freshman class. Often, the graduating class had only one-third of the size of the freshman class. This is normal in many locations and in many areas of education. This means that two out of three students did not graduate in the timeframe expected. Every semester costs money. Education is not just a degree; it is who you become as you pursue your goals.

How will this lesson help me?

Personal—If you are getting ready to start any personal endeavor and you started with the anticipation of never stopping because of your determination, then your finish line becomes easier to achieve. This may change the college you hope to attend. This may change your vocation. The marathon of your life may become a decathlon. Instead of just running through life, you can accomplish and finish ten different goals. Success is yours! It awaits you at the finish line. Don't stop until you hear these words...

Matthew 25:21, *"His lord said unto him, Well done, thou good and faithful servant: thou hast been faithful over a few things, I will make thee ruler over many things: enter thou into the joy of thy lord."*

Marriage and family—This may change your wedding plans and your dating habits. This book has not been created to give you dating advice. However, if you are dating and you think a marriage proposal might occur, you must determine if you can fulfill a lifetime commitment. Through much prayer, if you do not believe that the Lord wants you with this individual "as long as you both shall live," then seek counsel or discuss this with your partner, your parents, or your pastor at your earliest convenience.

Church—When you anticipate being determined to do something as a church, it is vital that you finish what you have begun by faith. I have heard a number of pastors say these words, "Never quit in fear what you started in faith." Perhaps you are going to send your youth group to camp. Be sure to complete that and fulfill their dreams. Perhaps your church decided to accomplish something larger than what they had dreamed that the Lord would allow. If the Lord said to do it and you started in faith, you can anticipate that determination will make the project successful.

Proverbs 13:12, *"Hope deferred maketh the heart sick: but when the desire cometh, it is a tree of life."*

Community—When you announce something is happening in your church, then the members will start telling their friends and their families. If the church fails to complete the project, the community may not be as likely to believe in a future goal or dream from your church.

This is also important on a personal basis. When you, as an individual, say that the Lord wants you to accomplish something and then you fail to accomplish it, then others might blame an omnipotent Almighty God for the failure. They might not believe what the Lord can do. The community will lack the substance of your faith.

Hebrews 11:1, *"Now faith is the substance of things hoped for, the evidence of things not seen."*

Don't Quit!

Don't quit!
When life goes wrong, as it sometimes will,
And you wonder which way to turn,
When you just got a "D" on that important exam
On a subject that you want to learn,
When you just lost your job that you need so much
For the college money you needed to earn…
Don't quit!
When you feel so bad because your body is hurting
From football, track, or phys. ed.,
When your heart is hurting from sad news
Because some false words about you were said,
When your stomach is feeling nauseous
From some food that you have been fed…

Don't quit!
When your homework comes in heavy
From teachers who really do care,
When you miss catching a pass for a touchdown
And the fans began to boo and stare,
When you just want to give up on learning
Because life just doesn't seem fair…
Don't quit!
When you play the wrong note in the concert
And everyone hears that strange noise,
When you begin to step outside of your comfort zone
But you are laughed at by some of the boys,
When you stumble in the school hallway
And you lose all your glamour and poise…
Don't quit!
When the walk to school is over a mile
And you step outside into the snow,
When your mind is challenged by a major exam
And you don't know what answer to show,
When you get the word that cancer has come
To a family member or friend you know…
Don't quit!
Your life may be full of challenges from the cradle to the grave,
But you can overcome such challenges because of the way you behave,
For you behave like a leader should—your greatness is about to appear;
Don't quit now, or we will never realize what a great leader we are near!
You are tomorrow's leader whom the world has yet to meet!
You are the one who marches to the drummer of a different beat!
Don't quit right now even though you sweat and cry and bleed!
Please don't quit now because you motivate the rest of us to succeed!

Wes Waddle
June 12, 2014
(altered with written permission from Dr. Jack Hyles)

THE ACCEPTANCE OF DETERMINATION

This step to your success is both powerful and comforting. It is powerful to you because you have just "accepted" the idea that you are now "de-termined." You are saying to yourself, "I can't quit!" There is no terminal. There is no end.

Luke 14:28, *"For which of you, intending to build a tower, sitteth not down first, and counteth the cost, whether he have sufficient to finish it?"*

Accepting your determination will take some preparation. Later in this book, we will discuss mentorship and how your wise contacts can help you to see the proverbial "light at the end of the tunnel." In business, this is when deals get done and contracts get signed. In your life as a student, this is when you can see that you will graduate during a specific semester. In marriage, this is when the term "as long as you both shall live" becomes a reality. This will help you through the decathlon of life (many different races and trials back to back).

Some people anticipate their determination before they start any large project. However, when trials come and difficult events occur, that anticipation becomes marred by reality. At this point, the acceptance of your determination will become your new reality.

A great example of this in the Bible is David and Goliath. When David suggested that he would confront Goliath, David anticipated his determination. However, when he picked up the stones, he activated the acceptance of his "de-termination."

First Samuel 17:45, *"Then said David to the Philistine, Thou comest to me with a sword, and with a spear, and with a shield: but I come to thee in the name of the LORD of hosts, the God of the armies of Israel, whom thou hast defied."*

Many decisions are made at churches on Sunday with the anticipation of changing some part of your life. As we make those decisions, we may need to pray about them every morning and accept that change to be determined to follow that decision on a daily basis. That is why daily devotions are so important. Temptations come when we least expect it. Sometimes we need to forget the past and look for the future.

Philippians 3:13–14, *"Brethren, I count not myself to have apprehended: but this one thing I do, forgetting those things which are behind, and reaching forth unto those things which are before, I press toward the mark for the prize of the high calling of God in Christ Jesus."*

But wait! You might not be able to do it all by yourself. It might wear you out. You then learn how to transfer that acceptance of determination to others. You build a team of like-minded individuals. You mentor them to accept that same determination in their lives. You keep going, and you build your own company. You build a culture of other great minds who accept the determination that will bring success to each person.

You will not use your people to build your church or your company. You will use the acceptance of your determination to build your people. Use your different ministries to build great Christian leaders. Build your people by helping them to accept the vision of what God desires so they can be the best of His servants.

Once each participant accepts the determination to work together and individually to be their best, everyone wins! Success is as close as you determine it to be. Accept the determination today.

How will this lesson help me?

Personal—Each of us wants to do our best in this world. However, each of us is tempted to do less than our best. You know what happens in your life when you are most vulnerable. It is at those times when you need to remind yourself that you are determined to succeed in overcoming the temptation. You know those times when you feel alone, but you need comfort in some manner.

John 14:18, *"I will not leave you comfortless: I will come to you."*

Marriage and family—Accepting your determination as you become engaged (before you are pronounced husband and wife) is a life-changing decision. When this happens, you begin to make plans and commitments that will last a lifetime. You have to decide who will be your best man and the maid of honor. These memories will be with you forever. These friends will help you on this important day. They will also be with you later in life as you reflect on this important day.

Proverbs 18:24, *"A man that hath friends must shew himself friendly: and there is a friend that sticketh closer than a brother."*

Church—Throughout my life, I have seen many church revivals. They are a wonderful time in the Christian life! Perhaps your church has a small type of revival meeting regularly where people make decisions that will change their lives. These changes bring joy into the lives of your members. As human beings we often lose focus of what is important to us; therefore, we sometimes lose our joy in our daily lives. Let's encourage one another every time we meet.

Psalm 51:12, *"Restore unto me the joy of thy salvation; and uphold me with thy free spirit."*

Community—The neighbors of every one of your fellow church members need encouragement. We need to be good to everybody because everybody is struggling. If we accept our determination to encourage and benefit our community, we may be able to lighten the burden of our current and future leaders.

Hebrews 13:2, *"Be not forgetful to entertain strangers: for thereby some have entertained angels unawares."*

THE AUTHORING OF DETERMINATION

As you author (write about) your determination, your mindset may change what you envision as your success. Think about the idea of writing and visualizing the idea that you will not allow yourself to stop. There is no end. There is no termination. You have "de-terminated" your success. Whether your destination is a great marriage, a race, a championship game, a successful organization (as a church or a nonprofit), or a great company, you cannot stop until it is achieved. Your determination is solid.

I was reminded recently about a race that I ran back in my senior year of high school. We had to run the cross-country path, which, at that time, was two and one-half miles. We were in the state of Ohio. It was around 9:00 a.m., which meant the dew had set, and the grass was wet. About two hundred yards after the beginning of the race, there was a turn. As I ran around that turn, my left foot slipped on the grass, and my left knee hit the asphalt pavement. I fell. That moment changed my life!

Picture this. I am on the ground with my left knee bleeding. I looked up, and every other runner was traveling away from me on the path to completing the course. I hesitated for five seconds feeling the pain and not wanting to risk more injury. Another five seconds passed, and I realized that either I could limp back to the coach (who would have been very patient and understanding), or I could immediately stand up and sprint to "the pack" and finish the race. I did not have even one minute (sixty seconds) to think. Was I going to activate my determination? I decided to stand up and sprint. To this day, when I "fall" during any endeavor, I think about that moment. I had already written my goal and authored my future. I was determined to finish.

As you read this book, you will want to jot down (author) a few ideas that will help you when it comes time to activate your determination. The best way to do this would be to take a few minutes right now as you are reading this lesson and use some of these techniques. Authoring and scripting your determination does not take many words. You may want to use "sticky notes" to remind yourself of your determination and what action to take. Sometimes, just one or two words on a "sticky note" will be sufficient.

Psalm 51:3, *"For I acknowledge my transgressions."*

A simple, short "love note" can author your determination to liven up your relationship with your sweetheart. Sometimes, just a note on a dashboard or a dresser that says, "I love you… See you tonight" is enough to remind each of you (the writer and the recipient) of your determination to have a wonderful, long-lasting relationship.

Sometimes, a handwritten card to a friend or coworker reminding that person that you care and that God loves them can brighten their lives for many days. Authoring determination is easy. Reminding yourself to author it on a regular basis for the benefit of all people takes more effort.

Colossians 4:18, *"The salutation by the hand of me Paul. Remember my bonds. Grace be with you. Amen."*

How will this lesson help me?

Personal—This lesson can change your life starting today. Sending out a love note to the person you love and reminding them of your dedication to your relationship may be exactly what they need today. Maybe it is your brother or sister who needs a reminder. It could be about the church member that you see on a regular basis who you know is going through a trial. Perhaps they need just a simple reminder that you care. As you write the note, your heart will change as you think of the words to say.

Perhaps you are a teenager. Have you written a love note or a letter of appreciation to your parents recently? Quite often a parent will keep such a note as long as they live.

Marriage and family—This lesson could change your marriage and your family relationship in such a dramatic way starting today. We all learn and react differently. Some of us are auditory, which means we love to hear the words "I love you." Others of us are visual, which means we need to see reminders of that love. Some of us are kinesthetic, which means we need to feel the love. This feeling can be enhanced by what we see. Love notes to your sweetheart and your family will be lasting reminders to the sender and the receiver. These love notes might never be thrown away. Make them special.

Philippians 4:8, *"Finally, brethren, whatsoever things are true, whatsoever things are honest, whatsoever things are just, whatsoever things are pure, whatsoever things are lovely, whatsoever things are of good report; if there be any virtue, and if there be any praise, think on these things."*

Church—Often little reminders on church bulletin boards reminding the members to pray or to work together on a specific project are all that is needed. Little reminders can work miracles together.

Sometimes, love is so strong in the church that even little disagreements can become difficult. It is important in these relationships to restore fellowship as soon as possible. This is especially true with marriages in the church. A church with strong marriages is a blessing to the community.

First Peter 3:7, *"Likewise, ye husbands, dwell with them according to knowledge, giving honour unto the wife, as unto the weaker vessel, and as being heirs together of the grace of life; that your prayers be not hindered."*

Community—Writing a love note to your husband or wife may not have an immediate impact. Sending a "thank you" card to a coworker may not be acknowledged immediately. However, when others see those notes or your spouse mentions it, others may follow your example, and friendships and marriages may be saved.

Matthew 5:23, *"Therefore if thou bring thy gift to the altar, and there rememberest that thy brother hath ought against thee."*

Ephesians 4:26, *"Be ye angry, and sin not: let not the sun go down upon your wrath."*

THE ACTIVATION OF DETERMINATION

As you read the last lesson on authoring your determination, you probably made a few sticky notes, wrote a few love notes, or wrote a note in this book to remind you what to do today (or this week) and in years to come. Now is the time to activate that determination.

For instance, if you wrote a note that says, "I love you," now is the time to prove that. It doesn't have to be a large gift or an extreme and complicated project. Proving your love to your spouse or parents may be as simple as taking out the trash, doing the dishes, or cleaning up the house.

If you are determined to be a great parent or a great leader, your actions may do more than help build teamwork and camaraderie within your family or group. As you sit and read this book, remember that determination takes no physical action. The decisions you make through quiet meditation, which reflect your past and project your future, have brought you to your current and present situation. The same thoughts that have brought you to the current situation will need to be analyzed as you prepare to activate your determination for the future.

By authoring your determination as you did during the last lesson, you will probably continue to write about your determination as you read through this section. The reason for that is that your mind keeps going and thinking about the "what-if" scenarios.

For instance, if you are a student and you determine that a certain college will be right for you, you will mentally envision your future as a graduate of that college or university. What will it feel like as you get your diploma from high school and then an advanced degree from that university? How will that change your life? Who will you meet? What opportunities will come to you by reading this book, meditating on your future, and activating your determination to make that happen? You have an exciting life ahead of you with a great deal of opportunity. It is up to you to make it happen.

Second Timothy 1:7, *"For God hath not given us the spirit of fear; but of power, and of love, and of a sound mind."*

Perhaps you are a pastor, and you feel that the Lord has called you to a different ministry. This is an exciting time! Activating your determination as a resolute decision to move forward will change the lives of many people at your present location and in your future ministry. Be sure to walk with God as you move forward.

Matthew 1:23, *"And they shall call his name Emmanuel, which being interpreted is, God with us."*

Perhaps you are a coach or a business leader; activating the determination of your team is crucial to success. If you help your people to author their determination by writing small notes to themselves and to their comrades, these notes will be reminders to each individual of the vision and the desired outcome for their team. Part of activating the determination may be as simple as a smile, a look in the eyes, or other body language, such as how a person walks.

Let's discuss body language for a moment. As you move toward success, your demeanor will change. What that means is you will smile differently. You will have more confidence in yourself and your team. You will be more proactive for the success of those who surround you. As you are determined to be successful in all aspects of your life, you will start smiling at things that benefit others who surround you. Likewise, you will find that you do not smile at actions or words that harm or discourage others. That is what a successful Christian life is all about.

Isaiah 50:7, *"For the Lord GOD will help me; therefore shall I not be confounded: therefore have I set my face like a flint, and I know that I shall not be ashamed."*

In the same manner as your smile, your eyes will reflect much of what is happening in your spirit. You know that look that came from your mother when she was displeased. We have all seen it. You also saw the look in her eyes when she was proud of you. It is our duty as believers in Jesus Christ to walk in the

Spirit. As you look at the actions of others who are helping you and surrounding you as you move toward success, you will be observant, and that will bring you to your objective. With the help of the Holy Spirit, you can actually encourage yourself by changing your actions, your body language, and your paradigm (how you view life and the world).

First Samuel 30:6, *"And David was greatly distressed; for the people spake of stoning him, because the soul of all the people was grieved, every man for his sons and for his daughters: but David encouraged himself in the Lord his God."*

Activating your determination will also be indicated by the way you walk. We have all seen it. When somebody is happy, they hold their head high, look people in the eye, and smile or nod with a sense of respect and admiration for the other person. Likewise, you have seen individuals who were not having a good day and would not look you in the eye. This attitude will also be present in their stride as they walk. A person who has just had good news will carry themselves differently than a person whose heart is broken and sad. As a believer, your obligation is to encourage fellow human beings to do what is right and honorable for them, society, and the kingdom of heaven.

Luke 24:17, *"And he said unto them, What manner of communications are these that ye have one to another, as ye walk, and are sad?"*

First Timothy 4:12, *"Let no man despise thy youth; but be thou an example of the believers, in word, in conversation, in charity, in spirit, in faith, in purity."*

If you are a church leader, Sunday school teacher, or even somebody who is admired at your church, it is important to remind yourself daily that your eyes, your smile, and even the way you walk can significantly impact somebody's day. This happens not just on Sunday but throughout the week while you are in school, in the community, or in business meetings. Can you imagine how Jesus Christ would look at a person and not say a word? That idea of activating your determination will change your life.

How will this lesson help me?

Personal—Changing the way you walk, smile, and look at people will change your life. Conversely, by changing your mindset, you will begin to walk, talk, smile, and look at people differently. This will help you to be determined to be all that God has asked you to be. There is a reason you are in this world right now. There is a reason that the great Creator has put you in your current location and has given you the opportunity to be determined to succeed in your desires. Remember desire comes from the Father. If you and your Heavenly Father had decided the outcome, then there is nothing stopping you from succeeding because your Father created the outcome for you before you asked.

Matthew 6:8, *"Be not ye therefore like unto them: for your Father knoweth what things ye have need of, before ye ask him."*

Marriage and family—As you activate the determination in your marriage and family, you may begin to have the happiest relationships of your life. These relationships will be fulfilling and rewarding as you give your attention to those who are most important in your life. These relationships will begin to be honest with one another. They will also be forgiving of one another. Nobody is perfect! We all make mistakes and disappoint one another from time to time. Activating your determination will bring unity.

Acts 2:46, *"And they, continuing daily with one accord in the temple, and breaking bread from house to house, did eat their meat with gladness and singleness of heart."*

Church—Activating the determination at your church can be as simple as motivating one teenager. Maybe you are that teenager. The influence of one young person can be beneficial because of the spirit which they carry. An energetic, vibrant young person who prays and walks with God will affect the teenagers and the adults. This will also encourage the toddlers who look up to this person as a future leader.

First Timothy 4:12, *"Let no man despise thy youth; but be thou an example of the believers, in word, in conversation, in charity, in spirit, in faith, in purity."*

In like fashion, a church is influenced by its music minister. Music is so powerful that it is used to activate the determination of military forces. Yet, it is used in churches to help people of every age to make life-changing decisions. If you cease to provide encouraging Christian music to yourself and to those who surround you, it might be easy to become discouraged and lose your focus on your determination.

Lamentations 5:14, *"The elders have ceased from the gate, the young men from their musick."*

Community—By activating your determination throughout your community, your community will change. Sometimes, you will be determined to help the homeless or underserved populations of your community. In some instances, you will want to start a rescue mission or a food shelter where others will see that you believe the principles that Jesus Christ taught when He was asked, "Who is my neighbor?"

Matthew 19:19, *"Honour thy father and thy mother: and, Thou shalt love thy neighbour as thyself."*

Matthew 22:37–39, *"Jesus said unto him, Thou shalt love the Lord thy God with all thy heart, and with all thy soul, and with all thy mind. This is the first and great commandment. And the second is like unto it, Thou shalt love thy neighbour as thyself."*

THE APPRECIATION OF DETERMINATION

As you complete your project and that which you were determined to make happen, you can now sit back, relax, and appreciate the determination that you had to put forth in order to succeed.

Psalm 40:3, *"And he hath put a new song in my mouth, even praise unto our God: many shall see it, and fear, and shall trust in the LORD."*

Psalm 23:4, *"Yea, though I walk through the valley of the shadow of death, I will fear no evil: for thou art with me; thy rod and thy staff they comfort me."*

Due to your determination, you have come through trials and tribulations, which only required you to walk to get to this destination. You did it! You did it through the help of the Holy Spirit, with Jesus Christ, who said He would never forsake you, and with the help of God Almighty. Congratulations! You have made it to success. You have completed the task. By remembering the word "determination" as you went through your goal, you did not terminate or quit. You completed the high calling that God has placed before you. You are an amazing servant. Well done!

Philippians 3:13–14, *"Brethren, I count not myself to have apprehended: but this one thing I do, forgetting those things which are behind, and reaching forth unto those things which are before, I press toward the mark for the prize of the high calling of God in Christ Jesus."*

How will this lesson help me?

Personal—As you finish every worthy task in life, you can sit back and enjoy your success. For many of us, this will be having completed a phase of education, whether that be a high school diploma, a college degree, your postgraduate work, or a special certificate. For some readers, it was the winning score of last week's ballgame. You won because you were determined not to quit. You didn't quit during practice. You did not quit when the other team was winning at halftime. You were determined to win, and you did. Congratulations!

Second Corinthians 4:1, *"Therefore seeing we have this ministry, as we have received mercy, we faint not."*

Marriage and family—When you get the chance, take a few minutes and talk to an older couple who have been married for a significant amount of time. Ask them for ideas that have helped them in their determination to keep their marriage together. I am not suggesting that you take all of their advice. However, they may be able to give you some advice on how to talk to your spouse and even your brothers and sisters so that family reunions will have pleasant memories.

Psalm 133:1, *"Behold, how good and how pleasant it is for brethren to dwell together in unity!"*

Church—Congratulations! As a church, you finished the project. That project may have been to increase your attendance, build a new building, start a new rescue mission, or something in your community. It might even be to start a new church locally or on a foreign mission field. The world will see what you have done. The world will be changed because you have completed the task. Be sure to thank your people! Thank your teenagers for their energy and their prayers! Thank the families of your church for continually striving, praying, and giving as needed to complete the tasks! You have an amazing church! Be sure to thank them in some mighty way. Show your appreciation and remind them that God has used them in the past and will continue to use them in the future.

Community—Your community will appreciate your completed project. The members of your church help to make up your community. As your members interact with other members of the community, they will appreciate the determination that your congregation has united and completed together. Many of you, as you read this book, sit on a board of directors. Some of you are on the deacon board. Some of you are on the local school board. Others of you are on the board of directors of a company or corporation. You understand the significance of the completed project. Your decisions have been a key element in your success. Congratulations!

Second Timothy 4:7, *"I have fought a good fight, I have finished my course, I have kept the faith."*

Isaiah 40:31, *"But they that wait upon the* LORD *shall renew their strength; they shall mount up with wings as eagles; they shall run, and not be weary; and they shall walk, and not faint."*

THIS PAGE HAS BEEN LEFT BLANK SO THAT YOU CAN MAKE
NOTES ABOUT DETERMINATION

DECISIONS (YOUR BONUS "D")

The title of this book talks about (only) three DIMES, but I like to give more than is expected. Therefore, I had to include one more important word. This action is used many times during each minute of life. This action is the mental exercise of "decision-making."

Since you started reading this book, you have made many decisions. Some decisions you have written down. Some decisions were fleeting thoughts that you didn't write down, but you should have. The next time these decisions come to your mind, be sure to have a piece of paper or electronic device in your pocket ready to capture that important thought.

Your decisions change your current life and the outcome of your life on a daily basis. You could be doing many things right now, but you realize that reading this book and making certain decisions are going to help you change your life as you pray, as you speak to others, as you smile, and even as you look at others. People will be encouraged because of the decisions that you have made. Lives will be helped because of the decisions you have made.

Sometimes, as I teach about the word "decisions," I discuss how a decision is similar to an "incision" (a clean, clear cut). An incision separates the skin. A skilled surgeon will make an incision so that he can first separate the skin. Then, he will make another incision beneath the skin, which will improve your health in the future. Both incisions and decisions are used to separate. Both incisions and decisions are critical and valuable.

Decisions are similar to incisions in the fact that every decision can separate you from outcomes that you don't want. For instance, if you decide to eat a large piece of birthday cake in the afternoon, you may not want to eat properly at supper time. If you make the decision to study for your final exam instead of going out to eat with your friends, you are separating yourself and may be recognized for academic achievement after graduating.

Some of the decisions that you make may separate you from good people who do not agree with every decision that you make. That is not a problem. It may actually be a blessing.

Luke 6:22, *"Blessed are ye, when men shall hate you, and when they shall separate you from their company, and shall reproach you, and cast out your name as evil, for the Son of man's sake."*

If scientific research is true, you could make about a thousand decisions in the next hour. You have a great mind. You have a great God. Ask the Holy Spirit to be with you as you walk in faith every hour of every day! Use the mind of Christ to help you as you make every decision so that when you stand before Him, He will be able to say, "Well done, good and faithful servant."

What decision do you need to make today? Knowing the answer to that question will change your life! Remember these two truths have the same words but in different order…

"One day will change your life!"

"One day your life will change!"

The decision is up to you as to what day that will be!

How will this lesson help me?

Personal—Having the ability to make decisions is a powerful tool in life. Earlier in this book, you read about the anticipation of desire and what you want to make happen. We discussed your dedication and determination to fulfill your dreams. Everything in your life will change because of the decisions that you make.

First Thessalonians 5:16–18, *"Rejoice evermore. Pray without ceasing. In every thing give thanks: for this is the will of God in Christ Jesus concerning you."*

Marriage and family—The daily decisions that you make with your family will determine how successful you are as a family unit and as an individual. Learn to pray with your family. Learn why your family members make certain decisions. Some of the decisions that they make will be because of how they view the world and how they view their family. If you learn to understand how others make decisions, you may be able to make better decisions for yourself and for your family.

Church—The decisions that your church makes will change the lives of each member, each visitor, and the community as a whole. Remind each person in your youth group, on your board, and throughout the congregation that their daily decisions made with careful prayer and walking with God will bring them a fulfilled life. Sometimes we will use the term "preaching to the choir" as if saying that we are being redundant and we shouldn't need to be reminded. However, each of us needs to be reminded on a regular basis about how powerful our God is.

First John 1:7, *"But if we walk in the light, as he is in the light, we have fellowship one with another, and the blood of Jesus Christ his Son cleanseth us from all sin."*

Community—Many of us reading this book right now will have an influence on the decisions that are made in your community. It is important to remember that you do not need to be the mayor or sit on the city council to change your community. However, the city may need you as the mayor. You may think to yourself, *But I'm just a high school senior.* That is fine! Do you realize that in many areas, you can be elected mayor at the age of eighteen? If you run for mayor and lose, you will be a better person because of the decision that you made.

First Timothy 4:12, *"Let no man despise thy youth; but be thou an example of the believers, in word, in conversation, in charity, in spirit, in faith, in purity."*

THIS PAGE HAS BEEN LEFT BLANK SO THAT YOU CAN MAKE
NOTES ABOUT DECISIONS

INSPIRATION
THE ANTICIPATION OF INSPIRATION

For some of us, this may be the most enjoyable exercise that we will do in the near future. What inspires you? What puts you in the spirit of success? We all love being inspired, yet we all are inspired by different things at different times and in different ways. That is what makes us individuals.

Most of us have five senses. We can see. We can hear. We can smell. We have the ability to taste. We can touch and feel. Some people will only have four of the senses, yet they can be inspired by using any of these. As you anticipate what will inspire you today, tomorrow, or in the future, let's look at each of these and how you can use them for your benefit. For right now, you may just want to think about different things. However, you may want to start writing down your inspiration, which you will use to succeed. Anticipate and look forward to being inspired.

Seeing—If you can see, certain pictures will inspire you. Take some time and anticipate what will inspire you when you see it. If you cannot physically see, you may be able to produce vivid images. That is why television and billboards are so profitable. You may have heard the term, "A picture is worth a thousand words." If I show you a picture of something that inspires you from your past, you may be able to talk for an hour about that experience.

For many of us, the picture of our sweetheart is so inspiring that it will cause us to excel and accomplish more than we ever thought possible. The love we feel while looking at (or a picture of) our loved one will affect the outcome of our day. Every member of the military understands this as they often keep a picture of a loved one with them. Why? Because of the anticipation of inspiration. Each person understands that they are going to need to be inspired to take action. That picture inspires them!

Perhaps you are a teenager on the sports team. Just before you go out to the basketball court, the football field, or the sports arena, you look at the picture of the one that inspires you. You want that person to be proud of you! You want that person to smile the next time they see you because of the inspiration that they have been able to help you achieve.

What picture inspires you? What site inspires you? Perhaps it is the home that you live in or have lived in. Perhaps it is a picture of Jesus Christ. Perhaps it is a picture of a beautiful sunset or sunrise. Many of us have an accolade or certificate hanging on our wall to inspire us. Your past can inspire your future! Many little successes accomplished over and over again become large successes. Every college class you take helps you become a little closer to that college degree. Every high school class that you pass will get you closer to your diploma.

Everything you see can inspire you if you view it as a miracle! Can you imagine being able to see your future? Would that inspire you?

Mark 8:24, *"And he looked up, and said, I see men as trees, walking."*

Vision—We discussed "seeing" (as a sense) above. In order to succeed to your maximum capacity, you will need to go one step beyond physical seeing and get a mental vision of who you will be when you become the success you envisioned. Every dream is a vision. Whether you daydream or dream in your sleep, your mind produces a vision. Take a few minutes and anticipate what vision will inspire you. Can you see yourself crossing the finish line? Can you see yourself crossing the goal line? Can you see yourself becoming a military officer? Can you see yourself marrying someone like that beautiful person you admire? You may have such a strong vision that you cannot share it.

Matthew 17:9, *"And as they came down from the mountain, Jesus charged them, saying, Tell the vision to no man, until the Son of man be risen again from the dead."*

God has given you a powerful mind! If you know what puts you into the "mind of success" and you can anticipate what inspires you now and what will inspire you in the future, success will be nearer than you can imagine. Your mind can conceive and can realize the future. That is how the future happens. Earlier in this book, we discussed your decisions. What you envision inspires you to reach the successful outcome of those decisions and will make success increasingly possible for you.

Mark 8:18, *"Having eyes, see ye not? and having ears, hear ye not? and do ye not remember?"*

Hearing—Do you like music? When you anticipate what will inspire you in the future, be sure that music is part of it. We all know how this works! You may have chosen your church because of the music program. You may enjoy your church because you sing in the choir or your loved one sings in the choir. Many churches are built around their music.

Perhaps you are in high school. You probably have your school fight song memorized. Your school may also have another song that is used to inspire the pep rally. If you are a coach, you are familiar with the anticipation of inspiration, as that is what gives your team the motivation to come back with a winning score.

Perhaps you are in the military. You have certain songs memorized. These songs will help you to be inspired and build camaraderie through difficult times. Sometimes, you will hum the songs without even realizing it. This inspiration will help you make it through the day.

Perhaps you are a concertgoer. I love gospel music! What do you enjoy? What inspires you today? What music do you anticipate or think may inspire you in the future? Is it a particular style of music? Is it a particular singer or band? Perhaps hearing the instrument that you played in the high school band still inspires you today. Music is so powerful.

Other than music, what other sounds inspire you and will inspire you in the future? Is it the sound of the birds singing? Perhaps it's the sound of a train whistle or a semitruck horn. Perhaps it's the sound of your mother's voice. Do you remember the voice of someone you love who passed away? When you hear a recording of that voice, does it inspire you?

Sometimes, you may be inspired by unusual noises. For instance, my father worked with trees. Therefore, the sound of a chainsaw inspires me. Since I fly airplanes, I love the sound of a small airplane flying high. I ride motorcycles; therefore, the sound of (some) motorcycle engines inspires me.

Perhaps you are deaf or hard of hearing. I had the privilege of working with the deaf and hard of hearing for over ten years. You can still feel the vibration. Every sound is a series of vibrations. There are certain "sounds" that can inspire you.

Think about what sounds inspire you. Think of what you can do in the future when you can hear those sounds again.

Think about your favorite Bible teacher, minister, or preacher and how that person has inspired you in the past. You remember what they taught you. You can still hear their words.

Luke 11:28, *"But he said, Yea rather, blessed are they that hear the word of God, and keep it."*

Smell—What smell inspires you? If you live on a farm, certain smells will inspire you every morning. If you're in the military or are a hunter, you probably are inspired by the smell of gunpowder. If you work around airplanes, you may be inspired by the smell of aviation fuel. What perfume or cologne inspires you?

For most of us, you can anticipate that you will be inspired when you walk into your home and smell your favorite food being prepared. Be sure to thank those who created it. Perhaps it is the backyard barbecue that inspires you. As you move forward with your life, you may either want to have a backyard barbecue or live near a park, or you can bring back such memories that will help you stay inspired.

For many of us, that first cup of coffee in the morning puts us into the spirit to keep moving. Sometimes, this smell can also be enhanced by the smell of the perfume or cologne of the loved one who is handing this to you. This is a powerful combination!

Every restaurant receives a certain amount of income because of the fragrance that is produced. You know the smell. When you walk into the pizza restaurant, you start getting hungry before you even look at the menu because of the wonderful smell of the kitchen. When you walk into the steakhouse and your mouth starts watering because you know how good it's going to taste, you are inspired to order more food so you can take it home for leftovers. That may put you into a certain spirit that you have enjoyed before. As you look toward the future and anticipate where you plan to go to college, you can remember those smells.

Hosea 14:6, *"His branches shall spread, and his beauty shall be as the olive tree, and his smell as Lebanon."*

Taste—What do you like to taste? When it comes to food, do you like Italian, Oriental, Mexican, or fast food? What will inspire you while you are in college or away from home? Maybe you just like the taste of freshly made bread. Will that put you in the spirit of success? The wonderful thing about taste is that you can eat or drink little amounts and enjoy the flavor. Your mouth may already be watering because you can anticipate the flavor. Imagine tasting something sweet right now.

Proverbs 24:13, *"My son, eat thou honey, because it is good; and the honeycomb, which is sweet to thy taste."*

Psalm 34:8, *"O taste and see that the LORD is good: blessed is the man that trusteth in him."*

Touch—Things that you touch might inspire you. Things that touch you can inspire you. Whether it's the clothes you wear or the furniture that surrounds you, each of these can inspire you. Twenty years from now, you may see an old picture of a room in your house that will bring back great memories and inspire you for the future. Be sure to remember how you feel as you touch each object.

Sometimes a great book can inspire you. Thank you for reading this book so far. As you read through this book, I pray that you will be inspired for greatness because of your ideas as you read. Great books inspire great decisions. Even the Bible itself is inspired!

Second Timothy 3:16, *"All scripture is given by inspiration of God, and is profitable for doctrine, for reproof, for correction, for instruction in righteousness."*

Throughout your life, make wonderful memories. By doing that, you can anticipate what will inspire you in the future. Stay inspired, my friends!

How will this lesson help me?

Personal—You know what inspires you today. By knowing that, you can anticipate what will inspire you in the future. You can make arrangements now to have that inspiration available to you when you need it. Since you know that you will need to be inspired in the future, make plans now to surround yourself with visions, sounds, smells, and feeling of inspiration.

Job 32:8, *"But there is a spirit in man: and the inspiration of the Almighty giveth them understanding."*

Marriage and family—You probably have some type of Christmas decorations in your house somewhere. These are used to help you to be inspired for the Christmas season. As you anticipate which decorations will go where you will begin to understand what the anticipation of inspiration is all about.

Perhaps you have a loved one who is about to graduate or receive an award. That person will be inspired as they complete their accomplishment. You will want to anticipate their inspiration so that you can celebrate accordingly.

Church—If you have an inspired church, there will be such a spirit that when visitors walk into the church, the visitor will feel the presence of the Holy Spirit that you have brought into the church. Let's pray that the Holy Spirit is with you always. Whether you are a young person, a church leader, or the pastor, take some time to anticipate what will inspire others in your church. This will build such church unity that many visitors will want to join in and be a part of this inspiration.

Second Timothy 3:16, *"All scripture is given by inspiration of God, and is profitable for doctrine, for reproof, for correction, for instruction in righteousness."*

Community—Most people love inspiration in their community. That is why we have parades. It is so that we can march those in front of us who have the spirit that they bring with them on that special day. Whether you are involved in a Veterans Day parade, a Thanksgiving Day parade, or another special event, inspiration in the community can unite and inspire the members of the community.

You can be a special blessing to your community when you anticipate and help to orchestrate that which will inspire your community. This is what "community service" (and politics) is all about. You may want to meet with your church leaders or your colleagues and become a leader for such an event.

Hebrews 10:24, *"And let us consider one another to provoke unto love and to good works."*

THE ACCEPTANCE OF INSPIRATION

As you read through the previous section of this book, did you think about all the different ways you can be inspired for good and for success for the rest of your life? As you read through that lesson and thought about each of your senses, did you realize the importance of each sense? Inspiration is so powerful! Almost everything you do throughout the day can inspire you to achieve more. Think for a few minutes about what puts you in a certain mood. If it is not the mood that you want, use something else that you know will inspire you in a different way.

Now that you have anticipated what will inspire you, go back through your thoughts and accept the things that you know will put you in the right spirit for success in the future that will not harm you or anybody else.

What action inspires you to be close to the Holy Spirit? We are commanded to pray without ceasing.

First Thessalonians 5:16–17, *"Rejoice evermore. Pray without ceasing."*

First John 1:7, *"But if we walk in the light, as he is in the light, we have fellowship one with another, and the blood of Jesus Christ his Son cleanseth us from all sin."*

Take some time and accept the ideas that you have had. Some things may inspire you for a short time. Other inspirations will last a lifetime. Accept those inspirations that will be beneficial to you throughout your life. Keep them close to you. Ponder them! Think about them carefully. Think about scriptures that put you into a certain frame of mind.

Psalm 119:11, *"Thy word have I hid in mine heart, that I might not sin against thee."*

Micah 6:8, *"He hath shewed thee, O man, what is good; and what doth the LORD require of thee, but to do justly, and to love mercy, and to walk humbly with thy God?"*

How will this lesson help me?

Personal—If you personally commit to knowing what will inspire you to take action at any given time, you can be blessed beyond measure. If you are able to accept that inspiration, then you are able to understand the comfort of the Holy Spirit and portray it to those in need at any given time.

John 14:18, *"I will not leave you comfortless: I will come to you."*

Marriage and family—Each of your family members is inspired in a different way. Each person has different experiences with different people for different activities that put them in a particular spirit. If you are a parent, each of your children will be inspired differently. Accept those different ideas and activities that inspire your children, your spouse, and your parents. By doing this you will know how to help each person to live an inspired life.

Church—Whether you are having a church revival or a funeral, your church will have a special spirit about it. As you thought about the different ways to create spirit and inspiration, you were able to analyze what will bring a certain spirit within your church. Many people get inspired by food at church. Some churches have potluck dinners. Some churches have a chili cookoff. I love watching God's people celebrate and be inspired as we go through this world. Find out what inspires your church and how you can recreate that same spirit wherever you live for the rest of your life.

Community—Perhaps it's Christmas time and you want to invite the general public to come to your Christmas program. When they arrive, they will feel the choir's spirit, smell the fragrance in the air, and hear the sounds of joy of the Christmas season.

Luke 2:10, *"And the angel said unto them, Fear not: for, behold, I bring you good tidings of great joy, which shall be to all people."*

In each area of the countries around the world, different cultures have different ways to create inspiration in their local community. It is important to hold your principles but be able to relate to different types of people. You can be an influence in their lives. Think about these words from apostle Paul:

First Corinthians 9:19–23:

For though I be free from all men, yet have I made myself servant unto all, that I might gain the more. And unto the Jews I became as a Jew, that I might gain the Jews; to them that are under the law, as under the law, that I might gain them that are under the law; To them that are without law, as without law, (being not without law to God, but under the law to Christ,) that I might gain them that are without law. To the weak became I as weak, that I might gain the weak: I am made all things to all men, that I might by all means save some. And this I do for the gospel's sake, that I might be partaker thereof with you.

Job 32:8, *"But there is a spirit in man: and the inspiration of the Almighty giveth them understanding."*

THE AUTHORING OF INSPIRATION

As we began the idea of inspiration, we discussed the different senses that the human body can use to be inspired. That was a long discussion because of how many ways each of us can be inspired. This is your opportunity to author and write down all of the ideas and types of inspiration that are specifically meant for you.

Take some time to write everything that inspires you as you smell them. You will begin to smell different restaurants. Write down the ones that make you feel the way you want to feel as you travel on the road to success. You may want to eat in similar restaurants often, or you may want to save that restaurant for a special occasion. It is totally up to you. (You may want to buy that restaurant franchise.)

Some of us will begin to "mentally smell" our favorite meal cooking in your kitchen. You know the smell. Your mouth begins to water as you walk into the room. Write these down. Maybe it's your mother's recipe. Go make a copy of that recipe and put it somewhere in a scrapbook that you will find in ten or twenty years. When you make that recipe, great memories will be produced.

You will also begin to smell perfumes, colognes, and different fragrances. Sometimes manufacturers will quit producing a certain fragrance. You may want to write down the names of fragrances that put you into a certain mood or inspire you.

Make a list of items that you can taste, whether it's a beverage or food item. The list can go on and on. You may want to make two lists, one list that you know that you can get at any location. You can buy certain beverages almost anywhere in the world. However, maybe the restaurant that inspires you is a small restaurant in your neighborhood with specialized food. I remember a restaurant where I worked years ago has gone out of business. Are you that way? Do you have a particular restaurant that you miss? Can you remember the smell and flavor of the food?

Make a list of items that, as you see them, you are inspired. If you take the time right now to make a list of items that inspire you, different ideas will come to you as you write them down. Keep this list in a safe place like a scrapbook that you could pull out and look at in a few years. This list will inspire you now and for years to come.

How will this lesson help me?

Personal—As you look around your house right now, you will probably see things that inspire you. You will probably see pictures of people that make you feel good. These may be relatives or friends that help you to have a good time. You might see many inspiring items and mementos that bring back great memories. These can be powerful for encouragement in good times and bad. Keep them handy!

Philippians 2:2, *"Fulfil ye my joy, that ye be likeminded, having the same love, being of one accord, of one mind."*

Marriage and family—As you create this list, you may change your marriage and family life because you will learn from each person and write down a list of items that you can keep handy that will inspire each person. Quite often we know what will create a great deal of inspiration in our spouse or brother or sister, yet we forget about or neglect the small items that inspire each person. If you have a family member who is middle-aged or older, they probably have a song they remember as a teenager that inspired them. If you can write down the name of that song and play it at a special event such as a birthday or graduation, this could be very inspirational and create lasting memories.

Church—This is a great exercise for your church or a group in your church. This is really important for your youth group. In my first book, I wrote a chapter entitled "When High School Seniors Take Over." It is amazing what a group of inspired teenagers and young adults can do together if they are all inspired at the same time. Making a list and knowing what inspires your teenagers will help you to know what type of activities will bring more teenagers to your church and help the work of the Lord in the next generation.

Acts 2:1, *"And when the day of Pentecost was fully come, they were all with one accord in one place."*

Community—What activities inspire your community? Is there a parade in which your church can get involved? Is there an activity supporting your police or firemen with which your church can get involved? As you get involved with activities that inspire your community, your teenagers will see their friends from high school. Your adults will see their coworkers from the factory, which will probably provide you an opportunity to meet more people in the community and invite them to your church.

Luke 9:50, *"And Jesus said unto him, Forbid him not: for he that is not against us is for us."*

THE ACTIVATION OF INSPIRATION

When is the best time to activate your inspiration? That answer would be every day. For some of us, we will answer, "Many times every day." When the Bible says in 1 Thessalonians 5:17, "Pray without ceasing," that means we should always walk and talk with God Almighty throughout the day. Many of us have sung the famous hymn, "In the Garden" (written by C. Austin Miles in 1912), which has the familiar words:

And He walks with me and He talks with me
And He tells me I am his own,
And the joy we share as we tarry there
None other has ever known.

With those words in mind, why should we ever need to activate our inspiration? The reason is that we are all human beings. We all need to be reminded every day of the words Emmanuel and "God with us."

Matthew 1:23, *"Behold, a virgin shall be with child, and shall bring forth a son, and they shall call his name Emmanuel, which being interpreted is, God with us."*

Have you ever had a time in your life when you were speaking and you looked at somebody and said, "I didn't think you heard me"? Isn't it good to know that you never have to do that with the Holy Spirit? The Holy Spirit wants to inspire you throughout your day (every day) until you meet with Him at the gates of heaven.

Since we are still on earth, sometimes we will need to use the reminders that you wrote down during the "authoring your inspiration" lesson. When you arise in the morning, have something near you that will inspire you to take action. It may be just a simple plaque with the words "I'm blessed" on it. Perhaps there is a picture of a loved one right beside it that will help you to activate your inspiration even before you get out of bed.

Some of us have responsibilities that require us to stand in front of a group of people. This could be a new opportunity in school. If you haven't given a book report or a speech to your class, you will need to activate your inspiration before you stand up. Don't be alarmed! Many speakers who speak in front of hundreds or thousands of people at one time have to activate their inspiration in the same manner. The only difference is that it is a larger audience. This may help you to understand why it was so important for you to write down what inspires you.

Perhaps you are a chaplain or a hospice worker, and you have to visit somebody who will be in heaven soon. This is an important time to activate your inspiration in a different manner because it is a different spirit that is needed when you walk into the room. The amazing thing is that the Holy Spirit understands each situation. I am always amazed as I read the Bible and study the life of Jesus Christ that He was able to have compassion in solitude as He raised a young girl from the dead right after the others laughed at him. And yet He was also able to stand in front of the multitudes and speak to them as one having authority.

Matthew 7:28–29, *"And it came to pass, when Jesus had ended these sayings, the people were astonished at his doctrine: For he taught them as one having authority, and not as the scribes."*

Many of us activate our inspiration without even knowing it. This actually helps to inspire those around us. A typical example is somebody singing or humming a song when they think nobody is listening. Music is inspirational. Music is used in every part of the world. If you want to change your life, start changing the music you listen to today. Your life can change simply by changing the radio station buttons in your car. You can actually be inspired without knowing it because as the music plays in the background, you will hear inspiring words and thoughts that will help you.

Do you listen to Christian music throughout your day? Do you listen to inspiring music and calm music throughout the day? Christian music does not have to be boring. Much of it will inspire you and help you to walk with the Holy Spirit throughout the day, which will be beneficial to both you and the people around you.

Since you authored your inspiration as we did in the last segment, take those notes out right now and look at them. If you are about to get into a car, think about what will remind you of each of your inspirational notes. This has a double effect on you, reminding you of what you wrote and inspiring you. This can also be a good testimony for you if you have other people in the car who you want to inspire and encourage. Your family members and your friends need encouragement and inspiration. You may be the one person that the Holy Spirit can use to influence their life!

First Corinthians 11:1, *"Be ye followers of me, even as I also am of Christ."*

Philippians 3:17, *"Brethren, be followers together of me, and mark them which walk so as ye have us for an ensample."*

How will this lesson help me?

Personal—If you start each day being inspired by the notes that you have written or the music that you listen to while the Holy Spirit walks with you, there is no power that can defeat you! Even when things go wrong and you become discouraged, you can stay inspired because of the actions, the notes, the music, and your prayers!

Psalm 23:4, *"Yea, though I walk through the valley of the shadow of death, I will fear no evil: for thou art with me; thy rod and thy staff they comfort me."*

Marriage and family—Activating the inspiration within your family can be an exciting opportunity to help your family as you move through hard times like the death of a loved one or through wonderful times like a marriage or graduation. Now that you know what inspires each person and you understand what inspires you, you have the ability to learn leadership. Leaders inspire their followers in such a way that the entire family wants to do better and help each one to succeed now and in the future. Even in your home, sometimes it only takes a smile to inspire. This may be a great family tradition to start. Have each person smile at every other person individually (not as a group) at least three times every day. This may change your life!

Romans 14:22, *"Hast thou faith? have it to thyself before God. Happy is he that condemneth not himself in that thing which he alloweth."*

Church—I sometimes have the opportunity to speak with music directors in churches. Each director has an opportunity to inspire the congregation, the pastor, and even the choir. Maybe you are involved in some manner with the music of your church. You may sing in the choir. You may sing a solo. You may play a musical instrument. You may run the sound booth or the public address system. Each position can inspire your members and visitors to the church or meeting location. Activating the inspiration before people walk in the door for any activity is an important position.

Luke 24:53, *"And were continually in the temple, praising and blessing God. Amen."*

Community—Often a church will be involved with the community because of a funeral or a wedding. Each of these activities will have a different spirit about them. The music for a funeral can inspire good memories of some of the attendees about times in their past when they attended your church or a similar church. Your opportunity to inspire can be life-changing. Weddings are the same way in that they are so emotional that if good memories arise, people will come to your church for many years because of the spirit they felt during the wedding.

Matthew 5:4, *"Blessed are they that mourn: for they shall be comforted."*

We often do not think about the spirit that we create with the help of the Holy Spirit that is within us. You may want to make it your goal to inspire yourself every morning so that you can be an inspiration to others throughout the day.

THE APPRECIATION OF INSPIRATION

This is a great time to sit back and appreciate all of the great inspiration that has led you to your current place in life. As you sit and ponder your thoughts, you may realize that you want to renew the spirit in your home, in your office, in your workplace, and within yourself. This is a perfect opportunity to appreciate the fact that you can appreciate your inspiration before you set this book down.

Think about that for a moment. You can appreciate whatever has inspired you in the past that has helped you to be successful and profitable to mankind and to your Christian faith. Maybe you have been influenced by the wrong people or the wrong music. Maybe that has inspired you to make the wrong choices about what you drink or act in a manner that would not benefit you in the future. You can change that today. Put all that behind you. Start today with new inspiration.

Philippians 3:13–14, *"Brethren, I count not myself to have apprehended: but this one thing I do, forgetting those things which are behind, and reaching forth unto those things which are before, I press toward the mark for the prize of the high calling of God in Christ Jesus."*

First John 1:7, *"But if we walk in the light, as he is in the light, we have fellowship one with another, and the blood of Jesus Christ his Son cleanseth us from all sin."*

Micah 6:8, *"He hath shewed thee, O man, what is good; and what doth the Lord require of thee, but to do justly, and to love mercy, and to walk humbly with thy God?"*

You might want to remember the words to that great hymn, "There Has Never Been a Friend Like Jesus," written by Ralph Carmichael:

We walk hand in hand through this pilgrim land
Here we linger for a day; but soon we'll leave
this land of night for that land so bright
There my friend and I will stay.

How will this lesson help me?

Personal—As you sit back and appreciate all the inspiration that has been given to you since you were born, you will begin to appreciate the individuals who have helped you survive and thrive thus far. Many of us may begin to appreciate our parents more. Many of us will begin to appreciate our teachers, our counselors, and our coaches more. You may want to write a short thank you note to people who inspired you years ago and let them know you appreciate the inspiration that they have given you. Think about your church leaders and spiritual leaders who have been an example and have inspired you.

Ephesians 5:20, *"Giving thanks always for all things unto God and the Father in the name of our Lord Jesus Christ."*

Marriage and family—Many of us do not appreciate enough the inspiration that we have received from our family members for all these years. If you are a teenager and your parents take you to your sports game or your school concert, appreciate the inspiration that they have given you. If they have helped you with your homework and inspired you because they knew that you could succeed, be sure to thank them. If you are a parent and your children have inspired you to do better or encouraged you in some manner, be sure that you let them know that you appreciate them for the inspiration.

Church—Your church should regularly take the time to let the members know how much their inspiration is appreciated. As members, we all inspire one another. As you attend church this week, be sure to thank your Sunday school teacher, your pastor, the music director, and others who keep you inspired week after week. Thank them for the inspiration. Make mental notes of things that occur at church that you can replicate throughout the week. Remember the smiles. Remember the handshakes. Remember the encouragement and pass that on to others this week.

Colossians 3:15, *"And let the peace of God rule in your hearts, to the which also ye are called in one body; and be ye thankful."*

Community—Maybe your church is working on the building program and the bank just approved your loan. You may want to have a few members write a short letter of appreciation to the banker, to the fire marshal, and to the other professionals in the community, letting them know how much you appreciate all the hard work that was involved. This will help to inspire the professionals so that when they have dealings with your church, they will be inspired to listen to the gospel.

Maybe your church has a softball team or other activity they do with other churches or community organizers. Let them know you appreciate the spirit and invite them to meet the Holy Spirit.

First Thessalonians 4:8, *"He therefore that despiseth, despiseth not man, but God, who hath also given unto us his holy Spirit."*

THIS PAGE HAS BEEN LEFT BLANK SO THAT YOU CAN MAKE NOTES ABOUT INSPIRATION

INTENT
THE ANTICIPATION OF INTENT

The word "intent" is a powerful word. When you intend to do something, you find your life's purpose! Why does God Almighty, the Creator of this great universe, have you on this earth at this time in history? What is the reason for your existence? God does not make mistakes! God has a reason for you being here and being geographically located where you are at this time!

Romans 8:28, *"And we know that all things work together for good to them that love God, to them who are the called according to his purpose."*

This is an amazing realization! God had a reason for creating this universe. He even decided when there should be a beginning.

Genesis 1:1, *"In the beginning God created the heaven and the earth."*

Then, God decided that you are to be born at a specific moment at a specific location to specific parents for a specific intent. Your purpose in life is to find out what God's purpose was and is for your life.

Ephesians 2:10, *"For we are his workmanship, created in Christ Jesus unto good works, which God hath before ordained that we should walk in them."*

Just before Jesus Christ left this earth, He told His disciples to teach all nations. You may find another purpose in life, such as an occupation or calling, but one purpose will always be to teach as Jesus Christ has commanded us.

Matthew 28:18–20:

And Jesus came and spake unto them, saying, All power is given unto me in heaven and in earth. Go ye therefore, and teach all nations, baptizing

them in the name of the Father, and of the Son, and of the Holy Ghost:
Teaching them to observe all things whatsoever I have commanded you:
and, lo, I am with you always, even unto the end of the world. Amen.

What is your vocation? Is that your purpose in life? Should you change your vocation to match your or God's intent? Where do you work? As you go to work this week, think to yourself, *Will this job help me to fulfill God's purpose for my life?* Will that change your intent and put you on a new path that the Lord has just shown to you? If you are married, maybe God has been speaking to your spouse and some great ideas. Be sure to seek His guidance.

Psalm 119:105, *"Thy word is a lamp unto my feet, and a light unto my path."*

Are you a student in high school? Are you a student in college? That is fantastic! The Lord has surrounded you with other students, which will help you become what the Lord has brought you into this world to become. The Lord has also surrounded you with other students who you may want to teach about the great God that you serve. Maybe a professor or a teacher needs an encouraging word, and you may just be in the right place at the right time to change their life by providing a smile and a word of encouragement. That is an awesome opportunity and an awesome responsibility!

Earlier in this book, you were asked to author or write down certain things. You may want to look at those lists and those notes before you go to bed today and pray about them and ask the Lord what His intent and purpose was and is for bringing you into this world and having you at your current geographic location surrounded by the people who cross your path on a daily basis.

Once you discover, through prayer, God's intent to have you on the earth at this moment, then you will have a new reason and a clear vision of your destination. We serve an omnipresent God. You cannot go anywhere that He is not present with you. God loves you. God is perfect love. That means God wants you to love mankind as Christ did while He was here on earth.

First John 4:8, *"He that loveth not knoweth not God; for God is love."*

As you anticipate and think about what the Lord has as a purpose for your life, it should be your intent to work toward that goal every moment of your life.

First John 1:7, *"But if we walk in the light, as he is in the light, we have fellowship one with another, and the blood of Jesus Christ his Son cleanseth us from all sin."*

As you read through this book, your intent will become clearer to you, and you will meet certain people who will help you to become what the Lord has intended for you.

How will this lesson help me?

Personal—When you find your intent and your purpose in life, your entire life may change as you read different books, speak to different people, and make new friends. You will find a mentor who will help you. You will study finances differently. You will take different courses in college or study different ideas about your occupation. You will also have more energy as you walk with God and with the purpose that He has given you. You will intentionally pray and walk with God, and He will walk with you in every step of life.

Marriage and family—This may be a good exercise to do with your family on a yearly basis (or more often). You may want to do this at the end of each school year, which will help each child prepare for sports or activities for the next year. This will also help each student to prepare for different classes in high school and prepare for college. Where do your children intend to go to college? Would your parents like to go to college?

Some families prefer to do such exercises during the holidays and call them a New Year's resolution. Every year, your life will change in some manner. If you are older, your lifestyle will still change in a different manner as your body ages. The Lord will give you the direction to go so that you can be a blessing to others until you meet Him in paradise.

Luke 23:43, *"And Jesus said unto him, Verily I say unto thee, Today shalt thou be with me in paradise."*

Church—Can you imagine if every person in your church, from young people to senior adults, knew what the Lord had for them? Some may become doctors and serve as part-time missionaries, changing lives worldwide. One young person may become an attorney (maybe you) and become a legal missionary to help churches nationwide. A few may become professors (maybe you). A few may start a new company that will benefit mankind worldwide. Whether you are young or old, ask a few people at church about their purpose.

Community—Maybe your occupation puts you in the community throughout the day. Maybe you are a teacher, and you know that is your purpose in life. As a teacher, you have the amazing responsibility to help guide your students to find out their purpose. You teach more than just subject matter because your students watch you. You may want to take a class period or part of a class period to help each student think about what they intend to do for their life. Here's why…

If a student has no purpose or can see no vision for their life, they may not be motivated to learn. However, if a student says, "I think flying airplanes would be fun and easy. I can do that without going to the college." As a teacher, you can agree with that student. That is true! It is fun! They do not have to go to college! However, now the student has a reason to learn math. They have a reason to study geography. They have a reason to understand social studies. They have a reason to study science and physics. They may even like school. You are an amazing teacher! You have amazing students!

You may be the student whose life is changed by reading this book! You may even want to start a book club. One of the reasons for writing this book was so that your book club or a class project could exchange great ideas. Whether you are in junior high school or a senior citizen, the world will be better as you work to fulfill your purpose.

Romans 8:28, *"And we know that all things work together for good to them that love God, to them who are the called according to his purpose."*

THE ACCEPTANCE OF INTENT

Now that you have anticipated your intent, do you accept the attitude that will be required to make your dream come true? This is an important question because your attitude toward what you intend while you are in school might be different if you are in college or building your business. Accomplishing your dream will be determined by your ability to successfully focus and pursue your destination.

Accepting your intent is one of the most important aspects of life. Why are we here on earth today? As each of us takes the time to pray and ask God why we are here, then we can determine what "success" looks like for each of us. Success is not about the acquisition of money. Success is determining what God wants you to be and completing that purpose.

Acts 26:16, *"But rise, and stand upon thy feet: for I have appeared unto thee for this purpose, to make thee a minister and a witness both of these things which thou hast seen, and of those things in the which I will appear unto thee."*

Accepting your intent with the right attitude internalizes it. This is very important! Acknowledging who you are in a beneficial way that will help mankind is important for your family, yourself, and those you surround yourself with. Your actions will determine the next generation and the generations to follow.

As you discover your purpose and intent, you will meet many people with the same purpose. However, you are an individual whom God loves, and it is your purpose to walk with Him through this life. Your coworkers or the students who sit in class with you may be studying to complete the same project. However, your family and your home life will be affected differently. The student sitting next to you or the person working beside you may be there because they have a relative working there and they see a purpose in their life. However, the other reasons could be true. That person may be there because of a blessing that they received, which now allows them to sit beside you. In either case, we are here to tell them how great our God is!

Ephesians 6:22, *"Whom I have sent unto you for the same purpose, that ye might know our affairs, and that he might comfort your hearts."*

In aviation, we have a motto that reads, "Your attitude will determine your altitude." The word "attitude" in aviation is determined by whether you are pointed up or pointed down. If your airplane is pointed in a higher direction with enough momentum, you will increase in altitude because you have a positive attitude. However, if you have a negative attitude and you are accelerating, you are likely to have an unfavorable end result as the ground rapidly approaches. As you move toward your purpose, accept that God is with you at all times.

Philippians 2:5, *"Let this mind be in you, which was also in Christ Jesus."*

Accept your intent. Accept your purpose. Keep the right attitude as you progress. If you are in college, each class will provide a different atmosphere, a different feeling, and a different environment. Each year will change your attitude. However, your purpose does not change. Keep your vision alive.

If you feel that the Lord is leading your life in a different direction and you need to change jobs, classes, friends, or churches, you are free to make that change, following the leading of the Lord. Your closest mentors might determine your success as these mentors become your friends and influence your life. Choose your friends accordingly. Use wisdom! Every person with whom you interact will have a different vision for their life. Each person is as individual as their purpose might be. Not all of your goals will align with all of your friends' goals.

You may have just one primary intent or purpose in your life. However, if your team, sports team, business team, or sales team has accepted a different intention, you may need to change teams. Nothing is more successful than a unified team that has accepted the same intention. Nothing might cause more frustration than being on the wrong team that has a different goal or intent to proceed.

If your intentions align with your team, then success may not be far away. Persistence is the key to success. Keep doing what you're doing. Keep the right attitude. The vision of your success is coming closer every day.

How will this lesson help me?

Personal—In the previous segment about intent, you were asked what you anticipate or what you think you believe God wants for you in this life. In this segment, you are asked to accept that as being what the Lord wants. Are you sure? If so, you are on your way to a great life!

First Corinthians 14:33, *"For God is not the author of confusion, but of peace, as in all churches of the saints."*

Marriage and family—This lesson will be very important for your family life, whether you are the parent or the child. If you are the parent and you accept your intentions after much discussion with your spouse and loved ones, you may be moving to a different location. This will affect your children and your grandchildren as they meet new people and date different people. They may be married in a different environment. Be sure that your intentions will help you to fulfill God's purpose in life.

If you are a teenager and your parents move or change churches, it may be because God will be leading you to speak to new people and be involved in different activities so that your life and the lives of your children will be affected. If your parents change churches or move to a different location, trust that God is in control.

Romans 8:28, *"And we know that all things work together for good to them that love God, to them who are the called according to his purpose."*

Church—This is an important lesson for the church as a whole and for each individual who attends your church. Accepting the intent that God has put on the hearts of your people can keep the church unified with the great spirit as you watch the children grow and as the saints go to heaven because you know that God can say, "Well done, My faithful servant." Your pastor is a visionary. By this I mean the pastor will help the church to have a vision for where they will be spiritually and financially in the months and years ahead. What is the purpose of your church? Why does it exist at this time in history and at this location?

Proverbs 29:18, *"Where there is no vision, the people perish: but he that keepeth the law, happy is he."*

Community—Can you imagine if every young person in your church understands their purpose and intent in life? They will be eager to learn from their teachers. They will do better in school. They will want to help others in school. They will grow up and be outstanding members of the community and your church! As adults, business leaders will be ethical because of what is taught in your church. A few of them may be politicians and become the mayor, the governor, or even the next president. This is all because you help them to see what God can do with their life. Just as King David did years ago, your young people may be recognized and asked to rule.

Second Samuel 5:3–4, *"So all the elders of Israel came to the king to Hebron; and king David made a league with them in Hebron before the LORD: and they anointed David king over Israel. David was thirty years old when he began to reign, and he reigned forty years."*

THE AUTHORING OF INTENT

In my first book, *Overqualified/Underqualified*, I wrote a supplement called "The Life Planning Session." Some of the questions that were asked in that exercise are the same as the questions that are being asked in this exercise. These questions were also asked earlier in this book under the topic "The Authoring of Desire"; however, in this exercise, you are being asked to think about the possible consequences of your answer. Write the answers to these questions:

Who am I? You know your name. Do you picture yourself as rich or poor? Are you close to God, or do you feel lost in this world? Who are your friends?

Luke 19:10, *"For the Son of man is come to seek and to save that which was lost."*

Proverbs 18:24, *"A man that hath friends must shew himself friendly: and there is a friend that sticketh closer than a brother."*

Where am I? You know your geographic location. Where are you in relation to your desired physical health? Are you staying fit? Where are you financially? Are your credit rating and bank account exactly what you want? Where are you spiritually? Do you walk with God and pray without ceasing? Where are you socially? Would it be wise to walk alone or in a different environment? Take some time right now and write your answers.

Why am I here? If you are a teenager living at home, there is a reason God has you at your current location. Learn to enjoy your surroundings. You are meeting certain people at this time of life so that God can direct you in the future.

As an adult, you have the opportunity to follow God's leading. If God has led you to your current location, then the answer to the question "Why am I here?" has already been answered. However, if you feel led by God to move, do not question His leading. You may think you are at a certain location because of your job, but God may have you there because He needs your children to meet certain people, or He needs your spouse to be involved in certain activities that will change the direction of future generations.

As you write your answers and understand your "why," this exercise may have you thinking about different aspects of your life. Do not try to rush this exercise. This may be life-changing.

Where am I going? This is always an important question that you can ask yourself on a regular basis. Where are you going in life? What does your future hold? How do you visualize your life in one year or five years? In what country will you live? Where will you retire?

Take some time and write some ideas as to what location (which community, city, state, or country) you might want to have a career or retirement. God can use you anywhere in this world. Think about the possibilities!

The most important answer is to know where you will spend eternity!

Why am I going there? If you can answer this question with a clear vision of the outcome, then you can create a great future because of your focus. You can plan your life like you would plan a cross-country trip. You know your destination, and you keep moving in that direction because the destination has benefits or rewards for you when you get there.

Write a couple of paragraphs or a few pages so that you know why you have chosen this as your life's destination. Keep this paper handy so that you can look at it periodically and pray for guidance from your Heavenly Father.

Another important question is, *"Who is going with me, or am I going alone?"* There are consequences to every action. How will others be affected by your decisions? Consider how this will impact your friends and relatives. Should you take them with you?

This segment will help you at any level of success that you have attained or that you will attain. Authoring or "writing down" your intent is so important that it will change your life. The act of writing your intent will help you to visualize. It can help you to remember your purpose with the right attitude as you keep your goal in mind.

Many of us have heard the expression "New Year's resolution." The reason for a New Year's resolution is that it is an aiming point or a starting point to restart your intent. However, it has been proven that New Year's resolutions do not often succeed. But *you* are different. If you have read this far in this book and have completed the previous "authoring" exercises, you have more than just motivation. You have the Holy Spirit, who is willing to walk with you every step of the way.

Every day starts a new year for you. You can create a new future starting today. Maybe today is your birthday, so start your future today. Write about your new future today! Maybe today is the first day of a new month. Instead of a "New Year's resolution," you are so successful and so focused that you can start your "new month's resolution." Start today!

Maybe you feel "lost" in this world. Maybe you need to find your purpose. Maybe you wish that you could simply start life all over again. I understand! I've been there, and so have many of the people you know. Jesus Christ had a conversation with a man named Nicodemus in the book of John chapter 3.

John 3:1–7:

There was a man of the Pharisees, named Nicodemus, a ruler of the Jews: The same came to Jesus by night, and said unto him, Rabbi, we know that thou art a teacher come from God: for no man can do these miracles that thou doest, except God be with him. Jesus answered and said unto him, Verily, verily, I say unto thee, Except a man be born again, he cannot see the kingdom of God. Nicodemus saith unto him, How can a man be born when he is old? can he enter the second time into his mother's womb, and be born? Jesus answered, Verily, verily, I say unto thee, Except a man be born of water and of the Spirit, he cannot enter into the kingdom of God. That which is born of the flesh is flesh; and that which is born of the Spirit is spirit. Marvel not that I said unto thee, Ye must be born again.

Don't be afraid of the phrase "born again." Jesus was simply explaining to Nicodemus the facts. You may want to read that passage again and think about your current situation. How's your spirit? Does your spirit dwell with the Holy Spirit? Do you need to be born again? In the same chapter (John 3), we are reminded…

That whosoever believeth in him should not perish, but have eternal life. For God so loved the world, that he gave his only begotten Son, that whosoever believeth in him should not perish, but have everlasting life. For God sent not his Son into the world to condemn the world; but that the world through him might be saved.

John 3:15–17

As you author your intent, I recommend having different short-term goals in life. Your purpose is that overall expectation of what you envision as the success that God has for you. Your goal will lead you to that intent. It will lead you a step closer to your success. That is why goals are important. Not that the goal is the ultimate finish line, but your goal will bring you closer to the finish line.

I enjoy running. I have spoken to many runners. Quite often the goal while you are running a 5K race isn't to finish the 5K race. It is to make it to the next telephone pole or to the next intersection. Every short-term goal will help you to get closer to your intended outcome.

As you author your intent, your intent and purpose will become clearer as you move forward. Keep every goal in mind. Pass every subject in school with the highest score possible.

Who does God want you to meet? Where does God want you to go? What do you want to accomplish? Remember:

Psalm 37:4, *"Delight thyself also in the LORD: and he shall give thee the desires of thine heart."*

Celebrate every goal! It is important that you celebrate along the way. As you accomplish each goal, you will ultimately be in the attitude of success throughout your life's journey, your career, your retirement, and your eternity.

How will this lesson help me?
Personal—By authoring your intent, you are writing up a promise to God. God is inspiring you with the words to write. God is also watching you write those words. He is also trusting you that you will keep your purpose in mind

throughout your life. He may give you extra work or extra projects to do while you are working on your purpose and intent. The notes that you write as you read this book have changed your life and will change the lives of others. Stay focused! Get a vision, focus, and succeed as the Holy Spirit leads you!

Marriage and family—If you are a parent, you have probably written the intentions of your family. You may not have sat down and created a journal, but you may have a job application or a bank statement. You may have paid a few bills and written a few letters showing your intentions for the future. You may have taken your family out to dinner and shown them how much you care. You may have helped your spouse or your children get a better education and advancement in life. Take some time and write down what you feel your Heavenly Father intends for your family.

If you are a teenager, you may want to get a vision of where you intend to go to college or what profession you feel God has placed before you, either in your hometown or somewhere else in your country or another country. Remember the last instructions that Jesus Christ gave before He departed the earth.

Matthew 28:19–20, *"Go ye therefore, and teach all nations, baptizing them in the name of the Father, and of the Son, and of the Holy Ghost: Teaching them to observe all things whatsoever I have commanded you: and, lo, I am with you always, even unto the end of the world. Amen."*

Church—This exercise may be so powerful for your church! As each person, including the pastoral staff, writes their purpose and their intent, they will view the church in a way that will be beneficial to the local community. The young people will see a purpose in their personal lives, and the Scriptures will mean so much more to them as they make decisions!

Community—The community is about to discover some great leaders because of your church through the help of God Almighty. Your people now have a vision. Your people now have a purpose that will help their local community, help their country, and help the world. Let's encourage one another as we together are servants of God. What are your intentions for your community while you are in your community before you leave your community?

Acts 2:1, *"And when the day of Pentecost was fully come, they were all with one accord in one place."*

THE ACTIVATION OF INTENT

Activating your intentions could be one of the most fulfilling activities of your life. Activating intentions is not a physical act. It is purely a change of your state of mind. Many philosophers will talk about the subconscious and the ability of the subconscious mind to change the activities and results of your waking hours. Activating your intent will change your spirit, and it can change your entire philosophy of life as the Holy Spirit guides you.

We spoke earlier in this book about activating your determination. Now we are talking about activating your intention. The difference between the two activities is that determination means you will not stop. Activating your intention means that you are moving forward with purpose. They are two different philosophies. Think of it this way. You are driving a race car at high speed. You are on the last lap of the race, and you are in second place. "Determination" means that your car cannot stop. Intent means that you are focused on the finish line and know you can and will win at the checkered flag. One says you cannot stop; the other says that you have a purpose and will keep going. The difference is the mentality and the energy that it takes to reach your destination.

Hebrews 12:1–2:

Wherefore seeing we also are compassed about with so great a cloud of witnesses, let us lay aside every weight, and the sin which doth so easily beset us, and let us run with patience the race that is set before us, Looking unto Jesus the author and finisher of our faith; who for the joy that was set before him endured the cross, despising the shame, and is set down at the right hand of the throne of God.

Activating your intentions should be fun. It should give you energy. It should give you enthusiasm. (We will talk about enthusiasm later in this book.) Activating your intentions and your purpose should give you a vision of where you are traveling. That is why it is important to activate your intentions with a full understanding of what will be around you when you get closer to that success.

Remember this guideline:

Ephesians 5:15, *"See then that ye walk circumspectly, not as fools, but as wise."*

That means that with every step you take, you must look around as you move forward. You need to keep walking toward your success, but as you do, you will want to be able to look around at the entire circumference. Look around and understand what is surrounding that next step before you take that next step. Please do not wait until after you have taken the step before you know what is around you. Know where you are placing your activity before you get there. With God by your side, you can go through "the fiery furnace" and not get burned. This could be the key to your success.

An "overnight success" does not happen overnight. When you succeed and receive your high school diploma, people will think you have succeeded. That did not happen overnight. When you reach any educational level and you get another certificate or another degree, that does not happen overnight. Money and success can flow through you and to you if that is what God has intended it to happen. Don't make the acquisition of money your end goal. Money is only a tool for future success.

Ecclesiastes 7:12, *"For wisdom is a defence, and money is a defence: but the excellency of knowledge is, that wisdom giveth life to them that have it."*

Matthew 16:26, *"For what is a man profited, if he shall gain the whole world, and lose his own soul? or what shall a man give in exchange for his soul?"*

According to Newton's third law, "To every action, there is an equal and opposite reaction." Your action will be that God has led you in the right direction. The reaction will be that your mindset and intentions will change, and sometimes your friends will change. If you have close friends whose goals are aligned with your goals, those friends will become closer friends. However, if your friends have different goals, that is okay! Your friends have a different purpose and intent. God has your life going for a special purpose that only you can travel.

Your friends will find friends whose goals align with their goals. That does not mean you cannot be friendly with those individuals. It is only that your closest friends will have goals that are most closely aligned with your current and future intentions. By activating your intentions as your friends activate their intentions, you'll be so closely in line that communication can exist without words being spoken.

First John 1:7, *"But if we walk in the light, as he is in the light, we have fellowship one with another, and the blood of Jesus Christ his Son cleanseth us from all sin."*

You probably have seen this happen in your own life. You've looked at somebody, and without saying a word, you have communicated either with a wink of the eye, a small gesture, or simply a look in the eyes. Communication and activating your intention can be a spiritual matter or an intuitive matter. This can be done without words or action. Sometimes, it's just a feeling or an energy level between the two individuals. By activating your intentions around others, you will form bonds of friendship that may last a lifetime.

How will this lesson help me?

Personal—Activating your intention will solidify your promise to God that you are resolved no longer to linger but to take action and move forward. It is like a new airplane ready to take off on a well-planned journey. You know where you're at. You know where you're going. You can draw a straight line to get there. God is your pilot. You hold the roadmap, but He already knows the directions and destination. Allow Him to take control, and you'll get to your destination as planned and on time.

Marriage and family—Activating your intention as a family may help you to create a family bond that will last for generations. You may create a business together that the sons and daughters will take over from the father and will give to the grandchildren. Many children (sons and daughters) will learn some type of lifestyle from their parents.

If you intend to become engaged to be married, this exercise may help to create a very loving bond of friendship and a vision for your future children and lifestyle. You may want to move to a new city, study together at college, or plan for similar occupations to benefit one another.

Church—A group from your church may read this book as a class project or even as a Bible study. Be prepared for a lot of activities. As each person realizes the destination that God has put before them, there will be a lot of activity and a lot of energy in a short amount of time. This can be an exciting time for you (whether you are young or old) as you and your friends fellowship and discuss great ideas.

Community—The activity that the people of your church start will impact the community at large. As your high school students communicate during class and in sports, the community will take notice of the focus and professionalism of your students. Likewise, businessmen will appreciate the diligence and professionalism of the people who work for them and with them.

Ecclesiastes 9:10, *"Whatsoever thy hand findeth to do, do it with thy might; for there is no work, nor device, nor knowledge, nor wisdom, in the grave, whither thou goest."*

Acts 4:28, *"For to do whatsoever thy hand and thy counsel determined before to be done."*

THE APPRECIATION OF INTENT

This could be the segment of this book that will bring the most joy to you throughout your life and throughout your retirement. This is where you sit back and say "thank you" to yourself. You thank yourself for the intentions that you had when you were younger. You have been a blessing to yourself. Your intentions have paid off by providing you a successful life.

You may still be in elementary school, and you can thank yourself that two years ago you started playing a musical instrument and you have been asked to play your instrument in the Christmas program at church. God is already using you! Appreciating your intentions as you look back at them at any age can bring you joy. With the right intentions of helping others and benefiting others as God has planned for your life, you can add friendships, opportunities, recognition, and awards throughout your life.

You may want to take a moment and remember some of the intentions that you had last month or last year that have brought you to a successful outcome. Appreciating and being thankful for your own intentions has brought you a certain amount of satisfaction. Your intentions have been helpful to others.

The following is just an example. It is not a recommendation…

I did not say that there will not be risks involved. When I decided to go skydiving for the first time, there was risk involved. Did I intend to go? Did I appreciate those intentions? Yes! Then, did I tell everybody that I knew that I was going to go skydiving? No! (Some people would have tried to talk me out of doing it!) However, that did not change my intent. Do I appreciate my past intention of skydiving? Absolutely! Maybe you are thanking God that He is impressing you to join the military. It may not be your intent to jump out of a perfectly good airplane, but the result will help you to become the military leader that He intends. Plus, you learn how to pray very quickly when you see the ground approaching you at such a high speed. Remember, if the parachute opens, it will be a great day. If the parachute does not open, plan to be in heaven in a few minutes. Then, it will be an even better day!

Again, this was just an example. It is not a recommendation...

(I love discussing the appreciation of intentions. It builds faith!)

Some things in your life will be the same way. You know that there are going to be risks. You know that some people will not agree with your decision. Appreciating your intentions, whether you are going to start a new business, going to start a new venture, going to start a new career, or going to start a healthy new relationship, is something to celebrate. Appreciate your past intentions because they are stepping stones toward your future intentions. Visualize those intentions with great expectations.

How will this lesson help me?

Personal—When you appreciate all that God has intended you to do and you look back, you will be so thankful for what He has brought you through. You may travel to certain places with the Lord by your side that you never expected to go, but He was there, and He needed you to be with Him so that you could record what He could do.

Marriage and family—As you look around at your beautiful family, you can appreciate all of the past activities that have brought you to your current status in life. Appreciate the fellowship and communication you have with your family. Help one another to succeed. If you are young, help your brothers and sisters to have a successful life. Encourage one another and appreciate one another.

If you are married, love your spouse and enjoy the home that you have created together. If you want a different lifestyle, appreciate the opportunity to communicate with your spouse and help one another to fulfill God's plan for your life.

Church—When you, as a church member or a church leader, look back at the past year, you will see that your members of all ages now have a clear goal and a clear intent of where the Lord wants them. You can look at the year ahead with great optimism, knowing that God is using your people inside the church and throughout the community. As you pray, you can be so thankful for how God used you to be a part of it all.

Community—Your community will be blessed as your people have worthy goals that will help the local community for many generations to come. You may want to work with your community schools and politicians to create intentions that will be beneficial. You will appreciate their appreciation for what you have accomplished. They may even build a bronze statue of you or name a community park in your honor and for your legacy.

Maybe you will decide to run for political office so that you can make decisions that the community will appreciate.

Proverbs 22:4, *"By humility and the fear of the LORD are riches, and honour, and life."*

THIS PAGE HAS BEEN LEFT BLANK SO THAT YOU CAN MAKE NOTES ABOUT INTENT

IMAGINATION
THE ANTICIPATION OF IMAGINATION

Imagination is one of the greatest tools that has been used throughout history to create the ultimate success stories. Every great philosopher and teacher has spoken about the idea of imagination or visualization. The art of imagination means that the individual will imagine or create an image (a vision) of what they would like to see happen in their life. Some of the most amazing verses in the Bible (in my opinion) are Genesis 1:1–2, which read:

"In the beginning God created the heaven and the earth. And the earth was without form, and void; and darkness was upon the face of the deep. And the Spirit of God moved upon the face of the waters."

Even when God Almighty, the Great Creator, took the time to create this world step by step, He could have just spoken it into perfection. Yet, He created it "without form." It was just particles, yet He had an image of what He wanted.

You have heard people say, "Can you imagine if…?" When you create an image in your mind of something that you want for the future and visualize that image, you begin to create an even larger vision. This little segment may be that portion that helps you become the success that you cannot yet imagine. Where can you see yourself in the future? Take some time and anticipate what you may want to imagine.

First Corinthians 2:9, *"But as it is written, Eye hath not seen, nor ear heard, neither have entered into the heart of man, the things which God hath prepared for them that love him."*

That is an amazing verse! When you compare the two phrases, "neither have entered into the heart of man" and "God hath prepared," it proves that mankind cannot even anticipate what God has already imagined. That is awesome!

First Corinthians 2:16, *"For who hath known the mind of the Lord, that he may instruct him? but we have the mind of Christ."*

The anticipation of imagination is an amazing thought. Earlier in this book, we talked about the anticipation of desire. Now, we are looking at the imagination and anticipating what you may wish you could imagine. This is a powerful tool. Think about this for a minute. What do you anticipate or think that you will want in the future to imagine for the future beyond that? Your life will be changed by the anticipation of visualizing or imagining what you will want in the future.

When you start anticipating what you might imagine, you may start to create a "vision wall" and post items of interest about which no person has ever thought. This is a vision of your future. Many business leaders will have images on their walls or on their desks of either family or success. It will reflect what they perceive their future will contain. Can you imagine the success that you will anticipate after you have already achieved success? Do you see how this can escalate? Every success that you can visualize is a stepping stone to your next success.

Anticipating what you will visualize after you succeed on your current journey will give you a larger visualization or scope of influence. For instance, maybe you like boats. So you visualize buying a thirty-foot houseboat. Then, because of the success that you have already visualized, you pay for that houseboat and decide to buy a larger boat. Later, because of your success, that boat gets paid off quickly, and you decide to buy a larger fishing boat. Soon, you buy a yacht. Can you anticipate your visualization of the yacht? Probably not yet. However, you can visualize the smaller thirty-foot boat. Once you achieve that and money starts rolling your way and success starts coming your way, then you can visualize how you can finance and make possible the larger vessel. Celebrate every small victory! It will not take long for you to have more influence because of your status.

Because of your anticipation of imagination, wealth should not be your end goal. Success is not necessarily measured in finances. It is measured in the many lives that have been affected. Some of the people who have affected the most lives are not the wealthiest of the world's population. If that were true, then every teacher would be very wealthy!

What can you imagine? What can you anticipate that you might want to imagine in the future? That is where this segment will lead you. Now is the time to visualize big, imagine big, and anticipate imagining bigger!

How will this lesson help me?

Personal—This segment will help you personally as you realize how powerful our God is. God is omniscient! God can do anything. God is omnipresent! He is everywhere. God loves you! With God as your Father, and He knows what you need before you ask Him, you will now start to ask and prepare for greater things in your life.

Matthew 6:8, *"Be not ye therefore like unto them: for your Father knoweth what things ye have need of, before ye ask him."*

Marriage and family—This would be a fun game to play some night with your family. Whether you are with your brothers and sisters, or you are a parent and you want to have a fun game with your children. Anticipate what you can imagine if you all work together as a family and create something together that would be beneficial for your life and for generations to come. You could create such a bond that it could strengthen your family relationship. Make this a fun event! Maybe do this a couple of times a year. Challenge each person's imagination and then try to figure out some method to make that image a reality.

Mark 10:27, *"And Jesus looking upon them saith, With men it is impossible, but not with God: for with God all things are possible."*

Church—As a church, when you get ready for your next building program, large event, or community activity, have your friends, your members, and your staff imagine that you already have everything that you have been praying for. Next, anticipate what you can imagine God will do for you in the future. That is the essence of faith.

Hebrews 11:1, *"Now faith is the substance of things hoped for, the evidence of things not seen."*

Community—Maybe you have been praying for something to happen in your community and you do not even think of it as possible. If someone were to call you tomorrow and say that they believe that you have been given the ability to complete that task and they will bring whatever funding is necessary to allow you to do that, are you prepared to step out in faith and make that happen? By using the anticipation of your imagination, what would you do after you complete that project? What would be your next goal or vision that you feel God would want you to accomplish? Imagine having that much faith in what you could do to change your community!

Hebrews 11:6, *"But without faith it is impossible to please him: for he that cometh to God must believe that he is, and that he is a rewarder of them that diligently seek him."*

THE ACCEPTANCE OF IMAGINATION

This segment of this book is written so that you might increase your faith. It will also increase the faith of those people who surround you. Think about this amazing truth: Jesus Christ said four times, "O ye of little faith" while He was talking with His disciples and followers.

Remember this example found in the book of Mark.

Mark 9:19–29:

He answereth him, and saith, O faithless generation, how long shall I be with you? how long shall I suffer you? bring him unto me. And they brought him unto him: and when he saw him, straightway the spirit tare him; and he fell on the ground, and wallowed foaming. And he asked his father, How long is it ago since this came unto him? And he said, Of a child. And ofttimes it hath cast him into the fire, and into the waters, to destroy him: but if thou canst do any thing, have compassion on us, and help us. Jesus said unto him, If thou canst believe, all things are possible to him that believeth. And straightway the father of the child cried out, and said with tears, Lord, I believe; help thou mine unbelief. When Jesus saw that the people came running together, he rebuked the foul spirit, saying unto him, Thou dumb and deaf spirit, I charge thee, come out of him, and enter no more into him. And the spirit cried, and rent him sore, and came out of him: and he was as one dead; insomuch that many said, He is dead. But Jesus took him by the hand, and lifted him up; and he arose. And when he was come into the house, his disciples asked him privately, Why could not we cast him out? And he said unto them, This kind can come forth by nothing, but by prayer and fasting.

This family could not even anticipate imagining that their child would be healed! Reread the verse "*Jesus said unto him, If thou canst believe, all things are possible to him that believeth.*" Then, through faith, allow yourself to accept this as your imagination:

John 14:12, "*Verily, verily, I say unto you, He that believeth on me, the works that I do shall he do also; and greater works than these shall he do; because I go unto my Father.*"

We, as believers, may be able to change this world with that one phrase, "*Lord, I believe; help thou mine unbelief.*" Can you imagine that feeling of awe that surrounded that place for the weeks and years that followed? Can you imagine what could happen in your life? What would happen if your church had such faith? What would happen in your community as a result of such faith?

You have a great imagination. Children often have a great imagination. If your child (or a child you know) can imagine something magnificent and you accept that imagination with faith, then it can become a reality.

Matthew 18:3, "*And said, Verily I say unto you, Except ye be converted, and become as little children, ye shall not enter into the kingdom of heaven.*"

Matthew 19:14, "*But Jesus said, Suffer little children, and forbid them not, to come unto me: for of such is the kingdom of heaven.*"

In fact, your imagination is more powerful than you can imagine. Are you in a similar situation as the apostles?

Luke 17:5, "*And the apostles said unto the Lord, Increase our faith.*"

I am sure when you were a child, your parents or somebody you know said you had an amazing imagination. You were just imagining things that could happen. Some people dream about what could happen. Amazing things can happen in the mind if you take the time to imagine what could happen.

Acts 16:5, "*And so were the churches established in the faith, and increased in number daily.*"

You may want to take a day, an entire week, or even longer just to start imagining the possibilities that could happen in your life. Then, accept that those ideas came through faith from your imagination. This is the real inner you.

These thoughts were given to you by your Heavenly Father. This came from inside of you. If what you thought about is beneficial to mankind and will help you succeed in the direction that you can imagine, accept that these ideas came from your imagination through faith. You may get ideas from other people's imagination. This is called brainstorming or masterminding.

Proverbs 13:20, *"He that walketh with wise men shall be wise: but a companion of fools shall be destroyed."*

As you brainstorm and mastermind with others who are using their imagination to enhance your imagination, then you have a foundation of great imaginations working together. (That is a lot of imagination!) Less than two hundred years ago, people imagined that they could fly like birds. They were ridiculed. They were laughed at. They were talked about. Yet they let their imagination work and tried different activities, which brought us to the current state of aviation today.

Your faith may lead you to ideas that other people will laugh at. But it is up to you to accept your faith, knowing that it is the power inside of you to manifest greatness.

As you accept your imagination, be sure that it is going to be beneficial to you, honest, and helpful to mankind so that your reputation and your integrity stay intact. Your imagination is a small example of the faith that God has given you. Surround yourself with others who have great faith, great integrity, and perseverance or success.

Galatians 6:9, *"And let us not be weary in well doing: for in due season we shall reap, if we faint not."*

How will this lesson help me?
Personal—If we as believers increase our faith, then Jesus could say "well done" to us also. Let us strive to make this our testimony!

Matthew 17:20, *"And Jesus said unto them, Because of your unbelief: for verily I say unto you, If ye have faith as a grain of mustard seed, ye shall say unto this mountain, Remove hence to yonder place; and it shall remove; and nothing shall be impossible unto you."*

Marriage and family—In our previous lesson, you were asked to create a game of anticipating your imagination with your family. You may want to expand on that game, exchange ideas with each participant in the family, and ask which of those ideas and images they are willing to accept as reality. Allow each person to visualize the outcome of their imagination by using their faith in God and the creativity that God has given them to make their faith a reality. You may want to do this game once a month every month while the children are growing up. You may want to do this every month with your spouse. God is a loving Father and wants to use you and your family for His kingdom. Enjoy His fellowship!

John 14:13, *"And whatsoever ye shall ask in my name, that will I do, that the Father may be glorified in the Son."*

Church—Can you imagine the power that could be produced by accepting our imagination, through faith, in what God can do with your church in the near future and in years to come by exercising that faith? Don't limit God in your personal life or the life of your church.

Acts 2:1, *"And when the day of Pentecost was fully come, they were all with one accord in one place."*

Community—If we, as believers, have the faith of which Jesus spoke, the world will change. We cannot even imagine what God could do if we fully trusted and asked Him through faith and believed Him for the results!

First Corinthians 2:9, *"But as it is written, Eye hath not seen, nor ear heard, neither have entered into the heart of man, the things which God hath prepared for them that love him."*

Matthew 21:22, *"And all things, whatsoever ye shall ask in prayer, believing, ye shall receive."*

THE AUTHORING OF IMAGINATION

The authoring of imagination, as you sit alone and think about it, may be very eye-opening to you. Have you ever sat and really imagined what you could do and then "authored" it and written it down? If you did this while you were in school, your teacher may have looked at it and accused you of daydreaming, but you believed that it could happen. As you look at what you had imagined, it may amaze you how great of a mind you have. You have a brilliant mind! You can imagine so much if you take the time to sit and think about it. You can author your imagination, but remember that Jesus is the author and finisher of our faith.

Hebrews 12:2, *"Looking unto Jesus the author and finisher of our faith; who for the joy that was set before him endured the cross, despising the shame, and is set down at the right hand of the throne of God."*

You may want to go to the library and look at book titles. If you have the time, you may leap through books or magazine articles. Doing an Internet search is beneficial, but looking at different categories of books and the different titles of each book will bring a different image into your mind. The image is what is important here. As you author or script your imagination, different words will mean different things. Use these images and ask Jesus to be the "author and finisher" of each.

Each person will use different words, which will create a different image in your mind, thus creating a greater imagination and different ideas that may be beneficial to you. Write down what you imagine. Before you go to bed at night, read what you have written. Take the time before you go to sleep to imagine more of what you have already imagined. Author it, create it, make it real in your life. Allow Jesus to finish the task with you.

You may want to set aside what you've written in this book and in this chapter. Look at it in a few days. It will bring back a different meaning a few weeks from now than it does as you write it down now. Writing down the different things that you imagine is what creates inventors, authors, composers, and technical industries. You can do this!

How will this lesson help me?

Personal—If you author what you imagine and you allow Jesus Christ to be the author and finisher of that faith, what is stopping you from changing the world starting today? Ponder that question this week. Write that question down and ask yourself what you and God can do together. Think about these words from Jesus Christ:

John 14:12, *"Verily, verily, I say unto you, He that believeth on me, the works that I do shall he do also; and greater works than these shall he do; because I go unto my Father."*

Marriage and family—This could be such a fun family project that while you are writing this down, you may create a brand-new game that will go worldwide and help create wonderful families and wonderful churches around the world as everybody starts imagining possibilities. Members of your family will go to school or to work and share these ideas with other like-minded families who may have time or money to make these dreams a reality. Your family may start new industries and help other families to have a closer relationship with your church.

Jeremiah 32:27, *"Behold, I am the LORD, the God of all flesh: is there any thing too hard for me?"*

Church—When each person who attends your church has the faith to move a mountain, can you imagine the energy that the Holy Spirit could have in the lives of the people of your church? You may want to do this as an exercise. Have your people write down the greatest accomplishments that they can imagine, then ask Jesus to be the author and finisher of the faith that will make this vision a reality.

Matthew 21:22, *"And all things, whatsoever ye shall ask in prayer, believing, ye shall receive."*

Community—As your community sees you as an individual walking in faith, they will see that you are getting your prayers answered. Therefore, if they see you in a hospital and they need prayer, they will probably approach you and ask you to pray for their loved one. That is amazing! Just as others would seek out Jesus, your community may seek you out because of the close relationship that you have with Jesus Christ. This may be beyond your imagination, but nothing too hard for the Lord!

Try this! Imagine different ideas that will help your community to be safer. Write down the different ideas that you can imagine. Next, imagine ways to make this a reality. Have faith that you can be a part of the solution. Then, take whatever action is needed to make it real!

James 2:26, *"For as the body without the spirit is dead, so faith without works is dead also."*

THE ACTIVATION OF IMAGINATION

The activation of imagination is one of the most interesting concepts in the world. That is the step just before activating your faith. Once you activate your faith and God starts working in your personal life and in the lives of those that surround you, you simply cannot imagine what will occur.

Ephesians 3:20, *"Now unto him that is able to do exceeding abundantly above all that we ask or think, according to the power that worketh in us."*

I love to listen to little children who have a vision and a vivid imagination. Just the activation of imagination brings so many pictures to the world. Imagination comes in so many different forms. Each of us is either primarily visual, auditory, or kinesthetic. Those of us who are visual appreciate art or pictures. We love to imagine what could be, and we appreciate those who have activated their imagination and can put that into different forms so that we can visualize.

Second Corinthians 5:7, *"For we walk by faith, not by sight."*

What will it take for you to activate your imagination and see the greatness that is inside of you? Can you imagine being the mayor of your city? Picture yourself as being a foreign minister to the president of the United States or another country. Sometimes, when I am speaking about leadership, I say to the audience, "If you were the homecoming queen last year, you could be the mayor of your city the next year. If you understand how to win an election, then winning can be a repetitive action." If you can visualize yourself winning an election, these two events have many commonalities. You may want to look around this week and see how many people would vote for you. In many areas of the country, you are permitted to be the mayor of your city or even a state representative at the age of eighteen. Many churches could use you as their assistant pastor or other staff member at the age of eighteen. I have referred to this verse before, but it is worth repeating,

First Timothy 4:12, *"Let no man despise thy youth; but be thou an example of the believers, in word, in conversation, in charity, in spirit, in faith, in purity."*

As you activate your imagination, use all of your senses. What do you see yourself becoming? What smells will you smell? Can you imagine hearing somebody tell you that you have just won the race? Maybe that race is a political race. Maybe that race is a half-marathon. Maybe that race is a triathlon. Maybe that race for you is the Indianapolis 500. Races require endurance. As you activate your imagination, you can see yourself winning the race, whatever that race may be! You have success inside of you. Activate your imagination! Win the race! Move that mountain! Remember these words…

Matthew 17:20, *"And Jesus said unto them, Because of your unbelief: for verily I say unto you, If ye have faith as a grain of mustard seed, ye shall say unto this mountain, Remove hence to yonder place; and it shall remove; and nothing shall be impossible unto you."*

How will this lesson help me?

Personal—If you and I activate our imagination and we walk with God and He can do more than we ask or think, then we can take this verse to its full meaning and use it daily to create miracles. Can you imagine having the faith to raise the dead or move mountains?

Matthew 11:4–5, *"Jesus answered and said unto them, Go and shew John again those things which ye do hear and see: The blind receive their sight, and the lame walk, the lepers are cleansed, and the deaf hear, the dead are raised up, and the poor have the gospel preached to them."*

John 14:12, *"Verily, verily, I say unto you, He that believeth on me, the works that I do shall he do also; and greater works than these shall he do; because I go unto my Father."*

Marriage and family—In this series of lessons on imagination, it has been recommended that you create this as a game or exercise for your family. You may want to use this verse, 1 Corinthians 2:9, each time you play this game and practice this exercise with your spouse and children. The words *"neither have entered into the heart of man"* are so powerful that miracles may occur.

First Corinthians 2:9, *"But as it is written, Eye hath not seen, nor ear heard, neither have entered into the heart of man, the things which God hath prepared for them that love him."*

Church—Think of the awesome prayers and brainstorming that could occur with your board of directors, your deacons, and the departments or committees of your church if they can imagine the greatness that lies within your congregation while each individual walks with God. If each person has the mind of Christ and each person brings one idea that will build the church, nothing is impossible! Action will be required! You have a great church. The world is looking forward to seeing what you can accomplish!

James 2:20, *"But wilt thou know, O vain man, that faith without works is dead?"*

Community—As you activate your imagination in the community, great things will happen! God's love is so powerful as it works within you. You will be able to build churches. You may build a new rescue mission. Where more people who follow the teachings of Jesus Christ, there will be fewer homeless and hungry in the community.

Luke 18:22, *"Now when Jesus heard these things, he said unto him, Yet lackest thou one thing: sell all that thou hast, and distribute unto the poor, and thou shalt have treasure in heaven: and come, follow me."*

Where there are more people who follow the teachings of Jesus Christ, there will be less destruction and violence.

Ephesians 6:12, *"For we wrestle not against flesh and blood, but against principalities, against powers, against the rulers of the darkness of this world, against spiritual wickedness in high places."*

Romans 13:10, *"Love worketh no ill to his neighbour: therefore love is the fulfilling of the law."*

THE APPRECIATION OF IMAGINATION

Imagination and visualization are somewhat synonymous, as they each benefit from a mental "vision" or "image." When you imagine something, you create an image in your mind; therefore, imagination is so powerful because you can see the future. Many people want to know what their future looks like. It is easy to get a picture of your future by looking at your imagination.

Now that you have worked with your imagination during these last few pages, can you appreciate how your faith has been strengthened and how you are more resolved to complete your project and your ministry successfully?

That is why you will appreciate your imagination as you reflect on your success. Remember it is your imagination. It is your visualization. It is your faith! I have interviewed many students and many college professors who have watched people succeed because that person could see themselves receiving a diploma or a certificate.

Appreciating your imagination will always come from two different viewpoints within yourself. The initial image now of looking forward to the success that you will have in creating that image. You will appreciate in yourself the reality that you can see that future. You can see what you are going to accomplish. You will keep that image in front of you during good times and times of struggle and difficulty. The appreciation of your imagination is also important as you look back on the small successes that created a large success to get you to where each step of your success will lead you.

Appreciation is so important in your life. Being able to say to yourself and to others "thank you" is vitally important. Every successful mentor will always tell you to be thankful. As you go through this life and you go through the different phases of your success, you will want to be thankful for each thing that has occurred.

Take some time right now and be thankful for the images that have brought you to a point where you were led to take action. Be thankful that you could visualize the activities that brought you this far in life. Also, be thankful that you can visualize your desires. As you are thankful, you can then build on that and appreciate that you can visualize the future to be even more successful.

Thankfulness is also known as appreciation. Imagination is sometimes known as visualization. These are the keys to moving forward. As we move on to the next lessons, keep your imagination open and be thankful for every healthy and helpful image that you create in your mind. Appreciate your faith!

First Corinthians 15:57, *"But thanks be to God, which giveth us the victory through our Lord Jesus Christ."*

How will this lesson help me?

Personal—As you read through this segment, you were given visions and images of what is possible in your life. Be thankful that your faith has brought you to the realization that you and God can change the world! Having that knowledge is so powerful. It is a new way to live life. It is actually who you are through Jesus Christ and the power of God Almighty that will help you as you move forward through life.

Mark 9:23, *"Jesus said unto him, If thou canst believe, all things are possible to him that believeth."*

Marriage and family—As you played the imagination game with your family and taught it to your children, could you appreciate the ideas they were able to visualize? Do you understand that your children may be able to change the world in a mighty way because you have taught them how powerful their Heavenly Father is? As you and your spouse pray together about your children and your marriage, realize that anything you imagine is possible.

Mark 10:27, *"And Jesus looking upon them saith, With men it is impossible, but not with God: for with God all things are possible."*

Take time to appreciate your imagination and work together to build a great family!

Church—If your church has studied this book in a class or in a book club format and you are reading it simultaneously, each of you may have been affected by the faith of others. Having faith and praying together at the same time will create miracles. Jesus Christ said in Matthew…

Matthew 18:19–20, *"Again I say unto you, That if two of you shall agree on earth as touching any thing that they shall ask, it shall be done for them of my Father which is in heaven. For where two or three are gathered together in my name, there am I in the midst of them."*

Community—Your community will be thankful for your faith as they will see lives changed. Crimes may be diminished. The streets may be safer. The power of prayer will influence your neighbors. People will be praying for one another. You will walk before the city leaders because you are diligent in your business.

Proverbs 22:29, *"Seest thou a man diligent in his business? he shall stand before kings; he shall not stand before mean men."*

Mark 9:23, *"Jesus said unto him, If thou canst believe, all things are possible to him that believeth."*

THIS PAGE HAS BEEN LEFT BLANK SO THAT YOU CAN MAKE NOTES ABOUT IMAGINATION

INTEGRITY (YOUR BONUS "I")

Integrity is more than just being honest and having strong moral principles. In the real estate industry, a building might be referred to as having "structural integrity." This means that it will stand the test of time. The building will stay intact when the winds blow. As the storms come, every person inside the building will stay safe. Jesus Christ gave this visual lesson as He taught what some people refer to as the "Sermon on the Mount" in Matthew chapters 5 through 7. During that lesson, He taught the "Beatitudes," the "Lord's Prayer," and other lessons. Yet, He summed it all up with a visual illustration of structural integrity, which is still effective today as He spoke in Matthew 7.

Matthew 7:24–27:

Therefore whosoever heareth these sayings of mine, and doeth them, I will liken him unto a wise man, which built his house upon a rock: And the rain descended, and the floods came, and the winds blew, and beat upon that house; and it fell not: for it was founded upon a rock. And every one that heareth these sayings of mine, and doeth them not, shall be likened unto a foolish man, which built his house upon the sand: And the rain descended, and the floods came, and the winds blew, and beat upon that house; and it fell: and great was the fall of it.

Notice the next few verses of that chapter (28–29) and understand the reaction of those who listened to Him speak.

"And it came to pass, when Jesus had ended these sayings, the people were astonished at his doctrine: For he taught them as one having authority, and not as the scribes."

Earlier in this book, we discussed your desires and your intent. Is that truly who you are? Are the thoughts that you have written truly your desire? Is that really your intent? Are you trying to be popular and "fit it," or are you "going with the flow"? Are you making those decisions because you do not want to be "left out"? Some people have referred to this as "FOMO" or "fear of missing out." Is that you? Are you surrendering to preach because your friend is surrendering to the mission field? Are you getting married because your friend is getting married? Are you saying that you are going on a diet because your friend is going on a diet? (Eating ice cream in secret may still cause an increase in weight.)

Integrity as we are using it today is to have "structural integrity" within yourself, your family, your marriage, and your church. This same integrity will flow into your community. How sincere are you and how true are you to the vision you have created and the words you have "authored" in previous chapters of this book? Be truthful to yourself right now. Your personal integrity now will determine your personal future.

As you read this book, nobody is challenging your vision! There are some ideas that you may not want to tell anybody for fear of discouragement or ridicule. Be true to yourself! If you believe that you can graduate from high school, then you can and will graduate from high school. If you believe that you can graduate from college, then you can graduate from college. It may take more perseverance for you to succeed than it does for others. That's fine. That is not a problem! Integrity is being true to your calling and your visualization to make your dream come true. Perseverance will keep you moving toward your destination.

I spent much of my career in banking and financial institutions. Each institution has integrity standards that must be followed. As you select which church ministry you build or which industry you build, visualize your success! Just as a bank has financial assets, you can use your integrity to build spiritual wealth and a bright future.

Think about which school you will attend to fulfill your dreams. As integrity relates to a school, it is important for every student to understand the school handbook on the first day of school. If your school is post-secondary (after high school), be sure to read the school handbook and policy procedure. You will be asked to sign the handbook agreeing to abide by all the rules and regulations of the school. When you sign the handbook, you agree to abide by those rules and regulations. The school is also agreeing to abide by the measures for the penalties that you have agreed to if you do not follow those procedures. Integrity works both ways. If you fail to keep the standards, they must take action.

As you look back on the integrity of your workplace or school, you will be able to appreciate that integrity as it brings you closer to success. Teach this lesson to your children as they are growing up. Each educational institution and company has rules, just like your home has rules.

Looking forward to the integrity of an institution allows you to realize the atmosphere and the environment that you are about to enter. It will help you to understand how you can adjust your "work-life balance." Some work environments and school environments require you to be at a certain location at a certain time for a certain amount of time. Other employment and other schools will allow you to adjust your time and schedule to meet your work-life balance. As you look forward to your career and your success, it is important that you "look at the big picture" of your life.

Perhaps you want to be a pastor. This means that you have a certain amount of freedom, but you also have some authority. However, in some situations (such as legal and financial) you may answer to a board of trustees or deacons. This also means that you may be called in the middle of the night when a loved member or friend is dying.

Matthew 23:11–12, "*But he that is greatest among you shall be your servant. And whosoever shall exalt himself shall be abased; and he that shall humble himself shall be exalted.*"

Success is not just in money or a title. However, your happiness, your health, and your outside activities, such as church or family time, are important to make your success worthwhile. Over the last few years, I have interviewed a number of people who were of retirement age. Some had attained great wealth but seemed unhappy and desired more. Others had not attained as much wealth or as high of education, but they look back on life as a success because they made a difference in the lives of others. Many grade school and high school teachers are in this position. They may have raised successful children and are now financially sound, but they never became wealthy. Remember this story…

Ecclesiastes 9:15–16, *"Now there was found in it a poor wise man, and he by his wisdom delivered the city; yet no man remembered that same poor man. Then said I, Wisdom is better than strength: nevertheless the poor man's wisdom is despised, and his words are not heard."*

In this example, the "poor wise man" had such integrity that he was able to deliver the city. Is that your situation today? Maybe you have not become as wealthy as others. However, you have the integrity within you to deliver the city! Perhaps you could find a way to deliver your city from homelessness, hunger, or poverty. Is that your calling?

How will this lesson help me?

Personal—Since we are all human, it is not uncommon for each of us to violate our own integrity. Maybe you have made a New Year's resolution and have failed to keep it. Maybe you have tried to diet and failed to lose the amount of weight expected.

Maybe you have planned to go to Bible college or seminary or start a ministry. Have you started it? Have you applied to the Bible college or seminary? Have you visited or written to the institution? Your actions in public and in private will determine your personal integrity. Nobody is faulting you if you fail. Do not be upset with yourself! You are still loved by Almighty God and by many people! You are still alive, and you have the ability to complete the project. Be true to yourself, take action, and fulfill your dreams as God had planned.

Philippians 3:13–14, *"Brethren, I count not myself to have apprehended: but this one thing I do, forgetting those things which are behind, and reaching forth unto those things which are before, I press toward the mark for the prize of the high calling of God in Christ Jesus."*

Marriage and family—Just a quick note here about integrity. Before you and your future spouse take your wedding vows, you must decide if you mean it when you say, "As long as you both shall live." Remember that before the minister says those words, the minister will ask, "Do you promise…'through sickness and in health' (even through cancer) and 'through poverty and in wealth' (even through bankruptcy)?" Integrity in the wedding vows will have a significant effect on your personal life, the lives of your loved ones, and your church.

Numbers 30:2, *"If a man vow a vow unto the LORD, or swear an oath to bind his soul with a bond; he shall not break his word, he shall do according to all that proceedeth out of his mouth."*

Church—When your church is founded upon a solid foundation of teaching and ministering, it is as if it were founded upon a solid cornerstone.

Matthew 21:42, *"Jesus saith unto them, Did ye never read in the scriptures, The stone which the builders rejected, the same is become the head of the corner: this is the Lord's doing, and it is marvellous in our eyes?"*

Community—Integrity in a community is vital! If you are a teenager, you are already getting an idea about who is honest in your life. If you are a small business owner, you are getting a reputation. Be sure you are hearing good words about your business. As you build your integrity in your community, remember these words…

Job 32:9, *"Great men are not always wise: neither do the aged understand judgment."*

Proverbs 22:29, *"Seest thou a man diligent in his business? he shall stand before kings; he shall not stand before mean men."*

THIS PAGE HAS BEEN LEFT BLANK SO THAT YOU CAN MAKE NOTES ABOUT INTEGRITY

MOTIVATION
THE ANTICIPATION OF MOTIVATION

Anticipating motivation is exciting. We live our lives around it. Every morning as you wake up, before you move, your mind anticipates and prepares for that first movement. If you are a new parent, you anticipate watching your baby take their first step. Perhaps you or a loved one has recently had surgery. Anticipating the first steps after a major accident is a life-changing incident. You look forward to it. You pray for it. You encourage and help the medical staff in every way possible to help you or your loved one to have a successful outcome every day.

Everybody loves the anticipation of motivation. If you are in sports of any kind, you anticipate motivated athletes preparing to create movement as they compete in the competition. How many of us gather around the TV set to watch the beginning of a football game, a basketball game, or an automobile race with great anticipation? Even a parade with all of the activities is an exciting time as we watch the movement occur.

Perhaps the movement is not physical but mental and psychological. Every day, millions of viewers watch a game show on television. They anticipate and are excited about the beginning of the competition. This is what your life is about to become. You can decide if your life will resemble a game show or a sporting event. As you get excited about your life and your future knowing that you're already a winner because Jesus Christ walks with you, keep these two verses in front of you at all times. This can be a powerful beginning to your new life as you prepare for the actions that are about to occur.

Hebrews 13:5, *"Let your conversation be without covetousness; and be content with such things as ye have: for he hath said, I will never leave thee, nor forsake thee."*

Romans 8:28, *"And we know that all things work together for good to them that love God, to them who are the called according to his purpose."*

Motivation creates movement. Do you like movement? Do you like to go on long walks with a friend or someone special? Do you love to ride horses? Do you ride motorcycles? Do you fly airplanes? Do you run 5K races? Motivation will prove your intention because the world can see where you will go next. If you are moving, you must look ahead and know where you are going. You will need to know what surroundings will be there when you get to your next location. Many of us who run races or run for pleasure understand that we always look ahead. We look at the road up in front of us to make sure we won't fall. We also look down the road where we will be running to make sure we can make it to that distance. When you drive a car, you do the same thing. You look far enough in the distance so you are aware of what will be surrounding you. When you fly an airplane, you might hear the term "keep your head on a swivel" because you will always have to know what is higher than you, what is below you, what is on your left, and what is on your right. In any vehicle, you will also need to know what is happening inside so that you do not get distracted. If you miss one of those elements, a tragedy could occur. How many of us have heard warnings about "distracted drivers"? That is why this verse is so powerful because you need to know what is surrounding you (and what will be surrounding you) at all times.

Ephesians 5:15, *"See then that ye walk circumspectly, not as fools, but as wise."*

As you anticipate your motivation and look forward to your future, this could be a very important factor in how quickly and completely you succeed in every area of life. It is easy to become a distracted driver. It is also easy to become distracted in life. That is where many of us delay our success. We do not stop moving forward, but we slow down in the "traffic jam of life." Is that where you are today? The key word to reaching your goal more quickly is "focus."

You are about to become engaged in a new venture, a new game, or a new race that you can call "My Motivated Life." This is going to be exciting. Fasten your seatbelt, adjust your mirrors, prepare to start your engine, and tune your radio to the "success" channel. Be sure you have enough fuel for you and everyone you want to take with you. Have your maps prepared. You may even want to have a snack available because this could be a long journey. Are you ready? Let's start!

How will this lesson help me?

Personal—As you anticipate being motivated about your future, your adrenaline will start to secrete. Your muscles will start to flex. Your mind will start to produce new thoughts and create new ideas about different areas of your life in the world that surrounds you. You may begin to have more energy as you wake up in the morning. You may begin to smile more and have a more positive attitude as you take this new journey, whether you are alone or with your family and friends. Be prepared. Stay excited. Enjoy the journey!

Marriage and family—If you are preparing for marriage, there will be a lot of motivation as you adjust to your new life. Anticipate the fact that there will be many changes that will need to be worked out together. If you are a growing family and have children, you already understand part of the motivation. Every year your life changes. Look forward to the next year and make plans with your spouse, your children, and your loved ones. Plan ahead with excitement. You have made a lot of notes while reading this book. Review your notes in the same manner as you would review your checklist for a long vacation. Be sure everybody is ready. Be sure you pray together before you start the engine!

Church—This is going to be an exciting time for your church as you anticipate the next season of your church. You can use this excitement to increase attendance, create a new ministry, or help your community in some mighty way. It is going to take energy and motivation from your young people, your families, and your senior citizens. You will need to work with church leadership, church staff, and different members as you move forward. Be sure to pray with each group and show them how the Lord can use them as you move forward!

Community—If you work in your community in any part of your life, you can get excited about the anticipation of motivation. If you are involved in the schools, there is always activity and motivation. Keeping the right motivation is one of the hardest jobs in the world, yet it can be the most rewarding as you watch young people create their lives. It is important for each of us to be active in the community as we teach the lessons from the life of Jesus Christ!

Matthew 28:18–20:

And Jesus came and spake unto them, saying, All power is given unto me in heaven and in earth. Go ye therefore, and teach all nations, baptizing them in the name of the Father, and of the Son, and of the Holy Ghost: Teaching them to observe all things whatsoever I have commanded you: and, lo, I am with you always, even unto the end of the world. Amen.

THE ACCEPTANCE OF MOTIVATION

This is really an interesting topic. Think about this for a minute. Internally, when you are ready to accept the amount of motivation that is going to take for you to complete a project, just the mental act of accepting that amount of motivation might be half of your battle. By accepting the motivation that it is going to take for you to complete the project successfully, you have determined in your own mind how much energy, time, and money it will take for you to see your vision come true. Accepting this fact will enable you to move forward on a daily basis until you reach your goal.

Remember in Matthew 28:18–20 when Jesus Christ spoke?

Focus on the words, *"All power is given unto me in heaven and in earth. Go ye therefore... and, lo, I am with you always."*

In reality, the words of Jesus Christ should be enough for us to accept the motivation required to complete any project that He has set before us, yet we are frail and sometimes lack faith. We often use these words...

Mark 9:24, *"And straightway the father of the child cried out, and said with tears, Lord, I believe; help thou mine unbelief."*

Yet, we could (and should) as easily use these words as our life's verse...

Acts 27:25, *"Wherefore, sirs, be of good cheer: for I believe God, that it shall be even as it was told me."*

Think of a big goal and the motivation that will be required for success. Accept it! Think of it like a mountain. As you look at the mountain, the first couple of steps are easy. By walking closer to the mountain, each step is a little steeper. Every step gets a little bit harder to take. If you climb a mountain when it is one hundred degrees outside (100°), you need to take extra water and dress appropriately. However, as you climb a mountain, the air gets cooler as you climb higher. You must be prepared for the future of the climb.

Once you accept your motivation, you have internally committed yourself to that success throughout every day until it is completed. You will need to wake up with that motivation to succeed. You must eat healthy meals to prepare your physical body for what is about to occur. You must prepare your mind to sleep well enough to wake up and become motivated. Your entire being will be needed as you have prepared to accept the motivation and create the dream of your visions.

Accepting means to internalize, visualize, and actualize each goal and desire that you have determined to create in your life. Accepting determination typically involves others around you. There is an old phrase that says, "No man is an island unto himself." Another proverb says, "You will be the average of your five to ten closest friends." Each of these proverbs states that it takes others to help you accept your motivation.

Proverbs 18:24, *"A man that hath friends must shew himself friendly: and there is a friend that sticketh closer than a brother."*

Surround yourself now with the people that you will want to surround yourself with when you become successful. You will receive encouragement and energy from those with whom you have surrounded yourself. You will also give energy and encouragement to those who surround you. This must be a "win-win" situation.

How will this lesson help me?

Personal—As you accept the amount of motivation it will take for you to succeed, you will want to prepare yourself for an exciting journey. You will want to pray more. You will want to eat correctly and exercise so that you can sleep well. You will want to read the right books and stay in touch with your mentors. If you are a teenager, this is a perfect opportunity for you to get a vision for where your life is going to take you. The Lord wants to use you in a mighty way. Be sure to read your Bible and follow the guidance of the Holy Spirit. If you are a pastor or a leader in the community, many people will be affected by your decisions. Accept your motivation, but never become too busy to be a blessing to others!

Marriage and family—As a family, you have discussed your motivation and all of the activities that will soon surround you. Now is the time to accept that and be prepared for the days, months, and years ahead. You may be preparing for a new job, a new house, a new career, or your next college degree. Each member of your family will be affected. It will be important to have a loving relationship with each person in the family and your relatives.

Church—As your church accepts this motivation, different members of your church will want to take part because it will be an exciting event in their lives. Different church leaders will need to be involved as different members have different activities in your community. If each church leader is excited about the outcome as it will be beneficial to their children and their community, this will give the Holy Spirit the opportunity to work through your people into the lives of others and build your church and goodwill for the future.

Community—When you have a new project in your church, your church will change. Some new people will join your church. Some of the neighbors will be affected by these changes. Keep a friendly relationship with the neighbors who surround your church. Some of this motivation may also affect your mayor, the police, and the political leaders. Be sure to be able to show how important this new activity is for your community.

THE AUTHORING OF MOTIVATION

This is your opportunity to write down the ideas and the actions that will help you as you internalize what it takes to motivate you for your success. During this exercise, you only need to write down what it will take. The authoring of your motivation will be different from the authoring of your determination. Here's why! Remember that determination means that you will not stop. However, motivation is what keeps you moving forward. There is a difference. You may want to distinguish the difference between speed and power.

Earlier in this book, we discussed your five senses. These are sight, smell, hearing, seeing (vision), and touch or physical feeling. This list for motivation could be different than your previous lists from earlier chapters. Some things that will inspire you and put you in the spirit of success may not cause you to move and physically take action when that success is near.

Mark 14:38, *"Watch ye and pray, lest ye enter into temptation. The spirit truly is ready, but the flesh is weak."*

Have you ever heard of the term "cramming for final exams"? This means that a person has not been motivated to study many times throughout the semester. But just before the final exam test for the course, the student realizes they do not have all the knowledge needed to do as well as expected on the final exam. There may have been inspiration throughout the semester, but now massive motivation is required and is an imminent requirement.

Many of us tend to procrastinate. It is easy to do because we sometimes change our priorities. For instance, is it important to sleep? Yes! Is it important to eat? Yes! Is it important to study? Yes! Is studying urgent? How you answer this question will be determined by your motivation. So now is the time to write down what it will take for you to be motivated and take action at the needed times so that you can succeed as God has planned. God has been with you the whole time. Now is the time to pray for success as you study. Now is the time to research and prepare your mind to do excellent on the test.

Ecclesiastes 12:12, *"And further, by these, my son, be admonished: of making many books there is no end; and much study is a weariness of the flesh."*

Every area of your life has a different type of motivation! As you review your notes so far in this book, which include desires, decisions, inspiration, and imagination, you can circle or highlight those ideas that are most important to you. Each will help you stay motivated and take action until you complete the project. For some readers, this will be a quick exercise, but for others, you may want to think about it and discuss it with your family or friends. They may also be working on the same project. Many classmates will study together. Doing research together on any project can be very beneficial. Always work together and help each person to succeed. Write down what will be required for many of you to be successful.

Practice ideas as a family. What will motivate each person in the family to succeed at a particular project? This project could be something that is happening in the house, such as redecorating. Projects like this take action. Write down what it will take for each person to take action on their own accord without being pushed or retold what to do. We are a family. We have a Heavenly Father. Our Father wants unity in the family and fellowship with one another.

Practice ideas like this in your church. Large projects in the church that are successfully completed result from many members working together and being motivated to take action that they might not otherwise even consider. When a new building is built, many members get together to paint and clean the building. Other members, who are licensed professionals, handle the electrical work and can complete the project quickly because of the many volunteers who are available and excited to get the project completed.

Write down important words. Sometimes, just writing down the words "pot-luck dinner" or "chili cookoff" are all the words that are needed to motivate a group of men and women to accomplish great things in the church!

Revelation 1:19, *"Write the things which thou hast seen, and the things which are, and the things which shall be hereafter."*

Remember what we discussed previously and your personal integrity to yourself. As you write down the actions that will be needed to help you stay motivated, you may want to say these words to yourself...

Galatians 1:20, *"Now the things which I write unto you, behold, before God, I lie not."*

How will this lesson help me?

Personal—As you take the time to write down what is needed for you to take action and persevere, then you are headed toward success. Motivation is a personal matter. It is up to you to take action and create the motivation within yourself in order to achieve the outcome that you desire. With the help of others and God Almighty, this may inspire you. Other people may "inspire" you; however, you must "motivate" yourself.

Marriage and family—You may want to do this exercise twice. Once by yourself so that you know what will motivate you. Then, do it again with your family. This will let you know what will motivate each person in the family so you can be successful as a single unit. This may keep the family bond strong and exciting. Have each person write down ideas that they are willing to share. Have each person write down some Bible reference, if possible, that compares to their motivation.

Church—Whether you are a teenager in church, a worker in the church, or the pastor, only you can require yourself to take action. Other people might tell you what you should do. Other people might encourage you and inspire you. However, if you want to be a part of helping the church that wants to make an impact on God, you will want to stay motivated and take some action.

Many churches will have banners or bulletin boards throughout their facility, which will reinforce the upcoming programs that will benefit each member in the entire church. By writing these reminders, you might want to include a yearly "motto" or Scripture verse in order to keep the focus.

Community—Think of different verses in the Bible that you can use to motivate your people in the community that will be beneficial both in the short term and the long term as they relate to the adults and the children of your community. Maybe you would want to adopt the slogan or motto for your church, such as "the friendliest church in town," using...

Proverbs 18:24, "*A man that hath friends must shew himself friendly: and there is a friend that sticketh closer than a brother.*"

If you write this, could this be your motivation?

Matthew 11:4–5, "*Jesus answered and said unto them, Go and shew John again those things which ye do hear and see: The blind receive their sight, and the lame walk, the lepers are cleansed, and the deaf hear, the dead are raised up, and the poor have the gospel preached to them.*"

THE ACTIVATION OF MOTIVATION

You may think at first sight that the words "the activation of motivation" may sound a little redundant. You may have perceived that they are so similar that both words would not need to be used at the same time.

How many of us have tried to start a car or some other type of motor when it was extremely cold outside or extremely hot? Many times, in either extreme, the battery will not have enough capacity to start the motor. When this happens, we need to "jumpstart" the battery by using a different battery or outside power source. Even after the motor starts, there is still another action required to activate the motivation. You next have to put the car in gear. Sometimes, the transmission takes time to warm up. Then, you need to apply the accelerator and provide fuel to the motor so that movement will occur.

Use your life as an example. How is your motivation? Is everything working fine so you can take action today? Perhaps you have said to yourself, *I just can't get motivated today!* We all understand that. Maybe you need a jumpstart from an outside source. That is why you author what is needed to give you that jumpstart. Even after you get your jumpstart, you still have to "get it in gear." What happens if you are out of gas? Have you ever had one of those days? There is a reason why you have been asked to write down so much to get to this part of the book. By writing it down in your own words, you can go back and look at what you've written. This will help you to activate the motivation required to get you to your destination in a safe and comfortable manner.

The notes you have written while you have started reading this book will be so powerful for you for the rest of your life. You may want to come back and look at your own notes over and over again for the rest of your life. You may even want to buy extra paper and put extra notes in this book and keep it in a safe place where you can use it in good times and bad.

As was mentioned at the beginning of this book, your desires will come from your father or a father figure. Therefore, your grandchildren may benefit by knowing what will motivate you. You may be able to help activate the motivation of others through the help of the Holy Spirit.

Acts 11:15, *"And as I began to speak, the Holy Ghost fell on them, as on us at the beginning."*

As you begin to activate the movement required for the completion of any large project, be sure to make good plans and start with the end in mind. Many projects have failed to be completed not because of a lack of effort but because of the lack of planning with otherwise people who are available to you. As you start your motivated activity, keep this lesson from Luke chapter 14 in front of you.

Luke 14:28–30:

For which of you, intending to build a tower, sitteth not down first, and counteth the cost, whether he have sufficient to finish it? Lest haply, after he hath laid the foundation, and is not able to finish it, all that behold it begin to mock him, Saying, This man began to build, and was not able to finish.

Stay motivated, my friends!

How will this lesson help me?

Personal—Sometimes, activating your motivation could be as simple as getting a wink from that person you love. It could be all you need is a nod and a smile from your coach or your pastor. But how do you give that to yourself? This is the reason to be around the right social environment. For many of us, going to church is the motivating factor in our life each week. Some of us go to hear a sermon, hoping that will motivate us. Some of us go because our friends motivate us.

Surround yourself with the right people so you can stay motivated!

Marriage and family—While you are growing up, you will have an influence on your brothers and sisters. You also influence your parents. As a teenager, you have the ability to be a blessing. Be sure to read your Bible and ask God to keep your motivation active so He can use you now and in the future.

If you are a parent, there will be days when you will have very little energy because of all of the activity of your children, your spouse, your job, and other duties in life. Be sure to review the notes you took about authoring your motivation. Keep those notes handy for those rough days and for the good days. Always keep a good spirit in your home so that you can motivate your children and your spouse to be used by God.

Psalm 133:1, *"Behold, how good and how pleasant it is for brethren to dwell together in unity!"*

Church—Activating the motivation of a church may be like being the locomotive of a long train carrying different types of cargo. This may not be the easiest task in the world because each member (just like every train car) will have a certain amount of resistance, which includes gravity and friction. But remember, be strong and of good courage.

Deuteronomy 31:6, *"Be strong and of a good courage, fear not, nor be afraid of them: for the LORD thy God, he it is that doth go with thee; he will not fail thee, nor forsake thee."*

Community—When your community knows that you can become motivated when needed, they will reach out to you for prayer and for guidance. Your community needs you as an individual because you have integrity and you are in touch with God Almighty. The community needs your church because of all the wonderful people who attend and want to help in time of need because they know that the God you serve can calm the storms of life and bring peace.

Matthew 8:23–27:

And when he was entered into a ship, his disciples followed him. And, behold, there arose a great tempest in the sea, insomuch that the ship was covered with the waves: but he was asleep. And his disciples came to him, and awoke him, saying, Lord, save us: we perish. And he saith unto them, Why are ye fearful, O ye of little faith? Then he arose, and rebuked the winds and the sea; and there was a great calm. But the men marvelled, saying, What manner of man is this, that even the winds and the sea obey him!

THE APPRECIATION OF MOTIVATION

Now, you can relax! If you reached this far, you may feel like you just finished your first triathlon! You didn't get here overnight. It took years for you to get to the position you are in right now. You worked hard. You stayed up late. You woke up early. Sometimes, your motivation has taken priority over your own enjoyment, but you made the right decisions and you have finished your course. You understand what the apostle Paul meant when he penned the words:

Second Timothy 4:7, *"I have fought a good fight, I have finished my course, I have kept the faith."*

There are three parts of your life, including your home life, your church life, and your studies or work life. Whether you are still in school, in college, raising a family, or a senior citizen, you can now sit back and enjoy the movement, motivation, and inspiration it took to get you to where you are today.

Are you tired yet? The amazing part of life is that every time you finish a goal, whether it's a new job, a different career, a newer car, or a bigger house, a new goal or opportunity will appear. You will have the privilege of accepting a new challenge or simply relaxing and appreciating the motivation that got you this far in life. Only you can make the decision through much prayer what is right for your life.

Let me take a minute right now to assure you that there may be a time at some point in your life when you are satisfied with all that you have accomplished. That is the ultimate point in life where you can enjoy all that you have done thus far in life. This is the gift of God!

Ecclesiastes 3:13, *"And also that every man should eat and drink, and enjoy the good of all his labour, it is the gift of God."*

Remember that wisdom is the principal thing that is needed most.

Proverbs 4:7, *"Wisdom is the principal thing; therefore get wisdom: and with all thy getting get understanding."*

That is why this next parable is so important. Remember what Jesus Christ spoke in Luke chapter 12.

Luke 12:15–21:

And he said unto them, Take heed, and beware of covetousness: for a man's life consisteth not in the abundance of the things which he possesseth. And he spake a parable unto them, saying, The ground of a certain rich man brought forth plentifully: And he thought within himself, saying, What shall I do, because I have no room where to bestow my fruits? And he said, This will I do: I will pull down my barns, and build greater; and there will I bestow all my fruits and my goods. And I will say to my soul, Soul, thou hast much goods laid up for many years; take thine ease, eat, drink, and be merry. But God said unto him, Thou fool, this night thy soul shall be required of thee: then whose shall those things be, which thou hast provided? So is he that layeth up treasure for himself, and is not rich toward God.

It is also important to remember the words of Jesus Christ as He spoke in Mark chapter 8.

Mark 8:36–37, *"For what shall it profit a man, if he shall gain the whole world, and lose his own soul? Or what shall a man give in exchange for his soul?"*

Appreciate your motivation. Be aware and careful of your motives.

How will this lesson help me?

Personal—If you are headed to your goal or working on a project and you remain motivated every morning, you are blessed! Appreciate the motivation that surrounds you. Be thankful for it and the people who helped to make that motivation to continue in your life. Stay humble and thankful for all of the Lord has provided you! Your motivation will help you to fulfill your dreams.

First Chronicles 23:30, *"And to stand every morning to thank and praise the LORD, and likewise at even."*

Marriage and family—As you motivate your family to complete the tasks that God has placed in your path, appreciate each individual family member. Remember that God is love. Keep that love with each person in your family so that they can show that love to others in their church and in their community.

First John 4:16, *"And we have known and believed the love that God hath to us. God is love; and he that dwelleth in love dwelleth in God, and God in him."*

Church—When you have the opportunity, take a few minutes and sit in your church without saying a word and appreciate all the motivation and all the movement that it takes from so many people every week to keep your church active for the members and the community. Appreciating each individual and praying for them may be the greatest blessing they receive this week. I always feel blessed when I hear somebody say these words to me, "I'm praying for you!"

First Samuel 12:23, *"Moreover as for me, God forbid that I should sin against the LORD in ceasing to pray for you: but I will teach you the good and the right way."*

Community—There are many people who are active in the community who are required to stay motivated for the protection of the people. As you pray for your community leaders, firemen, police, and your mayor, let them know you appreciate them. Sometimes a simple thank you note will make their day better. Maybe you should get involved more in your community. Explore opportunities to be a blessing to others so that you can introduce them to your church and to the Lord Jesus Christ.

Ephesians 1:16, *"Cease not to give thanks for you, making mention of you in my prayers."*

THIS PAGE HAS BEEN LEFT BLANK SO THAT YOU CAN MAKE
NOTES ABOUT MOTIVATION

MOMENTUM
THE ANTICIPATION OF MOMENTUM

Do you remember the first time that you went unusually fast in any type of vehicle? Do you remember the first time you went on a roller coaster? What happened the first time you went fast on your bicycle? Do you remember the first time you drove on an expressway at speeds over 50 mph (miles per hour)? Now, you may (legally) travel faster than 80 mph in some areas. Before you go faster than your normal speed, you must anticipate the momentum and be prepared for how quickly things will change their appearance.

Before you started your educational journey in college, did you realize how fast you would be required to finish your math lesson while you finished your English lesson and tried to finish your other lessons? Everything happened so fast that if you were not prepared, you might fall behind.

When you decided to get married, did you realize how quickly your life would change? As soon as you get married, you quickly get busy with your spouse, then a new job opportunity comes in, then you find out you are having a baby, and then morning sickness occurs. What's next? You look for a bigger apartment, or you buy a house. Then, you have more children. Next, there are school activities and church activities, birthdays and holidays, sickness and health. Soon there will be high school sports and graduations. Next is your children's college and career, then your retirement. Now, you understand what this verse is about...

James 4:14, *"Whereas ye know not what shall be on the morrow. For what is your life? It is even a vapour, that appeareth for a little time, and then vanisheth away."*

It is all about momentum. Are you prepared? Can you anticipate the momentum that is about to occur when you ask that beautiful woman to marry you or you accept the proposal?

Let's think of more momentum and faster movement. Some of us are pilots. We love speed! Some of us ride motorcycles. We love speed! Some of us ride horses. We enjoy a slow walk on horseback, but we also love to gallop. We love speed! Some people reading this book will be NASCAR fans. We love speed!

Engineers are constantly finding new ways to create speed for every vehicle. In real estate, we use the term "time is of the essence." This is true in every successful endeavor. The emphasis of that time is the anticipation of how that momentum will change with every challenge. For your success, you must anticipate the amount of momentum that will be required to complete your task or your endeavor in a timely manner.

Now, let's bring this idea to your situation. How can we make this practical in your life? What does the anticipation of momentum mean to you? If you are in junior high school and preparing to be on the basketball team, you must plan on how much action it will take to keep your grades up, go to basketball practice, and be on the winning team. Massive action will be required. You must anticipate the amount of momentum it will take for your success.

If you are in high school and preparing for the cross-country team, you must anticipate the amount of momentum it will take in different areas of your life. In school, prepare to keep your grades up. If you are on the cross-country team, you must prepare for all the exercise, calisthenics, and practice it will take to complete the cross-country race. During the race, you have to anticipate the momentum it will take to move your physical body faster than any other physical body of your competition! You must anticipate the momentum and prepare for it accordingly. You must eat right. You must get enough sleep. You must study, and you must exercise just to be on the winning cross-country team. There are many Christian athletic associations where you can find fellowship and prayer partners. Be aware that other athletes may need your encouragement and support as they are going through similar trials.

If you are eighteen (18) years old and you like momentum, you may want to try going one hundred miles per hour. Activities such as aviation allow for momentum. Do not break the speed limit on the ground! Momentum is good, but it must be controlled. Is that what you would consider success? How would you like to be a pilot as a missionary for the work of the Lord? When Jesus Christ said, "Go ye into all the world…" did you take that as a personal challenge? Pray about it!

In college, prepare in a similar fashion. You must anticipate the amount of work and the speed at which life will occur in your freshman year of college. Will you have to work while going to college? Will you have a family while going through college? You will still need to study. You will still need to exercise and stay healthy. You will need to complete all of the outside assignments that will be required for that passing grade. You may want to schedule each activity and "time block" because of the amount of momentum that will be required. By anticipating the amount of momentum that will be required, your stress can be reduced or relieved because you know each task will be completed in a timely manner.

There will be some projects that you will have in your lifetime with a specific time for completion. Sometimes, we call that a "deadline." If you are building a house, there is an expected completion time. If you are building a road, there is a time of completion. Because there is a deadline, you must anticipate the momentum it will take to complete the project on time, as planned, and on (or below) budget. If there is no deadline and life gets in the way, that will hinder you from accomplishing the goal as quickly as planned. You may need to use perseverance to carry you across the finish line.

Too many people rush through goals and plans. That affects their personal lives with their families and loved ones. Be sure to anticipate the momentum so that you can appreciate your fulfilled desires.

How will this lesson help me?

Personal—Many great people drop out of college, technical schools, and flight schools because they do not anticipate the momentum of how quickly their financial reserves will diminish. At the same time, their time would be required for study.

As parents, many of us do not think about how quickly our children will soon be teenagers and soon be married. We all realize that there are twenty-four hours in each day. We realize that there are twelve months in a year. Yet, on every birthday, we ask ourselves how the year went by so fast. Plan for it!

Marriage and family—Many of us know someone who has had a family member who passed away at a very young age. As you anticipate the momentum of life, you must be prepared for others to go to heaven and wait with the Lord for you to arrive. As you go through your daily life right now, you may not be thinking about how quickly you and those around you are growing older. It is important that you anticipate how quickly life passes.

James 4:14, *"Whereas ye know not what shall be on the morrow. For what is your life? It is even a vapour, that appeareth for a little time, and then vanisheth away."*

Church—As you help your church have more influence in the community, your church will grow! Plan for more weddings! Plan for a larger nursery. Plan for more funerals. Anticipate the needs before they arise. It will happen quickly!

Things change quickly in the life of a church. People grow older and pass away. New babies are born. Marriages occur. Pastors retire or move to a new ministry. Are your deacon board or church leaders prepared for the momentum?

Community—Your community might change more quickly than you had imagined. Perhaps a new factory will come to town. Perhaps a major employer will leave your area. Things also change when different public officials are elected. You might want to consider having someone from your congregation elected to public office. When I was a young man, I remember that the county recorder was a prominent member of our church. Think about the possibility of changing if you were elected to a political office.

Psalm 105:21, *"He made him lord of his house, and ruler of all his substance."*

THE ACCEPTANCE OF MOMENTUM

Now that you have anticipated a certain amount of momentum, can you accept that as being real in your life? This is where many of us begin to fall behind. We have thought about and planned for the momentum, but we fail to accept it when it surrounds us.

Here is an example. You sign up to run your half-marathon (thirteen-point-one-mile) race. When your race is half complete, if you do not accept the momentum, you will "break stride" (stop running) or drop out.

Galatians 6:9, *"And let us not be weary in well doing: for in due season we shall reap, if we faint not."*

Life is that way. In your personal life, while you are planning for your high school final exams, if you do not regularly study, you will need to cram for final exams because you did not consider how quickly this semester would end.

Procrastination is in direct proportion to the acceptance of momentum!

As you prepare for college, use this same lesson, as it will be accelerated during your first semester in college if you take a full load.

Many good students such as yourself will never receive their diploma or degree because we all fail at some time to understand how quickly things will change. In many professions, you will be required to take a number of different types of tests in order to complete your education. There may be physical tests to verify you are physically fit for the position. There will be written tests. There may be an oral test or an extensive interview required. Then, there is often an internship or a practical test in order to make sure that you can complete the work unassisted.

The better you accept the momentum, the greater the leadership positions that will be offered to you. For instance, an emergency room doctor might have an entire room full of patients within minutes if an accident occurs. As a mother or father, you might have to handle supper on the stove, an injured child, and the phone ringing at the same time. Either of these examples might have the same amount of momentum and action taking place. Each of these situations requires focus on many things at once. Are you prepared?

What happens if you are the emergency room physician (or nurse) and you are a mother or father? Then, you might relate to the apostle Paul, as he wrote…

First Corinthians 9:19–24:

For though I be free from all men, yet have I made myself servant unto all, that I might gain the more. And unto the Jews I became as a Jew, that I might gain the Jews; to them that are under the law, as under the law, that I might gain them that are under the law; To them that are without law, as without law, (being not without law to God, but under the law to Christ,) that I might gain them that are without law. To the weak became I as weak, that I might gain the weak: I am made all things to all men, that I might by all means save some. And this I do for the gospel's sake, that I might be partaker thereof with you. Know ye not that they which run in a race run all, but one receiveth the prize? So run, that ye may obtain.

How will this lesson help me?

Personal—On a personal basis, you may want to start while you are in junior high school to think about all the things in your life that are required for you to complete your current grade successfully. You have your family and your chores at home. You have activities or obligations at church. You have test scores in every class at school. Plus, you want to try out for sports or marching band. This will help to prepare you for college.

Perhaps you are a parent and you want to go back to college or get involved in a community activity, such as politics or the board of directors of a nonprofit organization. Do you have the time, and can you anticipate all of the activities and accept the responsibilities that will be required to complete that project and keep a successful family life?

Marriage and family—If you are a parent, thank you for taking the time to read this book! Your life is so full and busy that it sometimes becomes difficult to take the time to sit and read anything that is not required. You become busy with your spouse and children because of your love for them. You have accepted the speed and momentum of life. Congratulations! You are surviving and improving your life. Enjoy these days of haste, but prepare for the future.

If you're still a student in school and you think life is going by slowly, prepare yourself for final exams. If you have more time, start studying for the next school year. In many areas, you are permitted to take "dual enrollment," which means you can start your freshman year of college during your junior year of high school. I know a gentleman who received his associate degree from college one day before graduating high school. Is that what the Lord wants for you?

Second Timothy 2:15, *"Study to shew thyself approved unto God, a workman that needeth not to be ashamed, rightly dividing the word of truth."*

Church—As you think about your church, consider how it was two years ago. Do you see all of the things that have changed? New people are coming to your church. Perhaps a few people have passed away. Maybe your church has started a new ministry. Churches are typically not stagnant. They evolve quickly! You might have a new pastor or staff member who is beneficial to the church's future. Embrace the change!

Community—In many cases, your community is changing much more quickly than you had anticipated. Many of us will visit a place where we spent time in the past. Maybe you moved away from the city, and you went back to visit a few years later. You noticed that many things have changed. Buildings are built. New employers come to town. New stores are coming to your area. People grow older. Your church will adapt as the people in your church change with new ideas. However, God never changes! In all of the momentum and velocity, always remember that God walks with you.

Hebrews 13:8, *"Jesus Christ the same yesterday, and to day, and for ever."*

THE AUTHORING OF MOMENTUM

This may be a critical element to your success in any endeavor. Whether you are preparing for college, a marriage, a professional life, or building a church ministry, you will want to take some time right now to write down some ideas about how quickly you will finish the task in front of you.

This is your opportunity to write down some of your thoughts about momentum. Take each of these examples and jot down just a few of your thoughts.

Perhaps you are preparing for college. What will you be doing for income to pay for your college degree? If you are not required to pay for college at this time because you were able to save up money, get a grant, or borrow the needed funds, what will you do immediately after college? Write these ideas down now so that you can mentally prepare for what is needed as you move on to your professional life.

While you are in college, you will also need time to relax and unwind. For some of us, that may require us to exercise so that we do not get stressed out and we can relax. For others of us, we just need to relax by going fishing and relaxing on the beach. Also, while you are in college, you will want to find different ways of studying. Some people listen to audiobooks. Some of us speed-read. Others of us have a study group and compare notes with our friends.

As you are authoring your momentum, decide what works best for you so that you can be prepared when the time comes that these techniques are needed. Whatever you do, do not neglect your time and activities at your church.

Perhaps you are preparing for the Christian ministry. You might want to make a list of other pastors and missionaries with whom you can talk on a regular basis. These professionals have gone before you and laid the foundation for your success. Their motto might be…

First Corinthians 11:1, *"Be ye followers of me, even as I also am of Christ."*

As you author your momentum, you will want to learn the techniques of time blocking. What this means is you will be able to take out a calendar and promise yourself that you will use every minute possible during a block of time toward your success. You will want to write down the hours you will study, and do not let anything interfere with that study time. You will also want to block out time to sleep. Do not let anything keep you from sleeping. Study time is important, but if you do not sleep well, you will not do well on your tests and other assignments. You will also want to block out some time for exercise. Be sure that you block out time to pray. Praying will be important. Be sure to spend time with your church family. Invite your friends with whom you study to go to church with you. You will build lifelong friendships. This is part of your education.

Hebrews 10:24–25, *"And let us consider one another to provoke unto love and to good works: Not forsaking the assembling of ourselves together, as the manner of some is; but exhorting one another: and so much the more, as ye see the day approaching."*

How will this lesson help me?

Personal—This lesson will help you throughout your entire life as you go through high school, college, family life, and business life. Learning how to prioritize your desires and your other activities will help you to complete more projects and have a complete and more balanced lifestyle. There will be many times throughout your life when you become busy. By learning this lesson, you will have time for your marriage, your children, and what is currently known as work-life balance.

Matthew 6:33, *"But seek ye first the kingdom of God, and his righteousness; and all these things shall be added unto you."*

Marriage and family—Whether you are a teenager, a parent, or a senior citizen, take this opportunity to write down all of the activities of each person in your family. This will be a great exercise. If you are a parent, write down the activities of each of your children. What do they do in school? What are all of their after-school activities? Look at how busy each of your children is so that you understand their need for your attention.

If you are married, have some idea of all of the things that your spouse does and where they may need your help. Do not neglect your spouse. Perhaps they work at a school or in an office where they are permitted to receive a fresh cup of coffee or a love note, which will make their entire day better because they know you care. Be careful not to take them away from their duties, but find ways that you can be a blessing to one another.

Ephesians 5:25, *"Husbands, love your wives, even as Christ also loved the church, and gave himself for it."*

Church—There are many times in the life of the church that the seven days between this Sunday and next Sunday will go so quickly that you may miss something that was needed. It may totally slip your mind because you did not author or write down how important it was. I learned many years ago to keep an ink pen and a sheet of paper folded in my shirt pocket. It is amazing how many times that piece of paper has come in handy so that I could jot a note to myself and remember to handle some priority that somebody mentioned to me as they crossed my path. There are so many actions that take place every week in church. Each one is important to somebody. Be sure to remember to write it down.

Matthew 5:18, *"For verily I say unto you, Till heaven and earth pass, one jot or one tittle shall in no wise pass from the law, till all be fulfilled."*

Community—This is a great lesson if you have any activity in the community. Maybe you work on a community project with other churches, with the school board, or with government agencies. There are so many things that happen so quickly that are important to other people in the community. If people in the community notice that you do not forget the details of an important activity because you were wise enough to write it down and remember to make the correct phone calls, people will look at you as a leader. In these following verses, even the apostle Paul used the term "first of all," which shows that he kept his priorities in order.

First Timothy 2:1–3:

I exhort therefore, that, first of all, supplications, prayers, intercessions, and giving of thanks, be made for all men; For kings, and for all that are in authority; that we may lead a quiet and peaceable life in all godliness and honesty. For this is good and acceptable in the sight of God our Saviour.

THE ACTIVATION OF MOMENTUM

Having written down ("authored") your momentum, it is now time to activate and actively use that model that you have created. Make this a fun but disciplined activity.

Have you ever watched a spaceship launch? That is the activation of momentum! That event can visualize your entire career. Think about the activation, the initial thrust, that is required to create the momentum, the speed to move that massive object into outer space. That is your life! When you activate the momentum that is required to help you reach that vision in front of you, you will then be able to have the right fuel on board, the right systems in place, and the right instructors and mentors at the controls for you to be ready physically and mentally to move at the speed that is required for your success.

As we discuss the activation of momentum, we must consider Isaac Newton's first law, also known as the "law of inertia." This law states, "An object in motion tends to stay in motion, and an object at rest tends to stay at rest." Every person who has ever driven a car, ridden a motorcycle, or flown an airplane understands the activation of momentum. When you hit the accelerator or open the throttle, action takes place. The more power the motor has, the more momentum will occur.

As you look back at your life and you look at your current situation, are you moving forward at a slow pace or are you moving quickly? Are you taking no action at all at this time? If you're already moving forward, and your inertia has started to accelerate your movement, then activating momentum will not be a difficult task. However, if you have been sitting dormant, meaning asleep, or taking no action and you try to launch a spaceship in your life, it will be difficult to create and activate all of the momentum that will be required without something breaking. Then, all of your systems for success must be in place. Maybe you need power in your walk with the Lord. If so, remember the words of Jesus Christ...

Matthew 28:18–19, *"And Jesus came and spake unto them, saying, All power is given unto me in heaven and in earth. Go ye therefore."*

Sometimes, a word to the wise is sufficient.

Matthew 10:16, *"Behold, I send you forth as sheep in the midst of wolves: be ye therefore wise as serpents, and harmless as doves."*

If you have analyzed every part of your current situation and considered every aspect of the goal that is in front of you, then you may have the ability to activate the momentum necessary to launch the task. However, if you've looked at the proverbial spaceship in your life and you do not understand how to activate that momentum by giving it full fuel and the thrust that is required, it will be more difficult for you to create the momentum necessary.

The activation of momentum will be a different discussion depending upon if we are talking about the words power, speed, thrust, propulsion, lift, or drag. For instance, a train locomotive has a lot of power; however, it may not have much speed or momentum. An airplane has to have speed to create lift to get off of the ground, but it must consider the amount of drag that will counteract that lift. As you activate the momentum in your life and in your goals, some things will drag you down. It will be up to you to create more lift than drag if you want to fly to your destination. Be sure to have enough power and enough energy for you to reach your goals. Eat right! Sleep right! Live right! Activate your momentum! I will meet you here, there, or in the air!

How will this lesson help me?

Personal—By activating your momentum, you are creating movement physically and spiritually. Many of us go to church every week and fill our lives with ideas and plans about how we will serve the Lord in the future. Compare these two verses:

Matthew 26:41, *"Watch and pray, that ye enter not into temptation: the spirit indeed is willing, but the flesh is weak."*

Mark 14:38, *"Watch ye and pray, lest ye enter into temptation. The spirit truly is ready, but the flesh is weak."*

Do you see the difference between these two? One says, *"The spirit indeed is willing,"* while the other reads, *"The spirit truly is ready."* Picture it this way. The first time I put on a parachute while I was on the ground, I was "ready" to skydive. When I stood up in the airplane, I tried to stop the momentum because I was not "willing"; however, the jumpmaster (note the word "master") was ready, willing, and able. We landed safely because the "master" had control.

How is your relationship with the Master? Are you walking with Him today?

Marriage and family—Activating your momentum as you are first married is different than activating your momentum when you have teenagers. There is a different atmosphere in the house and a different energy level both at home and the church. You will pray differently with your spouse when you were first married than when you have your children in the house. As you pray for your family and all of the activities that are occurring rapidly as the children grow, there is an energy level that the Lord understands. When the children are ill, the Lord can heal them. God is always watching over you. Throughout all of your activities, be sure to take time to talk with the Lord so that He can give you the comfort needed as you move forward with life. When life seems impossible, fear not!

Luke 18:27, *"And he said, The things which are impossible with men are possible with God."*

Church—Do you feel a "revival" coming on? Because your church has been praying (or is going to start praying) for something great to happen in your church through the power of God, who has all power, you have power like a locomotive or a jumbo jet with the speed and momentum of a supersonic airplane. Think about these two verses together…

Matthew 28:18, *"And Jesus came and spake unto them, saying, All power is given unto me in heaven and in earth."*

Mark 10:27, *"And Jesus looking upon them saith, With men it is impossible, but not with God: for with God all things are possible."*

Therefore:

Matthew 21:22, *"And all things, whatsoever ye shall ask in prayer, believing, ye shall receive."*

Community—Let's look at your life and the big community surrounding you. If you activate your momentum and help change your entire community in a good way and in a way that pleases the Lord, your community will recognize you. They may ask you to lead their committees. They may ask you to help in government or politics. They may ask you as an individual or your church to be recognized throughout the state because of what you individually have done. You may be more important to your community than you realize. Pray for your community. Stay active and be a blessing to your community.

First John 1:3, *"That which we have seen and heard declare we unto you, that ye also may have fellowship with us: and truly our fellowship is with the Father, and with his Son Jesus Christ."*

THE APPRECIATION OF MOMENTUM

As you look back at all that you have accomplished, do you appreciate how quickly it all happened? It seems like just yesterday when you thought about going to college, and now it's graduation day. Maybe it seems like just yesterday when you asked your beautiful wife to marry you, and now you are sitting around the Christmas tree with your teenage children. It went pretty fast, didn't it?

As you walk across the graduation platform and are handed your college degree, you may look back and think of the long nights of study and the many good times that you had in college. However, you will also look back and realize how quickly those years have gone. Appreciate the momentum, but also take time on a regular basis to appreciate how quickly the Lord is moving in your life. Maybe you have faced a few delays during your journey. You may think that things are not working out as quickly as you had thought they might. Since you love the Lord, you can expect things to turn out differently as God has planned.

Romans 8:28, *"And we know that all things work together for good to them that love God, to them who are the called according to his purpose."*

Perhaps you decided to go to Bible college or seminary to learn to start a new work as a missionary. Now, you're sitting at your church surrounded by many believers who are there because of all the actions that you have taken and the momentum of which you have carried out the task that the Lord has given you. Your church believes in you because you follow the Lord Jesus Christ. They are so grateful for how quickly you have helped to change their lives!

Perhaps you are a senior citizen already. Your children are already success-ful! You have grandchildren coming over for a holiday dinner. Life goes so fast! Appreciate every hug! Appreciate every smile! Appreciate the speed. Be thankful that you are prepared for heaven.

First Thessalonians 5:18, *"In every thing give thanks: for this is the will of God in Christ Jesus concerning you."*

Soon, you might hear the words…

Luke 23:43, *"And Jesus said unto him, Verily I say unto thee, Today shalt thou be with me in paradise."*

How will this lesson help me?

Personal—When you appreciate how quickly things change in this world, you will be amazed at how things work together for your good because you love God and are called according to his purpose. God does not make a mistake! Whether good things come to you quickly or difficulties arise, remember God has the power to bring people into your life and help people to cross your path as he feels is best. If you are ever in doubt, relax, pray, and allow his word to guide your path.

Psalm 119:105, *"Thy word is a lamp unto my feet, and a light unto my path."*

Marriage and family—Sometimes, when there are teenagers and children living with parents, you will hear phrases like, "I can't wait until I'm old enough to…" or, "You are growing so old so quickly." As your children get their high school diplomas, you realize how quickly time passes.

If you are in junior high or high school right now, you may think time is going slowly. It will seem that way sometimes. Do not be alarmed. Appreciate every day. Create many good memories with your friends. Each school year will be over quickly. Then, it will be time for college, the military, or some other job that will create a new career. Appreciate the momentum!

Church—If you have been in a church for the past few years, you will notice how quickly things have changed. There is a different excitement and a differ-ent feeling with the people. Typically, new babies have been born. In a similar fashion, a few people have gone to heaven. Yet God still remains the same.

God loves to hear the prayers of His people. Though things change quickly in a church, keep fellowship within your people. Keep these principles in mind.

Ephesians 4:32, *"And be ye kind one to another, tenderhearted, forgiving one another, even as God for Christ's sake hath forgiven you."*

Matthew 7:1–2, *"Judge not, that ye be not judged. For with what judgment ye judge, ye shall be judged: and with what measure ye mete, it shall be measured to you again."*

Community—Appreciate how quickly things change in your community. Be thankful to the leaders in your community. Let your church know how thankful you are for the leadership in the church and the community. Keep a good rapport with community leaders. Since all things work together for good to those who love God, the things that are changing in your community are for your good. Pray for your leaders as things change. Maybe God is calling you to be one of those leaders. Can you appreciate how quickly things would change if the high school seniors from your church began to run your city next year? Appreciate the momentum!

Acts 2:46, *"And they, continuing daily with one accord in the temple, and breaking bread from house to house, did eat their meat with gladness and singleness of heart."*

THIS PAGE HAS BEEN LEFT BLANK SO THAT YOU CAN MAKE NOTES ABOUT MOMENTUM

MENTORSHIP
THE ANTICIPATION OF MENTORSHIP

This may be the most important lesson in this book for many readers. As we begin to discuss the idea of mentorship, this lesson will reflect on the previous two lessons that you have read in this book. Allow me to give you a visual illustration of why mentorship is so important. The three lessons in this book that begin with the letter "M" can be compared to this lesson in your life. It is a lesson that I use in aviation; that is the words "motivation," "momentum," and "mentorship."

In order to get an airplane off the ground, it takes a lot of movement or motivation to get the airplane from the parking spot on the ramp or the gate to the runway. However, in order for the airplane to get off the ground, you have to include the second M, which is momentum. Without the needed amount of momentum, the airplane will not take off. (If you think you have the momentum and you do not, you will crash during takeoff). Once the airplane is airborne, you will need to have a mentor (or the teachings of a mentor) available to you. A mentor is a trusted advisor. If you are a student pilot, then your mentor is your flight instructor. If you are flying a large jet, your trusted advisor will be your first officer or your flight engineer. If you are flying alone, you still need to remember the words of your trusted advisor.

Colossians 3:2, *"Set your affection on things above, not on things on the earth."*

Your life is the same way. Your career is the same way. Up to this point, you have made a lot of movement and have had a lot of motivation. But until you get your life and your career to the runway where you can give it enough momentum, you will never get your career off the ground. Perhaps that's where you are today. You did not realize why you could not succeed. Now you realize that you need that mentor in your life. At this point, do you have a trusted advisor who is patient, understanding, and ready to help you become successful in the completion of the trip? Your mentor may be looking for you and will want to help you succeed.

First Corinthians 10:12, *"Wherefore let him that thinketh he standeth take heed lest he fall."*

We have all had teachers in our lives to help us to learn how to read, write, and study. You may have had an English teacher who would help you to understand how to use words in a productive manner. You may have had a math teacher to teach you how to use numbers to your advantage. Perhaps you had a music teacher who would teach you how to play an instrument or relate to others using music.

Each of these teachers could be a mentor at the discretion of each person involved (the mentor and the mentee). There is a distinct difference between a teacher, an instructor, and a mentor. As I was growing up, I heard the phrase, *"The teacher cannot appear until the student is ready." That means the teacher can only teach when the student is ready to learn.*

The title of mentor is new to many of us. A mentor often will provide guidance and direction in order to keep the mentee headed in the right direction for the intended success. The mentor has the knowledge of a teacher; however, through experience, the mentor/mentee relationship allows there to be significant influence to be used to transfer wisdom and understanding to the mentee.

Welcome to the world of mentorship. Often, a mentor is willing to help you and mentor you because they see that you have potential for success and have direction in your life to make that success a reality. Quite often, the mentor/mentee relationship will last a lifetime. You will develop mutual respect and admiration for one another. Your mentor will be an "overseer" and keep a watchful eye on your success. The mentor will advise but may also allow the mentee to make mistakes, which will provide more wisdom and experience. In many cases, the mentor is more than just "a trusted advisor."

Most of us have had a few mentors in our lives. Our current situation is a result of how we handled the relationships afforded to us. The mentor was successful in their career and wants you to attain the same or greater success. Since this relationship is voluntary for each person, there are no set requirements to be a mentor, but there are certain traits that will be exemplified. You will want to understand the difference between a coach, a teacher, and a mentor.

If you are in high school (or remember your high school days), you know the math "teacher." You know the football or basketball "coach." You may even know the student "advisor." Will any of those professionals trust you (and you trust them) enough to take you under their wing, "mentor" you, and watch over your activities until you succeed? A mentor may not be a "friend." Using the example I used a few minutes ago regarding aviation, if you are flying and an emergency arises that could be life-threatening, you probably don't want a friend in the cockpit that will make you feel happy about the situation. You need a trusted advisor to help you complete your trip successfully and safely.

Anticipate having a great mentor! Keep your eyes open. People want you to succeed. Let them help you. You'll be glad you did!

How will this lesson help me?

Personal—Since we know that all things work together for good to those who love God and we know that we have eternal life, let us all be aware that many people want to help you succeed and thrive. These wise individuals cross our paths quite often, and we don't even recognize that they were sent to us for a particular reason.

Proverbs 4:7, *"Wisdom is the principal thing; therefore get wisdom: and with all thy getting get understanding."*

Marriage and family—Watch for people who can help you to have a great family life. Many of these may be older couples in your church or in your community who are willing and able to pray for you and help you to keep perspective when you have difficulties in your marriage or family life.

If you are a teenager, be especially cognizant of the teachers and leaders that God has put in your path. Listen to wise counsel and be aware of sound doctrine. When somebody tries to give you advice, compare it to the words that are in your Bible. If you are ever in doubt, compare it to the words of Jesus Christ and ask the Holy Spirit to guide you.

Ecclesiastes 12:9, *"And moreover, because the preacher was wise, he still taught the people knowledge; yea, he gave good heed, and sought out, and set in order many proverbs."*

Church—If you are a teenager, can you imagine what you could accomplish if you had a great mentor who would watch over you and help you succeed while you are on earth? You have a Heavenly Father watching over you, and He will guide you, but God uses people in a special way to help you along your path. Use wisdom in every life-changing decision.

If you are in a leadership position at your church, can you imagine what would happen if every person of every age had a great mentor who had helped them through life to do whatever God has created them to do? If your church is filled with great men and women who want to help others become successful or do whatever God needs, your church will be blessed!

Second Timothy 2:2, *"And the things that thou hast heard of me among many witnesses, the same commit thou to faithful men, who shall be able to teach others also."*

Community—Your community has mentors. Your community has successful business owners and leaders who want others to succeed. Perhaps you will go to the doctor with your child, and the doctor will see great potential in your child and help them become a doctor or a leader in the medical field. Perhaps the doctor will see physical or emotional excellence, which can be used throughout your community or worldwide.

Your banker may be willing to be a trusted advisor for you or your children and guide your family to a successful financial future. Perhaps your banker could be a trusted advisor and help your child become a bank vice president, which will benefit you, your church, and the world for many generations to come.

Perhaps there are military leaders in your community who see the potential in you that you never expected may even exist inside you. That leader sees that you have wisdom and understanding through your studies at school and your studies of the Bible. If you have the opportunity to sit with the military leader and gain understanding from their experience, take the opportunity to gain wisdom about the possibilities of your future. You'll be glad you did!

Second Timothy 2:3, *"Thou therefore endure hardness, as a good soldier of Jesus Christ."*

THE ACCEPTANCE OF MENTORSHIP

This is a powerful concept. It is totally up to you if you will accept the mentorship of another individual. In the last section, we talked about the anticipation of mentorship. It is important to keep your eyes open to those who are willing to give you advice that will be profitable to you. Whether you accept that advice or not is totally within your power.

Accepting mentorship is more important than just accepting advice. Accepting mentorship is a relationship. Sometimes, these relationships are short term because of your location for the project on which you are working. The acceptance of mentorship can also be a long-term, lifelong friendship that can create business opportunities and philanthropic relationships.

Proverbs 1:5, *"A wise man will hear, and will increase learning; and a man of understanding shall attain unto wise counsels."*

Many people will go through life without a mentor. Sometimes, it is not because the mentor is unavailable but because they do not accept the mentorship. You have heard people say, "I can do it my way." They may also say, "I don't need your help." What they are saying is, "I will not accept what you have to offer." Many students in school will not accept mentorship. Quite often a teacher, instructor, or professor would like to mentor a bright young mind. However, it is up to the student to accept that mentorship, accept the leadership, and accept the opportunities that will be aligned by accepting the words and wisdom of that trusted advisor.

Proverbs 4:5, *"Get wisdom, get understanding: forget it not; neither decline from the words of my mouth."*

The acceptance of mentorship may not end at the end of the school year. Every student will either graduate or leave school. Many will become productive members of society. Every teacher is a productive member of society. Therefore, the student and the teacher may interact and benefit one another long after the school years have ended. Possibly, your teacher could mentor you and encourage you to discover a field of interest that could benefit you for a lifetime.

Oftentimes the student may become an expert in the subject, which the teacher may need. I am sure this happens every day all around the world. The teacher might teach the student in math or English, and then the student becomes a doctor, lawyer, or advisor to the teacher. Teachers can be (but are not required to be) great mentors. Students can become great mentors. When someone offers to become your mentor or your advisor and lead you into a successful career, take their expertise into consideration. Remember that every person knows something that you do not know; therefore, you can learn from everyone.

If you take that word of advice, your life can be greatly enriched. As a mentor of mine once said, "A word to the wise is sufficient." So accept the mentorship that is offered to you. But remember, "A mentor is a trusted advisor." Trust and good advice go hand in hand.

Psalm 119:99, *"I have more understanding than all my teachers: for thy testimonies are my meditation."*

How will this lesson help me?

Personal—Whether you are a young person, an adult, or a senior citizen, there may be someone who wants to help you to become successful. Watch for a trusted advisor as you read this book and throughout your life because other people want you to succeed.

Perhaps you are in high school or a young adult. You may decide to be a Little League coach. You may want to become a trusted advisor and mentor. At any age, you may be able to use your experience and knowledge to help guide others to seek wisdom and help them to become successful.

Marriage and family—This may be the lesson that will save your marriage. Whether you are just beginning your marriage or have you have been married for many years. Understanding from whom you should take advice and guidance will be the key to a long, happy, and successful marriage. Sometimes, this mentor may be a family member. Often, it may be wise to select a mentor who is a friend of the family and knows the characteristics of each. Sometimes professional advice is needed from your pastor or other professional. Be sure the advice given to you is biblical and unbiased. I would recommend always keeping this verse in mind, as it is the key to a great life.

Proverbs 17:28, *"Even a fool, when he holdeth his peace, is counted wise: and he that shutteth his lips is esteemed a man of understanding."*

Church—If you are a leader in your church, you probably want every person in your church to be successful and beneficial to the Lord's work for their entire lifetime. If you can picture every person having a trusted advisor or many trusted advisors, then the young people of your church will want to accept the wisdom of proven leaders. This means that in a few years, your church will be full of community leaders and mentors to help your church through the next generation.

Second Timothy 2:7, *"Consider what I say; and the Lord give thee understanding in all things."*

Community—Accepting the mentors available to you in your community takes great wisdom. Some mentors may be from a different socioeconomic (wealth) bracket than others. Some great doctors, lawyers, or businessmen who see that you have great potential will help you reach your full potential without trying to change your relationship with the Lord. Many of these great leaders will appreciate and admire your walk with the Lord and ask you to pray for them. Whether you are male or female, young or old, may this be your motto…

Proverbs 8:14, *"Counsel is mine, and sound wisdom: I am understanding; I have strength."*

THE AUTHORING OF MENTORSHIP

This will be an interesting opportunity for you to decide what qualities you would like to see in your mentor. I am sure that many readers will think that this is an impossibility; however, I have found that this is not only possible but also very likely to occur in your life in the near future.

I have had a few great mentors in my life who reached me unexpectedly. I did not know these people, but I wrote down certain aspects of a job description that I wanted, and I asked the Lord to provide experts in those areas to cross my path and allow me to gain their wisdom. I am always looking for great qualities in others from which I can learn or with which to partner.

If you take the time right now to write down the qualities of what you want to see in a mentor, your eyes and your mind will start seeing those qualities cross your path. Maybe you want to become a great leader of a Christian organization. If so, in the near future, you may be asked to attend a function or meet with the leader of such an organization, who will encourage you to follow the Lord's leadership so that you can run that same organization.

Perhaps your idea of a mentor is in the music business. You may soon have the opportunity to meet with or speak with a local radio personality who knows that same person. Write it down! Write down the type of people that you want to meet. What qualities does your mentor have? Maybe your idea of a mentor is your pastor or a deacon in your church. Maybe you want your mentor to be like your coach or your music director.

Perhaps you love studying history, social studies, and government. Maybe you would like to have your mentor be similar to the qualities that you see in your mayor or your governor. Have you met your mayor? Does the mayor know you by first name? Write down the qualities that you want to see in your mentor. The same qualities will be in front of you in the very near future.

I am constantly looking for highly qualified computer programmers with whom to exchange great ideas for the future. I enjoy "brainstorming" with great minds. In modern society, it is wise to understand technology and how computers affect your goals. As you watch for mentors, look for specific qualities.

Perhaps you are good at leading group discussions. Use this book and lead your group, book club, or organization to become the best leaders and mentors possible.

Proverbs 15:22, *"Without counsel purposes are disappointed: but in the multitude of counsellors they are established."*

How will this lesson help me?

Personal—By writing down what you would like to see in a mentor, you will start seeing these traits in the people around you. You will also see these in new people you meet. There are certain characteristics that attract our attention. There are different leadership qualities in each person. These traits start to be recognized at different ages. Stay aware of your surroundings and the people you meet.

Proverbs 13:20, *"He that walketh with wise men shall be wise: but a companion of fools shall be destroyed."*

Marriage and family—It will be important as you write down the qualities that you want to see in your marriage that you select possible mentors who have the same qualities. Consider the personalities of different marriages. They all have different lifestyles and different characteristics that you will either want to have in your life and your marriage or that you prefer to avoid. At the beginning of your marriage, there were circumstances surrounding the marriage proposal and the marriage ceremony. As the marriage progresses, you grow the love and admiration for one another. Write down the characteristics you would like to see in your marriage and compare those with your spouse. Build great memories together! Don't create undue "expectations" of one another. Have mentors who can advise you to have a long and happy marriage!

Hebrews 10:16–17, *"This is the covenant that I will make with them after those days, saith the Lord, I will put my laws into their hearts, and in their minds will I write them; And their sins and iniquities will I remember no more."*

Church—Your people might, individually, write down the types of mentors that will help them to succeed. If you are looking for a new church leader (like adding a staff member or a new pastor) God would use this new leader as a mentor to have your members succeed. Each person should aspire to greatness under this new mentor. Each group will begin to pray with more faith because of the vision that is set before them. They will be able to see the possibility that God can use them.

Second Corinthians 5:9, *"Wherefore we labour, that, whether present or absent, we may be accepted of him."*

Community—This activity could also help build the relationships of your people with their community. For instance, if your people see the qualities of a mentor in military veterans, the veterans who are in your church will be able to introduce your people to the leaders of their military organizations, thus building your relationship with the community and possibly raising the number of military veterans in your church. The mentoring possibilities are endless.

In like fashion, if the people in your community exhibit the traits of the police officers and firefighters in your community, then your young people may be able to save the lives of other community members because of the activities of your church. Through wisdom and understanding, your community can grow stronger.

Proverbs 4:7, *"Wisdom is the principal thing; therefore get wisdom: and with all thy getting get understanding."*

Ecclesiastes 9:14–15, *"There was a little city, and few men within it; and there came a great king against it, and besieged it, and built great bulwarks against it: Now there was found in it a poor wise man, and he by his wisdom delivered the city; yet no man remembered that same poor man."*

THE ACTIVATION OF MENTORSHIP

This will be a great test of faith within you personally and within church leadership. Now that you have authored and written those traits that are needed in your mentor, these traits will begin to appear.

Activating mentorship is actually different than choosing church leadership; however, they do have their similarities. When you choose leaders for your church, you look for certain qualities that will be spiritual and build uniformity inside the church for many years to come. Since mentorship is an individual quality on a person-to-person basis, each individual member of your church, including your pastor and your staff, can choose to be a mentor or can look for a mentor.

Pastors often need mentors; however, some may feel like it shows that they lack leadership. Compare these two verses:

John 15:5, *"I am the vine, ye are the branches: He that abideth in me, and I in him, the same bringeth forth much fruit: for without me ye can do nothing."*

Romans 11:18–20:

Boast not against the branches. But if thou boast, thou bearest not the root, but the root thee. Thou wilt say then, The branches were broken off, that I might be grafted in. Well; because of unbelief they were broken off, and thou standest by faith. Be not highminded, but fear.

Now that you have authored and written down those qualities that you want to see and each person wants to see in their mentor, you may go out into the community and ask those community members to become members of your church. Always be honest and let them know what your church believes and the direction that you want the church to go. See if they would like to be a part of this dynamic change that is about to happen in your church and in your community because of what your church is doing. It is going to be an exciting time to work and activate this mentor-mentee relationship. It will be an exciting time in the lives of each person, every group in the church, and the community in the near future. This will result in changes to your community as friendships develop within your community, which might not have been developed had you not taken the time to look at activating the mentorship and building relationships inside and outside of your church.

I have had a few mentors in my lifetime who were tremendous leaders in their community. One was a personal bodyguard to the president of the United States. I have been honored by these relationships. One of the goals of this book is to help you as you read to be able to find such a mentor or become such a mentor. This will change your life and allow you to be a blessing to others. Be sure to keep your list of mentorship qualities with you or someplace where you can reveal them or review them regularly. This will change your life!

How will this lesson help me?

Personal—By being aware of the qualities that you would like to see in a mentor, you will also desire those qualities within yourself so that you can become a great mentor. As you think of these qualities today, hold your head up and look people in the eyes, smile, and treat everybody with respect. Maybe that person who you did not know yesterday may become a member of your church next week. They may have their life changed and become your mentor. Possibly, they had been looking at you as a leader, and they did not know how to approach you. Now that they are going to your church, you have the ability to influence them for the cause of Christ. You can be a leader and change their life as they build respect and trust with you.

Proverbs 13:20, *"He that walketh with wise men shall be wise: but a companion of fools shall be destroyed."*

Ecclesiastes 9:17, *"The words of wise men are heard in quiet more than the cry of him that ruleth among fools."*

Marriage and family—When you activate this mentorship as a teenager, you will begin to recognize possible mentors and leaders in your life who will be beneficial for many years to come. These individuals will help you to succeed far more than you could have imagined. Be sure to compare their words with your understanding of the Bible. There were many great mentors in the Bible who helped younger men and women to become great leaders. God can use you as well!

As a married couple, when you begin to take the advice and activate this mentorship of others who have had great marriages, you might see your marriage improve in such an amazing way that you will begin to inspire others.

Church—As your church begins to gain mentorship within your church and with leaders outside of your church, you will be surrounded in the near future by civic leaders, community leaders, military leaders, and political advisors. This is going to be a great change in your church but a welcome change, as you personally (whether you are a teenager or a church leader) will be influenced by great minds who will help you. This will be beneficial for the church and bring more people to the saving knowledge of Jesus Christ. Are you ready for a great revival in the hearts of your church?

Proverbs 29:8, *"Scornful men bring a city into a snare: but wise men turn away wrath."*

Acts 2:46–47:

And they, continuing daily with one accord in the temple, and breaking bread from house to house, did eat their meat with gladness and singleness of heart, Praising God, and having favour with all the people. And the Lord added to the church daily such as should be saved.

Community—By having mutual mentorship relationships inside and outside of your church, you can expect that you will have such people attend your church. These leaders, such as doctors and medical staff, police and security personnel, lawyers and judges, and possibly sports heroes, will possibly become members. The community might want to become involved in your church and your new mentorship program because every person wants to feel respected and admired when they walk into a room. To create such a beneficial environment, your pastor and church leaders will need to stay humble and kind, using the teachings of Jesus Christ. When your community sees the Holy Spirit in your people, lives will change. The community will benefit, and more people will want to go to heaven and spend eternity with Jesus Christ and with you!

John 12:32, *"And I, if I be lifted up from the earth, will draw all men unto me."*

THE APPRECIATION OF MENTORSHIP

You will really appreciate having mentors for yourself and for others who surround you. Whether you are in high school or an adult at any age and you find a teacher or community leader who is willing to help you and guide you to have a successful life, you will want to treat that mentor with respect, kindness, and sincere appreciation.

Proverbs 8:33, *"Hear instruction, and be wise, and refuse it not."*

If you are in church leadership or business leadership, you will be able to appreciate the new respect that others gain toward you as they look to you for wisdom and understanding. That is one of the greatest unrecognized qualities of the mentor-mentee relationship. That is the respect and appreciation that each one has for the other. It is an amazing quality when a leader has mutual respect for you as an individual and the choices of your friendships.

If you are a leader, you will probably become a mentor and not even recognize it. That is a possibility. In a similar fashion, you may be a likely candidate to become a mentee simply because of the success track that you choose. If you are in the eye of the public, such as a radio announcer, a community spokesman, a politician, a police officer, or a television personality, you will need great mentors. Likewise, if you are in these positions, you will probably become a mentor to many people who look up to you with respect and admiration.

As a church leader, you will have the ability to change many lives while you teach the lesson of appreciation of mentorship. If you are a teacher in a public school or a private school and your students are permitted to learn the ideas of mentorship, they may start choosing different leaders in their lives. This will help change their personal day-to-day activities. Quite often pastors get involved with schools, and teachers get involved in the church where they attend. This symbiotic relationship is so valuable to the community as we teach the appreciation of mentorship; lives can be changed. You can start that change in many lives this week. There are many Christian organizations involved with public and private schools. Maybe a new Bible study or prayer group at your local school would be permitted. This is an awesome responsibility! My prayers are with you!

Proverbs 11:30, *"The fruit of the righteous is a tree of life; and he that winneth souls is wise."*

How will this lesson help me?

Personal—By appreciating your mentors, you will change your life as you immediately start to appreciate the qualities of the mentors surrounding you. Until now, you may not have even recognized all the qualities of individuals and leaders who have been wanting to help you to become successful now and in the future. Whether you are in high school, college, or in the middle of your career, somebody wants to help you. If you are a senior citizen, you still have a lot to offer; people want to help you. Appreciate the quality of the people that surround you! Starting today, smile more! Look people in the eyes and be thankful for the qualities that they possess. Many people want to gain respect, but they also want leadership. Many people want to surround themselves with great leaders so that they can learn to be great leaders.

Proverbs 1:5, *"A wise man will hear, and will increase learning, and a man of understanding shall attain unto wise counsels."*

Marriage and family—As you appreciate your mentors, your marriage will stay strong or possibly improve as you watch others who are happy. If the other couple smiles more, find out why. If other couples seem more friendly, you may want to watch them and see how you could do likewise. Sometimes the amount of money will have an effect. However, sometimes, they will have less money, but their attitude and use of money will be the determining factor regarding their happiness.

As you teach these lessons to your children, you will begin to see the fruits of the Spirit manifest. Often these mentors will show more peace and gentleness, which you can appreciate as you see those developed in young people.

Galatians 5:22–23, *"But the fruit of the Spirit is love, joy, peace, longsuffering, gentleness, goodness, faith, Meekness, temperance: against such there is no law."*

If you are a teenager, appreciate your teachers! Many of them want to become your mentor and help you to have massive success!

Church—As your church begins to appreciate all the qualities of the mentors that each person has written down in this exercise, the church will have more admiration for the leadership inside the church and the leadership in their community. Your church will benefit because they see the respect of the pastoral staff, the deacons, and the Sunday school teachers. Everyone will notice the wisdom and knowledge that they have regarding the Bible and Christian values. The church will also be able to influence others outside of the church because of the respect that they bring to each individual. That respect will be mutually beneficial for all parties concerned.

Acts 2:46, *"And they, continuing daily with one accord in the temple, and breaking bread from house to house, did eat their meat with gladness and singleness of heart."*

Community—The community will be changed as each person in your church is part of that community. As each person uses mutual respect for the others, this will not require your church to change its stance on any biblical standards! This will actually be beneficial as you explain what is in the Bible.

Acts 8:4–6:

Therefore they that were scattered abroad went every where preaching the word. Then Philip went down to the city of Samaria, and preached Christ unto them. And the people with one accord gave heed unto those things which Philip spake, hearing and seeing the miracles which he did.

THIS PAGE HAS BEEN LEFT BLANK SO THAT YOU CAN MAKE NOTES ABOUT MENTORSHIP

MINDSET (YOUR BONUS "M")

As you read this book, your mindset may change. Your mindset is typically a set of beliefs of what you have thought in the past. This book is not trying to change your principles. This book should not change your basic beliefs about your culture. However, as you read the Bible, you may want the Bible to help guide you as to what your Heavenly Father would like you to become and accomplish while you are here on earth.

One of the purposes of the book is to help you discover what has been holding you back from the success that you would like to have. Another purpose is to help you discover what God wants you to complete so that you will have a fulfilled life that will help others. You may not have believed that was possible for you, but with the help of God, all things are possible.

Matthew 19:26, *"But Jesus beheld them, and said unto them, With men this is impossible; but with God all things are possible."*

Mark 10:27, *"And Jesus looking upon them saith, With men it is impossible, but not with God: for with God all things are possible."*

One of the goals of this book is to help you to increase your faith. By looking at the different lessons in this book and reviewing some of the relative Scriptures, you have been able to be reminded of the power of your Heavenly Father.

Mark 9:23–24, *"Jesus said unto him, If thou canst believe, all things are possible to him that believeth. And straightway the father of the child cried out, and said with tears, Lord, I believe; help thou mine unbelief."*

Perhaps you have what is commonly known as an "entrepreneurial mindset." What this means is that you have the ability and the mindset to build a business.

This will help you if you are a business leader or a church leader because it will remind you about the business part of the church. In many areas of the world, a church is a registered business or corporation that must be recognized and will need an entrepreneurial spirit to help it grow.

If you have an entrepreneurial spirit and you are working with your community or assisting your church, each person can benefit from your mindset. Use wisdom in every area of your life. You have the ability, at any age, to have an entrepreneurial mindset and build a business, a church, or even start a college or university because of the lessons you have learned throughout this book. Share those great ideas with others.

If this book has changed how you think, you may want to help others by building a local book club or church group that can learn these lessons and "brainstorm" and come up with great ideas to help change your community and the world!

How will this lesson help me?

Personal—By changing your mindset and creating greater conversations between the great minds in your classroom or your book club, you will be able to create synergy. You may walk with a new demeanor and a new way of looking at life. You and your Heavenly Father, working with His Holy Spirit, may be able to create a new atmosphere in your classroom.

First Corinthians 2:14–16:

But the natural man receiveth not the things of the Spirit of God: for they are foolishness unto him: neither can he know them, because they are spiritually discerned. But he that is spiritual judgeth all things, yet he himself is judged of no man. For who hath known the mind of the Lord, that he may instruct him? but we have the mind of Christ.

Marriage and family—The mindset of your home will have a direct impact while you are away from the home. If you love going home because of the warmth and friendship inside, then your ability to be happy outside of your home will be affected. Your mindset toward your spouse will determine your desire to go home. Always try to make your home a haven of love and respect.

As a teenager, your mindset toward your parents and teachers may affect your ability to learn and succeed. This mindset will also help you as you grow older to be able to be in a leadership position because people can see that you have respect and are willing to work on projects with others.

Second Corinthians 6:1, *"We then, as workers together with him, beseech you also that ye receive not the grace of God in vain."*

Church—By learning some of the lessons that you read throughout this book, your church may have a new respect for each person and every visitor inside the church and in the community. There may be a new spirit of enthusiasm within your church. There may be a new respect for each person who comes in contact with members of your church. New relationships of excellence might occur as each person strives for excellence and humility simultaneously.

Nehemiah 4:6, *"So built we the wall; and all the wall was joined together unto the half thereof: for the people had a mind to work."*

Community—When people in your community have respect for one another, they also have respect for the police, the firemen, and even the homeless or underserved population in your community. Each person in your community deserves respect. Do not equate a person's financial status to their greatness in this world or the world to come.

Matthew 26:11, *"For ye have the poor always with you; but me ye have not always."*

Proverbs 13:7, *"There is that maketh himself rich, yet hath nothing: there is that maketh himself poor, yet hath great riches."*

THIS PAGE HAS BEEN LEFT BLANK SO THAT YOU CAN MAKE
NOTES ABOUT MINDSET

ENTHUSIASM
THE ANTICIPATION OF ENTHUSIASM

We talked about inspiration earlier in this book. Now we will discuss enthusiasm. There is a difference between the two. Inspiration means "in the spirit." It is thought to be mental stimulation that will control the mind for a short period of time. As your spirit changes, your inspiration may change. However, enthusiasm is derived from *theos*, from which we get our word "theology." Therefore, enthusiasm means "in God." Have you ever wondered where enthusiasm originates? It must be from God. It is more about your interest and enjoyment of something inside you that helps you fulfill your purpose in life through the power of God.

Are you really enthusiastic about your plan for success? Is it simply a passing idea that you would like to achieve? As you anticipate the amount of enthusiasm it will take for you to sustain your energy and your inspiration throughout the completion of your success, do you feel like the Lord will be with you as you proceed?

Hebrews 13:5, *"Let your conversation be without covetousness; and be content with such things as ye have: for he hath said, I will never leave thee, nor forsake thee."*

When you start looking at what you consider "success," you will naturally become more enthusiastic and energized by the probability that you will achieve your goal in the near future. Can you imagine carrying that same enthusiasm through the entire project until your success has formalized? If you can carry your enthusiasm and your energy level throughout the entire project, then nothing can stop you.

Since a common synonym for "enthusiasm" is "zeal," let's look at this passage...

Galatians 4:16–18, *"Am I therefore become your enemy, because I tell you the truth? They zealously affect you, but not well; yea, they would exclude you, that ye might affect them. But it is good to be zealously affected always in a good thing, and not only when I am present with you."*

In every area of your life, your level of enthusiasm will change your perspective and your outcome. Have you ever watched somebody who is enthusiastic about the same goal that you want to accomplish? Some people are enthusiastic about the same sports team. High school coaches know that the closer their team is to the playoffs, the more enthusiasm will develop. Professional team owners make large amounts of money by keeping the enthusiasm that surrounds their team.

Some people are enthusiastic about their hobby. If you mention boats to a fisherman, you may gain a friend for life. If you mention music and your type of music is the same or similar to others, you may be able to start singing the same tunes spontaneously. What are you enthusiastic about?

You may be like many of the readers of this book and be enthusiastic about your church. What is it about your church that you would like to have other people enjoy? Is it the music in your church? Is it the fact that the people in your church care about one another and pray for one another, which allows nonjudgmental, open conversations about situations that you would otherwise keep private? Let other people know how enthusiastic you are about your church. They may need exactly what you have, but they don't know that you have it. Share the gospel! Share your life experiences of how God has cared for you like no person ever could. Many people need to hear your testimony and share your enthusiasm!

Are you really enthusiastic about the visualization that you have created for success? If you can visualize the outcome and remain enthusiastic about that outcome, success will be achieved with much less effort because your success is the "real you." Since the word "enthusiasm" means "in *Theos*," or "in God," and the Bible says, *"With God all things are possible,"* then you cannot fail if God has designed your plan. Your situation may require more perseverance and more persistence than the next person's journey, but success is the journey that you travel. If you can anticipate the amount of enthusiasm that you will need for your journey to success, then during the rough times of those journeys, you will not look at the journey as a mountain to climb up. You will look at it as a stairway to success. Enjoy the journey!

How will this lesson help me?

Personal—As you anticipate having the enthusiasm that will change your entire life experience, your life will change. Many people go through life and just don't seem to be enthusiastic. You do not need to be bombastic or show outward expressions of enthusiasm. You may just want to ask the Lord to show you what the true purpose is for your life. Since you've read this far in the book, you have had several different ideas that may benefit mankind. If you're unsure which direction to go, take some time this week and ask the Lord to give you enthusiasm for some purpose, great or small. Maybe your life's purpose is simply to follow as Jesus Christ leads you to some great accomplishment.

Matthew 19:21, *"Jesus said unto him, If thou wilt be perfect, go and sell that thou hast, and give to the poor, and thou shalt have treasure in heaven: and come and follow me."*

John 10:27, *"My sheep hear my voice, and I know them, and they follow me."*

Marriage and family—If you are a young married couple, this could be a very interesting conversation to have some night after having dinner. Ask each other, "How could our marriage change if we had more enthusiasm?" Each person may have a different view of enthusiasm. One may consider it just energy, while the other considers that to be a closer relationship between each of you and God.

If you're a teenager, living with enthusiasm around school may help you to make it through some hard times because you know God is with you. Enthusiasm does not need to be extreme and flamboyant; it may just mean being able to inspire other students and your teachers. Try it for a few weeks and watch how it will help you and the Spirit in the classroom.

Church—Can you imagine if your entire church begins to live with enthusiasm when they are not at church? Many church services will bring lively activity. If the members of your church live with enthusiasm, they will talk with God in the morning and the evening. As the members of your church communicate with members of the community, they will be enthusiastic about what the Lord is doing in their lives and the life of the church.

First Thessalonians 5:15–24:

See that none render evil for evil unto any man; but ever follow that which is good, both among yourselves, and to all men. Rejoice evermore. Pray without ceasing. In every thing give thanks: for this is the will of God in Christ Jesus concerning you. Quench not the Spirit. Despise not prophesyings. Prove all things; hold fast that which is good. Abstain from all appearance of evil. And the very God of peace sanctify you wholly; and I pray God your whole spirit and soul and body be preserved blameless unto the coming of our Lord Jesus Christ. Faithful is he that calleth you, who also will do it.

Community—Enthusiasm is contagious. You cannot keep enthusiasm bottled up. Since enthusiasm means "in God" and we have a great big, wonderful God, people will see your enthusiasm and appreciate your enthusiasm as you share your testimony in a humble and professional manner.

Luke 2:10, *"And the angel said unto them, Fear not: for, behold, I bring you good tidings of great joy, which shall be to all people."*

Micah 6:8, *"He hath shewed thee, O man, what is good; and what doth the LORD require of thee, but to do justly, and to love mercy, and to walk humbly with thy God?"*

THE ACCEPTANCE OF ENTHUSIASM

The acceptance of enthusiasm will give you an entirely new life. It is important to understand that enthusiasm is available to you at any time and in every situation that you need. Accepting enthusiasm can be an entirely new lifestyle. You can be enthusiastic about every area of your life. You need to be enthusiastic about that which you have perceived as success. That will leave you with a mindset that will change your paradigm because you will view the world differently.

Second Corinthians 5:17, *"Therefore if any man be in Christ, he is a new creature: old things are passed away; behold, all things are become new."*

If you will accept enthusiasm as your lifestyle then you can help your children to have an enthusiastic childhood with positive energy surrounding them. Your lifestyle could possibly benefit from having an enthusiastic marriage and family life. I am not asking you to be energetic when you walk into the house, but I am suggesting that you look at your children, your spouse, and even your pets as gifts from God. Enjoy the spirit that each of these beautiful creations reflects back to you. Enthusiasm can come from looking into the eyes of both family and your pets that enjoy your presence.

For some people, this might be a new concept. Maybe you feel lost in this world. It may feel to you like nothing makes sense. You may wish that you could pause the world and start life all over again. The great news is that you can. Allow me to use the true story of a man named Nicodemus who met Jesus.

John 3:1–7:

There was a man of the Pharisees, named Nicodemus, a ruler of the Jews: The same came to Jesus by night, and said unto him, Rabbi, we know that thou art a teacher come from God: for no man can do these miracles that thou doest, except God be with him. Jesus answered and said unto him, Verily, verily, I say unto thee, Except a man be born again, he cannot see the kingdom of God. Nicodemus saith unto him, How can a man be born when he is old? can he enter the second time into his mother's womb, and be born? Jesus answered, Verily, verily, I say unto thee, Except a man be born of water and of the Spirit, he cannot enter into the kingdom of God. That which is born of the flesh is flesh; and that which is born of the Spirit is spirit. Marvel not that I said unto thee, Ye must be born again.

Later, in that same chapter we read the famous verse, John 3:14–17:

And as Moses lifted up the serpent in the wilderness, even so must the Son of man be lifted up: That whosoever believeth in him should not perish, but have eternal life. For God so loved the world, that he gave his only begotten Son, that whosoever believeth in him should not perish, but have everlasting life. For God sent not his Son into the world to condemn the world; but that the world through him might be saved.

I have been told many times that I am one of the most enthusiastic people that you will meet. I am not sure that is true. I have met many people who have more energy, but I have met few people who enjoy life more than I do. Every day is a gift. Everybody has twenty-four hours a day to decide what they are going to do with it. As you read through this book, it will be your choice on how much you accept your own enthusiasm. You can anticipate having enthusiasm and look forward to having enthusiasm, but until you accept it for yourself and live it day by day, you are missing a great part of life.

You will want to surround yourself with friends and others who have the same amount of enthusiasm that you wish to possess. Typically, these individuals will have the type of health or income that you are striving to achieve.

Proverbs 13:20, *"He that walketh with wise men shall be wise: but a companion of fools shall be destroyed."*

Enthusiasm comes in many different forms, as God reveals Himself to each person in a different manner. Enthusiasm creates energy! When you see somebody who is enthusiastic as they walk into a room, you will feel energy in that room. If you and I walk into a church or a social gathering of energetic people, we can feel the energy that fills the room. If you accept the spirit of that room and become a participant in that energy, you may realize how much of the atmosphere was created by enthusiasm. You will feel more energetic in these situations.

Have you ever seen an enthusiastic high school sports team? When I was a freshman in high school, our basketball team went to the state championship. It was a small country school of about 400 students. Every Friday when you walked through the hallways you could feel the enthusiasm that permeated the entire student body.

Is your life that way right now? At any point in life, you can decide what you want to be enthusiastic about. Is there something you are now doing (or thinking you would like to do) that you could be enthusiastic about for the rest of your life? You may want to go back to the list that you created when you started reading this book. All of the desires and aspirations you wrote down when you started writing in the lessons of this book will inspire you to some extent. Accepting enthusiasm as part of each of those desires will help you to reorganize and prioritize those desires that come from your Heavenly Father instead of an earthly father figure. Enjoy your enthusiasm. It is a gift from God.

How will this lesson help me?

Personal—When you accept the enthusiasm that is inside of you, you begin to realize that God surrounds you. When you accept Jesus Christ and the power of the Holy Spirit through God the Father, you realize the awesome responsibility it is to seek God's presence in your life continually. There are very few verses in the Bible that only have two or three words. Consider these two as they appear together:

First Thessalonians 5:16–17, *"Rejoice evermore. Pray without ceasing."*

When you accept your enthusiasm, these two verses will go hand in hand. You will rejoice evermore because you pray without ceasing. As you set this book down, renew your joy ("re-joy" or rejoice) with the knowledge that you can talk directly to (and with) God.

Marriage and family—When your family begins to accept the enthusiasm and understand that they can walk with God and that God is love, your family will begin to love others and care about others in your home, at church, and throughout the community. God will be able to work in you and your family, which will create great family bonds and wonderful memories.

Philippians 2:13, *"For it is God which worketh in you both to will and to do of his good pleasure."*

Church—When every member of your church begins to come to the realization that they can talk with God Almighty, the church body becomes more like a family. If we want something, let's go talk to our Father, and He will give us the answer and provide what we need to complete any project if it is within His will and good pleasure. We have a loving Father who delights in His children as they obey Him.

Luke 12:32, *"Fear not, little flock; for it is your Father's good pleasure to give you the kingdom."*

Community—As the people from your church are involved in the community and the community sees that your church is getting their prayers answered and that they walk with a new acceptance of the enthusiasm, the community will be able to recognize that your church is "different" in some manner. They may not be able to explain it or understand it until you help them understand who your Heavenly Father is and how they can join the family of God and understand the love that God has for them and the entire community.

John 15:7–9, *"If ye abide in me, and my words abide in you, ye shall ask what ye will, and it shall be done unto you. Herein is my Father glorified, that ye bear much fruit; so shall ye be my disciples. As the Father hath loved me, so have I loved you: continue ye in my love."*

THE AUTHORING OF ENTHUSIASM

This section might be the most fun you get out of this entire book. By authoring your enthusiasm, you are writing down those topics, those ideas, and those activities that most delight you in a positive manner and you can feel good about for the rest of your life. Take a few minutes after you read this section, grab a piece of paper and a pen or pencil, and write down those top ten items or ten subjects that would most give you enthusiasm for the rest of your life. Then, write down some Bible verses that you can use to remind you that you are in God and that God has provided those desires. Pray and be sure that it was God (and not man) who was leading you.

Psalm 23:1–4:

The Lord is my shepherd; I shall not want. He maketh me to lie down in green pastures: he leadeth me beside the still waters. He restoreth my soul: he leadeth me in the paths of righteousness for his name's sake. Yea, though I walk through the valley of the shadow of death, I will fear no evil: for thou art with me; thy rod and thy staff they comfort me.

For some of us, this means learning something new about music. You may want to make a list of hymns or songs that are sung in your church (or not sung in your church, but you hear them on the radio) that will remind you that God is always with you.

Psalm 96:1, *"O sing unto the Lord a new song: sing unto the Lord, all the earth."*

Psalm 33:3, *"Sing unto him a new song; play skilfully with a loud noise."*

Maybe your faith will have you writing music and creating great hymns that will be sung for many years. You have a song in your heart as you are speaking to yourself. Let others hear your music.

Ephesians 5:19–20, *"Speaking to yourselves in psalms and hymns and spiritual songs, singing and making melody in your heart to the Lord; Giving thanks always for all things unto God and the Father in the name of our Lord Jesus Christ."*

First Chronicles 15:16, *"And David spake to the chief of the Levites to appoint their brethren to be the singers with instruments of musick, psalteries and harps and cymbals, sounding, by lifting up the voice with joy."*

Maybe, by authoring your enthusiasm, you will want to write down different ways that you can reach other people in your community. The ultimate test of faith is accepting Jesus Christ as your personal Savior and trusting Him to take you to be with Him when your body gives up the spirit.

Luke 23:42–43, *"And he said unto Jesus, Lord, remember me when thou comest into thy kingdom. And Jesus said unto him, Verily I say unto thee, Today shalt thou be with me in paradise."*

Acts 4:12, *"Neither is there salvation in any other: for there is none other name under heaven given among men, whereby we must be saved."*

Here are some ideas that may help you to test your faith and possibly build your faith. As you write your ideas, use these verses as a foundation.

James 2:26, *"For as the body without the spirit is dead, so faith without works is dead also."*

James 2:20, *"But wilt thou know, O vain man, that faith without works is dead?"*

You may be interested in riding a motorcycle. There are a number of safety classes for beginners. Often, former military personnel and business executives will ride together for charitable organizations. You may want to be a chaplain for these riders.

Maybe you would be interested in a running club. I highly recommend staying healthy. There are many reasons to run, as it is personally beneficial for your body and for your spirit. People love to surround themselves with energetic people.

First Corinthians 9:26–27, *"I therefore so run, not as uncertainly; so fight I, not as one that beateth the air: But I keep under my body, and bring it into subjection: lest that by any means, when I have preached to others, I myself should be a castaway."*

You can decide if your enthusiasm would be enhanced by something spiritual, something physical, something mental, such as school, or something creative, like being an inventor, songwriter, or author.

What is it in your life that you would like to have in your life that you could be enthusiastic about every morning when you wake up? Perhaps your mode of transportation is a horseback ride in the morning, and you wake up early to go outside, saddle up the horse, and just enjoy God's gift of nature.

I have met many pastors across the country and around the world who enjoy what they do. They help others. Many nurses enjoy being able to take care of others. These same professions can be very tiring because of people's needs all night long. Don't mistake a tired body for not having an enthusiastic spirit. Quite often they are one and the same.

Take a few minutes right now and write down ideas for activities that will bring you enthusiasm throughout your life. Some of us enjoy reading. You have heard that "leaders are readers." This means that the more you read about a subject because it interests you, the more others will want to be around you because of the enthusiasm that you have for any particular subject, which will result in delightful conversations.

How will this lesson help me?

Personal—This lesson will change your life. As you begin to write down ideas that bring you enthusiasm and keep you closer to God, you can live an entirely different lifestyle without spending any extra money. You can walk with the new realization that God is walking with you in every area of your life.

Hebrews 13:5–6, *"Let your conversation be without covetousness; and be content with such things as ye have: for he hath said, I will never leave thee, nor forsake thee. So that we may boldly say, The Lord is my helper, and I will not fear what man shall do unto me."*

As you write down those activities and ideas that bring you closer to walking with God, you will be able to pray without ceasing and enjoy a closer fellowship with others who walk with you. You are God's child. Soon, we will walk together in heaven.

Marriage and family—This could be a fun family night project. Let each member of the family write down what will give them enthusiasm and something to look forward to as a fellowship with each other as they prepare for heaven. Life can really be fun when you know that the Lord is watching over you and all things work together for good because you love Him.

If your family is small, or maybe it's just a husband and wife, think of some things that will be enthusiastic and possibly provide the amount of money needed to do great service for Jesus Christ in your local area and around the world. You may want to take a trip to many countries and do it as a missionary trip helping missionaries and exploring the world at the same time. Would that give you enthusiasm? Jesus Christ commanded us to go into all the world and teach the gospel. Think about it. Enjoy the trip!

Matthew 28:18–20:

And Jesus came and spake unto them, saying, All power is given unto me in heaven and in earth. Go ye therefore, and teach all nations, baptizing them in the name of the Father, and of the Son, and of the Holy Ghost: Teaching them to observe all things whatsoever I have commanded you: and, lo, I am with you always, even unto the end of the world. Amen.

Luke 13:22, *"And he went through the cities and villages, teaching, and journeying toward Jerusalem."*

Church—I always try to remind people in church that we are a family. We are just children who have a wonderful Heavenly Father, and we are here to do His will together for a short period of time until we meet with Him for eternity. Let's enjoy living with enthusiasm ("en *Theos*").

Matthew 12:48–50:

But he answered and said unto him that told him, Who is my mother? and who are my brethren? And he stretched forth his hand toward his disciples, and said, Behold my mother and my brethren! For whosoever shall do the will of my Father which is in heaven, the same is my brother, and sister, and mother.

Community—This may be the one exercise in this book that will help to unify your church with your community and bring you blessings beyond your expectations. When Christ dwells in your heart and your community sees and feels your enthusiasm, they will be attracted and want to know why you have such a wonderful spirit. It is because of your enthusiasm through Christ! Share your enthusiasm!

Ephesians 3:17–21:

That Christ may dwell in your hearts by faith; that ye, being rooted and grounded in love, May be able to comprehend with all saints what is the breadth, and length, and depth, and height; And to know the love of Christ, which passeth knowledge, that ye might be filled with all the fulness of God. Now unto him that is able to do exceeding abundantly above all that we ask or think, according to the power that worketh in us, Unto him be glory in the church by Christ Jesus throughout all ages, world without end. Amen.

THE ACTIVATION OF ENTHUSIASM

How would a person "activate enthusiasm"? You might do it through prayer mixed with belief and expectation! Jesus Christ taught this lesson to His disciples.

Matthew 18:18–20:

Verily I say unto you, Whatsoever ye shall bind on earth shall be bound in heaven: and whatsoever ye shall loose on earth shall be loosed in heaven. Again I say unto you, That if two of you shall agree on earth as touching any thing that they shall ask, it shall be done for them of my Father which is in heaven. For where two or three are gathered together in my name, there am I in the midst of them.

I call this "The Original Brainstorming Lesson." Can you imagine if you and your brother have a wonderful relationship with your father and you ask each other, "What can we do together that would make Dad happy?"? If we rephrase that knowing that our Heavenly Father can fulfill any desire if it is in His will, what would you ask for if you could receive it from your Father who loves you?

This short lesson on "the activation of enthusiasm" teaches both enthusiasm and faith. These two subjects can be so intertwined in your life that you may not realize when you are going from one to the other.

First John 1:7, *"But if we walk in the light, as he is in the light, we have fellowship one with another, and the blood of Jesus Christ his Son cleanseth us from all sin."*

Hebrews 11:1, *"Now faith is the substance of things hoped for, the evidence of things not seen."*

Since these verses are true, when you activate your enthusiasm, you are doing so by using the faith of the possibility of your dream coming true.

If two of you read this book simultaneously, you might gain some synergy. This means that you are combining your actions with a purpose. If you understand that this short lesson may be the missing element of the teamwork in your office, your classroom, or your group project, then by using these lessons that Jesus Christ first taught, you can magnify the effectiveness of your activities.

Some readers of this book will be in management of some kind. Some readers will work in a church ministry or a nonprofit organization. By using this lesson to activate enthusiasm, you are also using this lesson for prayer and for brainstorming. What is brainstorming? It is the activity of working together and coming up with ideas for the benefit of all parties concerned. This will generate more enthusiasm. When one person in the group says, "I have an idea" and the other members of the group realize that the idea will produce the results needed, enthusiasm is generated.

Some businesses are built through enthusiasm. Churches are built through enthusiasm. Your life from this date forward can be built on enthusiasm. Suppose you can find one other person who is as enthusiastic about an idea as you are, and you activate that enthusiasm through prayer, meditation, daydreaming, and authoring or scripting that idea. In that case, your life can be different for the better every day for the rest of your life. Activate your enthusiasm today!

How will this lesson help me?

Personal—We discussed a little bit about how sports teams have enthusiasm. When we begin to treat life as a sport, we will build upon that idea and become active about our enthusiasm. We will step out in faith, knowing that God is working with us, and our faith will be renewed every morning.

Second Corinthians 4:16, *"For which cause we faint not; but though our outward man perish, yet the inward man is renewed day by day."*

Marriage and family—When a family starts to activate enthusiasm and live knowing that Jesus Christ is with them always, then each person can walk with the newness of life and a smile on their face as we greet one another. You do not have to be arrogant when introducing somebody to your brother. We have been adopted into the family of God. Jesus was the only "begotten" Son of God.

First John 3:2, *"Beloved, now are we the sons of God, and it doth not yet appear what we shall be: but we know that, when he shall appear, we shall be like him; for we shall see him as he is."*

John 3:16, *"For God so loved the world, that he gave his only begotten Son."*

In like manner, you would be able to introduce Jesus Christ and the Holy Spirit to everyone with whom you come in contact. Make God real in your family and ask the Holy Spirit to be with you and give you enthusiasm throughout the day.

Luke 18:27, *"And he said, The things which are impossible with men are possible with God."*

Church—As our churches become active, vibrant, and enthusiastic and we stay focused on the will of God, we will have the ability, through the power of God, to fulfill whatever He has asked us to do. We are His servants. He has a desire (from the Father) for your life. There are things that God wants done that He will allow you to do. People will be amazed that you did it. It is not because you are amazing but because you have an amazing God. Be sure to remind people that it was God who completed the work. He is only using you because you are His child.

Philippians 2:3–7:

Let nothing be done through strife or vainglory; but in lowliness of mind let each esteem other better than themselves. Look not every man on his own things, but every man also on the things of others. Let this mind be in you, which was also in Christ Jesus: Who, being in the form of God, thought it not robbery to be equal with God: But made himself of no reputation, and took upon him the form of a servant, and was made in the likeness of men.

Community—Your community needs you to be enthusiastic! Activate your enthusiasm! This will make a big difference in your personal life and the life of your community! The world wants to see what your God can do. Can you imagine what would happen if you took the challenge to make a difference in this world? God can use you! God wants to use you! Your community would love to see you being able to pray for somebody and allow God to heal them at the hospital. Your community would love to see you working with teenagers and helping them be directed toward your Heavenly Father.

Please remember that we do not have to be physically destructive or damage any property to see God work miracles and change the nation.

Ephesians 6:12, *"For we wrestle not against flesh and blood, but against principalities, against powers, against the rulers of the darkness of this world, against spiritual wickedness in high places."*

Matthew 5:38–40:

Ye have heard that it hath been said, An eye for an eye, and a tooth for a tooth: But I say unto you, That ye resist not evil: but whosoever shall smite thee on thy right cheek, turn to him the other also. And if any man will sue thee at the law, and take away thy coat, let him have thy cloak also.

THE APPRECIATION OF ENTHUSIASM

The last suggestion in every lesson of this book is appreciation. As you finish any activity and you look back on that activity, you will want to appreciate the enthusiasm that brought you to this point in life. What does it mean in your life to appreciate enthusiasm?

If we relate your life to our race, such as a marathon, a triathlon, or a decathlon, you will look back and realize the many times that you have sat and thought and possibly prayed as you traveled the distance. I have run a couple of half marathons and realize the enthusiasm that would be needed to begin the race. Throughout the race, I had to remind myself of the enthusiasm that it took to start it. I am sure many of us runners said to ourselves (during the race), "Lord, help me…"

Hebrews 12:1–2:

Wherefore seeing we also are compassed about with so great a cloud of witnesses, let us lay aside every weight, and the sin which doth so easily beset us, and let us run with patience the race that is set before us, Looking unto Jesus the author and finisher of our faith; who for the joy that was set before him endured the cross, despising the shame, and is set down at the right hand of the throne of God.

However, using the same amount of appreciation of enthusiasm, when I ran a triathlon, I had to appreciate the enthusiasm even more with each phase of the race. As you begin the triathlon race, you must prepare to swim, bicycle, and run. When I finished the bicycle portion of the race, I knew I had a long run ahead of me before the triathlon would be finished. At that moment, I had to appreciate the enthusiasm that it took to start the race and appreciate the enthusiasm that I knew that I would have at the end of the race.

Your life is this way! You have many different phases of your life that you can look back on and appreciate the success that you have had so far in life. You have succeeded at something. If you look back at your life right now and realize all that you have accomplished and all that you have completed, you will want to take a few minutes and just appreciate the inspiration and enthusiasm that you have used throughout your life. When you set this book down in a few minutes, you will want to stand up more enthusiastically, knowing that you and your God have accomplished this together. You are not alone!

When you brainstorm and pray in a group setting and you accomplish a goal together with other individuals, you can look back and appreciate that enthusiasm. When I was practicing for some of the races that I have run, I would often join up with a running club or exercise group as a test run for the actual event. If you are part of a church or a religious organization and you pray in a group, you can then recall the words of Jesus Christ, who speaks of the power of prayer in the group setting.

Matthew 18:20, *"For where two or three are gathered together in my name, there am I in the midst of them."*

Matthew 26:41, *"Watch and pray, that ye enter not into temptation: the spirit indeed is willing, but the flesh is weak."*

Matthew 17:20–21:

And Jesus said unto them, Because of your unbelief: for verily I say unto you, If ye have faith as a grain of mustard seed, ye shall say unto this mountain, Remove hence to yonder place; and it shall remove; and nothing shall be impossible unto you. Howbeit this kind goeth not out but by prayer and fasting.

Learn to appreciate those who are like-minded as yourself in any endeavor. That is called camaraderie. We sometimes would call those individuals "comrades in arms," as they have shared many of the same difficulties. This is how many groups, such as churches and nonprofit organizations, are formed. This is also how many great companies are created. This is how lifelong friends and great marriages exist throughout the world today.

How will this lesson help me?

Personal—When you take the time to appreciate all of your enthusiasm, you will appreciate having walked with your Heavenly Father through many trials and tribulations of everyday life. Life is tremendous when you walk through life with a tremendous Heavenly Father who is with you every step of the way, no matter what the trial is over when it occurs. You may be going through a tough time in life right now, or you have gone through hard times earlier in life. God was always with you. When we appreciate the enthusiasm that God has provided to us while we are here as his children on this earth, we can be a blessing to our brothers and sisters in Christ and to our communities.

Galatians 5:16–23:

This I say then, Walk in the Spirit, and ye shall not fulfil the lust of the flesh. For the flesh lusteth against the Spirit, and the Spirit against the flesh: and these are contrary the one to the other: so that ye cannot do the things that ye would. But if ye be led of the Spirit, ye are not under the law. Now the works of the flesh are manifest, which are these; Adultery, fornication, uncleanness, lasciviousness, Idolatry, witchcraft, hatred, variance, emulations, wrath, strife, seditions, heresies, Envyings, murders, drunkenness, revellings, and such like: of the which I tell you before, as I have also told you in time past, that they which do such things shall not inherit the kingdom of God. But the fruit of the Spirit is love, joy, peace, longsuffering, gentleness, goodness, faith, Meekness, temperance: against such there is no law.

Marriage and family—At the end of each day, you will be able to look back and appreciate the enthusiasm that you and your family have had throughout the day. Maybe you had a tiring day, but you will feel blessed to have been close to your family and close to the Lord throughout the day. You may possibly have a family member who is not as close to the Lord as you are, but by showing them how blessed they are and how blessed you are to be with them, you can show them how trusting in Christ in every part of life can bring them comfort.

Psalm 133:1, *"Behold, how good and how pleasant it is for brethren to dwell together in unity!"*

Church—When our churches appreciate being enthusiastic about walking in the Spirit of Christ, we will enjoy life as we fellowship with one another. When we can appreciate the enthusiasm for the work of the Lord and we have fellowship with one another, we will all be supportive of the work that the Lord is doing in each of our lives.

First John 1:7–9:

But if we walk in the light, as he is in the light, we have fellowship one with another, and the blood of Jesus Christ his Son cleanseth us from all sin. If we say that we have no sin, we deceive ourselves, and the truth is not in us. If we confess our sins, he is faithful and just to forgive us our sins, and to cleanse us from all unrighteousness.

Community—People love and appreciate enthusiasm! As your community begins to see you and your church walk with Christ, people from other churches with the same mindset will begin to pray. There may be many people in your community who love the Lord. Be willing to pray for others who are like-minded. Pray for others and ask the Lord for wisdom as you seek to do His will.

Mark 9:38–40:

And John answered him, saying, Master, we saw one casting out devils in thy name, and he followeth not us: and we forbad him, because he followeth not us. But Jesus said, Forbid him not: for there is no man which shall do a miracle in my name, that can lightly speak evil of me. For he that is not against us is on our part.

Anticipating and Appreciating Your Christian Life

THIS PAGE HAS BEEN LEFT BLANK SO THAT YOU CAN MAKE
NOTES ABOUT ENTHUSIASM

ENLIGHTENMENT
THE ANTICIPATION OF ENLIGHTENMENT

Have you ever said, "I am looking forward to figuring out how all of this works!"? If I rephrase your dilemma, we could say, "I am anticipating being enlightened on this subject." The word "enlighten" means to provide knowledge and understanding. Often this will happen by seeing the big picture and being enlightened through our eyes. There will be many different books available to read on your subject of interest. Be sure that you become familiar with your subject so that you can document your trusted sources and become an expert.

Second Timothy 2:15, *"Study to shew thyself approved unto God, a workman that needeth not to be ashamed, rightly dividing the word of truth."*

This may be one of the sections of this book that you will appreciate more because of the personal impact and the ability to use this for your benefit. It will help you with your classmates. It will help you with your friends. It will help you to choose your friends. You know which friends, the five to ten closest friends you want to be like. This will help you with your children and your spouse.

What is the anticipation of enlightenment all about?

The anticipation of enlightenment is the excitement of knowing that you are about to understand how "it" all works and how you have made it happen. You are amazing! By reading this far in this book, you have demonstrated that you want to understand what surrounds you and what you want to learn. This is one of the most exciting ideas of mankind. We all want to know more about the future, about "life, liberty, and the pursuit of happiness."

Have you ever heard someone say, "I don't understand. Could you enlighten me?"? What they are saying is, "Can you give me greater knowledge and understanding about a subject or situation?" Anticipation is expecting the realization in advance or giving intellectual or spiritual light to a matter, such as success.

Maybe you are saying to yourself such things as…

I am really curious! How can I really achieve success?

I am looking forward to understanding what all of this "success" really means.

Have I already achieved success and not even realized it? That is one of the greatest questions of mankind. What is life all about? Will the Bible help to enlighten me?

Proverbs 1:7, *"The fear of the LORD is the beginning of knowledge: but fools despise wisdom and instruction."*

Psalm 19:7, *"The law of the LORD is perfect, converting the soul: the testimony of the LORD is sure, making wise the simple."*

I am an instructor in aviation, mortgages, and real estate. I am married to a teacher. We often discuss these ideas over coffee in the morning. We love to talk about the idea of when we see the student's eyes "light up," and they say words like, "I got it!" or "Now, I get it!" or "Teacher, I finally understand! Thank you!" Some of these students are in high school. My students are typically adults. All of our students thank us for their new knowledge! That is where you may be today as you say words such as, "I want to learn more about (some topic) that will lead to success!" and "I am really anxious to understand the meaning of success, the idea of success, and the mindset of successful people. Please, enlighten me!" That is the anticipation of enlightenment!

You may have already passed success in your life journey and did not even realize that you had already achieved it. If you have read this far in this book, then you have already achieved some success as you have the ability to read and understand your language. You have proven to yourself that you still have the desire to learn more about success. Learn all that you can, but no matter how much knowledge or wealth you gain, be sure to stay humble!

First Samuel 2:3, *"Talk no more so exceeding proudly; let not arrogancy come out of your mouth: for the LORD is a God of knowledge, and by him actions are weighed."*

James 4:10, *"Humble yourselves in the sight of the Lord, and he shall lift you up."*

Success is both a journey and a destination. It is like a long trip with many shorter ones along the way. It is like driving across the country. You have to stop for gas and food. You will still see other travelers along life's journey who will inspire you and help you reach your goal. You will meet people such as bankers and financial advisors because you cannot reach any destination without finances to pay for food and necessities. Be aware of your surroundings. Many people will help you because we all want you to succeed. You may even cross the path of angels.

Hebrews 13:1–2, *"Let brotherly love continue. Be not forgetful to entertain strangers: for thereby some have entertained angels unawares."*

How will this lesson help me?

Personal—Anticipating enlightenment is like being a senior in high school and having what is known as "senior fever." This is an expectation of realizing that you have acquired the knowledge for the next phase of your life. This is even more exciting when you are in college and you are about to graduate. As you read this book, you are in a time of life as you are looking forward to the next step in your success. Enjoy this time. It is an important time in your life as you accept the understanding of whatever it is that you feel is success.

Marriage and family—You may be preparing to get married. You may ask yourself, *How does all this "happily ever after" really work?* You may be reading marriage manuals or asking your married friends how to stay happy for many, many years. As you anticipate your marriage and all of the activities, remember to take the time to learn together with your spouse.

If you are married and you do not understand something regarding your spouse, ask them to enlighten you and tell you their side of the story so that you can learn what their thoughts are behind the situation. Your spouse loves you enough to marry you. Concentrate on the love and friendship that brought you this far in life. Look forward to learning about each family background and what brought you together.

If you are still in high school, you can use this lesson with your brothers and sisters (and your parents) and solve many of the arguments in the house. Instead of arguing and forcing your opinion, learn to ask why the other person has their opinion. This will help you throughout your life to understand negotiation and how to keep peace in the world around you.

Philippians 1:20, *"According to my earnest expectation and my hope, that in nothing I shall be ashamed, but that with all boldness, as always, so now also Christ shall be magnified in my body, whether it be by life, or by death."*

Church—When your church anticipates enlightenment, you may be able to have a group of wise individuals in your church who will anticipate a new direction for your church. This will build your church in preparation for the next generation. Be sure that your decisions are based on Scripture. Be sure to follow the rules provided in your community. For instance, your local fire marshal has been enlightened on certain safety issues. Be sure to invite him regularly to be sure your buildings are safe. Other local officials should be treated similarly.

Hebrews 13:17, *"Obey them that have the rule over you, and submit yourselves: for they watch for your souls, as they that must give account, that they may do it with joy, and not with grief: for that is unprofitable for you."*

Community—As you anticipate enlightenment in your community, you will hope to see "the big picture" and how every part of your community can benefit from your faith and your willingness to help the community to be a better place to live for all individuals. Not everybody will believe like you believe yet. Through many prayers, they might soon want to know your Savior. Stay faithful. Do what the Lord requires of you to do.

Micah 6:8, *"He hath shewed thee, O man, what is good; and what doth the* LORD *require of thee, but to do justly, and to love mercy, and to walk humbly with thy God?"*

Mark 12:17, *"And Jesus answering said unto them, Render to Caesar the things that are Caesar's, and to God the things that are God's. And they marvelled at him."*

THE ACCEPTANCE OF ENLIGHTENMENT

When you accept enlightenment, you are actually accepting the fact that you now have the ability to understand and have full knowledge of how it all works in your favor and to your benefit. You cannot know everything. That is why the world is full of colleges and universities. Each professor and instructor has a realm of knowledge that differs from other disciplines. However, when you accept enlightenment in your area of expertise and achieve success in your life, then you begin to understand your own destiny.

Accepting enlightenment is similar to accepting your high school diploma or your degree from college. You accept the fact that you understand, and you are aware of "how it all works." Think about this concept. When an authority from your college confers upon you a college degree, it signifies that you have an understanding of your studies. When you accept that degree, you are accepting the fact that you understand the rights and responsibilities of that degree.

In many areas of expertise, you have the opportunity to receive a certificate or an endorsement. You have proven to have "been enlightened" and understand the industry. For instance, pilots receive a number of endorsements during their endeavor to receive their pilot certificate. That endorsement shows that an instructor believes that the student has the knowledge, understanding, and skills that are required for that endorsement. You get to decide what you feel is success or what you accept as enlightenment. Are you successful when you receive an endorsement? Are you successful the first time you fly the airplane alone ("solo")? Are you successful only after you receive your commercial pilot certificate? You must decide!

Every industry is similar. As a salesperson, are you successful with your first sale? Yes! You now understand what it takes to sell. As a teacher, are you successful after your first year? Yes! You survived, and you learned more about teaching. As a coach, are you a success after your first win? Yes! As a pastor, when does "success" take place? That answer is between you and God!

Will you succeed and "accept enlightenment" with a bachelor of science degree, a master's degree, a PhD, or an MD? Every doctor will continue to study and learn as technology advances.

When do you accept the fact that you know your area of expertise? You may feel that you want to continue to be enlightened. This action typically results in becoming an instructor or earning a "doctorate" degree. Enjoy being enlightened and learning as you still want to learn more about each subject. However, along your journey, help others to reach the success of their dreams. Leave a legacy for others to follow.

How will this lesson help me?

Personal—When you accept your high school diploma or college degree, you are actually accepting a document that says that you have been enlightened and understand what is required to receive the document. You have probably been tired many times from all the studying, but now you have achieved your goal and accepted that you have the knowledge that will benefit others.

Second Timothy 2:15, *"Study to shew thyself approved unto God, a workman that needeth not to be ashamed, rightly dividing the word of truth."*

Ecclesiastes 12:12, *"And further, by these, my son, be admonished: of making many books there is no end; and much study is a weariness of the flesh."*

Marriage and family—A good way to think about "the acceptance of enlightenment" with your family is to think about getting out the cookbook and learning a new recipe together. Think about it this way. When you look at a new recipe, you have to look at all the ingredients, how much of each ingredient, and the order in which it needs to be put together before it is "tried in the fire" and comes out of the oven to be enjoyed by the family. If the recipe turns out well, then you can accept the fact that you have all been enlightened, and you can enjoy the dinner together. If the meal did not turn out as planned, then you can work together to see how you can improve it the next time.

That is what marriage and family are all about. You are trying different ideas and different combinations before you go through the heat so that you know the outcome will be successful and you can enjoy it throughout your life. Years ago, if something was easy, a common phrase would be, "It's just a piece of cake." That is a recipe for a good marriage! Savor it together!

Proverbs 14:29, *"He that is slow to wrath is of great understanding: but he that is hasty of spirit exalteth folly."*

Proverbs 22:1, *"A good name is rather to be chosen than great riches, and loving favour rather than silver and gold."*

Church—As each church member begins to study and accepts the ideas of becoming enlighted about many intellectual subjects, your church may begin to develop study groups. Sometimes these groups will be of certain age groups, such as teenagers, college age, and adults. However, sometimes, these groups will be by subject matter. For instance, you may have a group in your church who all want to study financial matters at any age. In this group, you may have teenagers sitting next to a banking executive, a military leader, or a business owner. Each of these groups may have guest speakers who are knowledgeable. This may attract new visitors to your church with common interests. Be sure that these knowledgeable individuals are like-minded with the truths taught by your leadership.

Romans 15:5, *"Now the God of patience and consolation grant you to be likeminded one toward another according to Christ Jesus."*

Allow me to express one word of caution. Sometimes the word "enlightenment" is misconstrued improperly, as people mistakenly may consider themselves equal to God in some manner.

Romans 8:7, *"Because the carnal mind is enmity against God: for it is not subject to the law of God, neither indeed can be."*

Romans 16:17, *"Now I beseech you, brethren, mark them which cause divisions and offences contrary to the doctrine which ye have learned; and avoid them."*

Community—If you take this lesson as a personal challenge and become enlightened on a particular subject, you might become a pastor, a healthcare professional, a legal professional, a politician, or a business leader. When you accept that you have the knowledge and the leadership ability in any given field, you will become active in your community because your community will come to you for leadership and advice. Accepting enlightenment is an awesome responsibility. It may be used to show the world (starting with your community) how great faith is within the members of your church. Use this wisely!

Matthew 8:10, *"When Jesus heard it, he marvelled, and said to them that followed, Verily I say unto you, I have not found so great faith, no, not in Israel."*

THE AUTHORING OF ENLIGHTENMENT

This lesson will help you no matter your age or status in life. This exercise could take you a few minutes or a few hours. In preparation for this exercise, you may want to take a few days and think about all the different aspects of your life that you have written down since the beginning of this book. However, you may not need to take days because you have already been thinking about great ideas. Research shows that the average person has forty to sixty thoughts per minute. This may help you as you begin to author your enlightenment.

At what point in your life or the life of your career will you be able to say, "I understand how it all works!"? Let's think about different aspects of your life and consider "complete understanding" or enlightenment. How are you in your Christian life today? If a friend asks you about your walk with God, are you able to write down the scriptures? Will you be able to write your friend a letter and explain what God means in your life? What you may need to ask yourself is, *Can I author my enlightenment?* Can I write a letter to my best friend in simple terms and explain to them how they can meet me in heaven? That is an awesome responsibility! Try to write down how God is your Heavenly Father. God has an awesome Holy Spirit, which your best friend might see in you. You may want to use Scriptures or come up with personal illustrations of what God has done in your life.

Maybe part of your enlightenment is that God is directing you into a specialized field, such as being a missionary in a particular foreign country. This may mean that you have to study and master a language. You may also need to master the rules of transportation to get to that village. In some areas, you will need to use an amateur radio (also known as a "ham radio"). You may also need to learn a little bit about aviation, as you may be part of the team that will fly to that remote village. You may not need to master each of these techniques but only to write down ("author") what it will take for you to be enlightened on each subject.

What is it that God wants you to do? This answer will be different for each individual because each person may have a different idea of what they consider "success." Maybe you are a local business owner of a small restaurant or coffee shop. When you master your craft, you may have more influence in your local area as police officers and emergency workers may gather at your location. As you begin to write down ideas that will help to make you successful in being of benefit to your community, you will want to think of ideas that will be exciting and beneficial for the safety and operation of your city or local area. Think about how much influence you can have by helping your staff and workers learn about your great Heavenly Father. Think about how you can help your community and your family.

Write down ideas about how you can help direct people of all ages (and all walks of life) to come to you for spiritual advice. You may not have the title of pastor or chaplain, but you may be a greater influence on more people as they are influenced by what you are about to write down. Make this an exciting exercise. Write down those ideas that will help you to know how you were enlightened to your craft and also to the knowledge of the saving power of Jesus Christ. Teach those lessons to your community.

Matthew 28:18–20:

And Jesus came and spake unto them, saying, All power is given unto me in heaven and in earth. Go ye therefore, and teach all nations, baptizing them in the name of the Father, and of the Son, and of the Holy Ghost: Teaching them to observe all things whatsoever I have commanded you: and, lo, I am with you always, even unto the end of the world. Amen.

How will this lesson help me?
Personal—As you begin to write down those enlightenment ideas in your life, you will come across spiritual decisions. You will want to write down your testimony and stories that you can use that will be beneficial for the rest of your life. For instance, when I understood that I needed a personal relationship with

Jesus Christ, the pastor spoke on the one word "joy." There have been many times in my life that I have used that example so that I could help others understand the joy and how they can have that in their life.

Psalm 51:10–12, *"Create in me a clean heart, O God; and renew a right spirit within me. Cast me not away from thy presence; and take not thy holy spirit from me. Restore unto me the joy of thy salvation; and uphold me with thy free spirit."*

Galatians 5:22–23, *"But the fruit of the Spirit is love, joy, peace, longsuffering, gentleness, goodness, faith, Meekness, temperance: against such there is no law."*

Marriage and family—In our previous lesson, we looked at the "acceptance of enlightenment." You were to make recipes of what is working that created a successful outcome in your marriage and family. This is your opportunity to write down and create those recipes for a great marriage. What do you do first? How much of each ingredient needs to be added? Since you know that things will heat up as you go through the "oven" of life, you can be prepared that everything will turn out correctly.

If you are a teenager, you may want to write down ideas that will help you to have a successful outcome so that you can help others through the hard times of their life. Ensure your friends and loved ones know about the God that wants to walk with them. Help them to know that God is love and that He loves them!

Micah 6:8, *"He hath shewed thee, O man, what is good; and what doth the* Lord *require of thee, but to do justly, and to love mercy, and to walk humbly with thy God?"*

First John 4:8, *"He that loveth not knoweth not God; for God is love."*

Church—In some cases, you may want to make this a church project. Some readers will want to discuss this in their Sunday school class or their small group settings. Have each person write down (if possible) what happened in their life they can use as a personal illustration to tell others about what Jesus Christ has meant in their life. This may be an amazing time in your church and a wonderful time of fellowship and blessing as each person gains insight into the testimonies of others.

Mark 5:19–20:

Howbeit Jesus suffered him not, but saith unto him, Go home to thy friends, and tell them how great things the Lord hath done for thee, and hath had compassion on thee. And he departed, and began to publish in Decapolis how great things Jesus had done for him: and all men did marvel.

Community—As your church members begin to write their testimonies and discuss the things in this world that have helped enlighten each to the work of Jesus Christ in the power of God Almighty, there will be people who don't yet understand. These members of the community want to learn and understand why we are here on earth and how this God can love us. That is why you need to write down what has helped you to know the love of God in your life. Our responsibility is to deliver the message that Jesus Christ has given us. We can ask God to help others to understand His magnificence!

John 3:11–12, *"Verily, verily, I say unto thee, We speak that we do know, and testify that we have seen; and ye receive not our witness. If I have told you earthly things, and ye believe not, how shall ye believe, if I tell you of heavenly things?"*

THE ACTIVATION OF ENLIGHTENMENT

The activation of enlightenment is a unique term, as it can be expressed in so many different ways. Activation or activity is similar to what we discussed earlier in this book regarding motivation. Activation means there must be activity. Since activity can be physical, mental, emotional, or spiritual, then, it is different than pure inspiration.

We will be discussing enlightenment as expanded educational and professional knowledge. We will also discuss the expanded spiritual knowledge that you received from your Heavenly Father and how you can use this in combination with your other knowledge and activities.

Acts 4:20, *"For we cannot but speak the things which we have seen and heard."*

Acts 22:15, *"For thou shalt be his witness unto all men of what thou hast seen and heard."*

"Enlightenment" means that you have figured it out and you now understand what your subject is all about. Therefore, if you received a degree, a diploma, or similar recognition, then others feel like you are (and recognize you as) being enlightened to some extent. So how do you activate that? By working in the field of expertise and succeeding as expected when you receive your degree. You will now want to use the knowledge received in each of those classes that you took that will benefit mankind. Stay active with the knowledge and understanding of your profession throughout your life, for that is what activating your enlightenment is about. You will then be able to teach wise men about your profession and speak with them about your Lord!

Job 34:2, *"Hear my words, O ye wise men; and give ear unto me, ye that have knowledge."*

Typically, activating your "pure knowledge" is only temporary and will only be used during your adult working life. Many people do not use their degree or their vast knowledge after they retire. Therefore, let's go one step further and consider your spiritual knowledge and enlightenment. How do you currently activate the enlightenment that you share about your relationship with the Lord? What do you do to actively keep your walk with God alive, active, and vibrant? How often do you tell others of your faith in your Heavenly Father? Do you know where to turn for guidance?

Psalm 119:105, *"Thy word is a lamp unto my feet, and a light unto my path."*

Each of us could strengthen our testimony by knowing that we walk with the Heavenly Father with every breath we take. Some people reading this book will keep their testimony alive by singing in their church. Some people sing in the choir, while others sing in a praise group or ensemble. You may be one of these gifted individuals praising in a quartet in your church or other churches. However you sing, keep your testimony alive by keeping a song in your heart.

Acts 22:15, *"For thou shalt be his witness unto all men of what thou hast seen and heard."*

Psalm 95:1, *"O come, let us sing unto the LORD: let us make a joyful noise to the rock of our salvation."*

Maybe you will be active in your church through some ministry, Sunday school class, or small group sessions. This means that you study extra so that you can understand the message that the Lord is trying to give to you. This takes extra effort, and the Lord will bless you for it.

Matthew 5:6, *"Blessed are they which do hunger and thirst after righteousness: for they shall be filled."*

All of us who receive any post-high school education have a reason for pursuing that career path. No matter what your field of study is, you choose it because it interests you or you find it financially and socially rewarding. By keeping your activity in that profession or endeavor, you will meet new people and enjoy life because of those contacts as you benefit others.

We sometimes use the acronym "JOY" as meaning "Jesus, Others, and You" (in that order). By keeping Jesus first in your life and concentrating on what He once did for you, then you can be a testimony to others throughout your career. What you have learned through your career and studies may benefit others through their trials and tribulations. You will gain earthly friends and friends with whom you can spend eternity in heaven. Enjoy keeping your enlightenment and enthusiasm active! By doing so, many clubs and churches will ask you to return as a speaker because they appreciate your knowledge.

Acts 15:36, *"And some days after Paul said unto Barnabas, Let us go again and visit our brethren in every city where we have preached the word of the Lord, and see how they do."*

How will this lesson help me?

Personal—As you "activate your enlightenment" and use all of your knowledge, you can keep your testimony alive while keeping your work life, your social life, and your spiritual life active. You will be able to walk each day with such love and appreciation for all that the Lord has done for you. You may get tired by staying active, but the activity itself will be a blessing to you. Keep up the good work! Other people are watching you and admiring you as you walk with the Lord.

Micah 6:8, *"He hath shewed thee, O man, what is good; and what doth the Lord require of thee, but to do justly, and to love mercy, and to walk humbly with thy God?"*

Marriage and family—Now that you have created the recipe for success in your family and you have written it down, the most exciting part of marriage and family is to activate what you have learned. What that means is to do the activities that you now know will create a better marriage. Find things to smile about. Look at things that help you to smile and laugh at the same time. In some instances, find things that help you to sing together. Do these activities together so that you can build great memories.

If you are a teenager, whether you have older or younger siblings, find activities that will help you to laugh together. Don't laugh at or disgrace any other person. Have joy in your life and create smiles. Find ways to help each other succeed so that when you grow older, you will both live successful lives and have great family reunions.

Psalm 126:6, *"He that goeth forth and weepeth, bearing precious seed, shall doubtless come again with rejoicing, bringing his sheaves with him."*

Church—This will help your church to remain vibrant in your community. Your church will be excited by the activity of being able to express their walk with the Lord openly. They will find out how they can be a blessing or have been a blessing inside the church to members of the church. They have also been a blessing to others in the community. Your church may start gaining a reputation for being active as they walk every day with the presence of Jesus, who walks with them. Notice that James 1:27 does not refer to only people who attend your church. You have so much to offer. Your church is a blessing to your people, and they can bless others!

James 1:27, *"Pure religion and undefiled before God and the Father is this, To visit the fatherless and widows in their affliction, and to keep himself unspotted from the world."*

This is how "mission trips" start. Knowledgeable people in your church may volunteer to use their expertise to start a mission or help a missionary. They may also start a local rescue mission. Start with your community.

Community—Your community will be excited when you personally start using and activating your enlightenment of what you used in your post–high school education. When you stay active about the subjects with which you have been enlightened and study to help others and you do that with enthusiasm, people feel your energy and spirit when they walk into your business or your office.

For instance, if everyone who walks into your presence knows that you want to help them, are happy to use your knowledge, and are willing to teach them, you will be praised for enlightening others in a way that will benefit them.

Matthew 10:8, *"Heal the sick, cleanse the lepers, raise the dead, cast out devils: freely ye have received, freely give."*

In a similar manner, if you help others throughout your day to know what God can do for them as they walk daily with Him truly and humbly, people will begin to trust you and have a willingness to trust your Heavenly Father.

First Kings 8:61, *"Let your heart therefore be perfect with the LORD our God, to walk in his statutes, and to keep his commandments, as at this day."*

THE APPRECIATION OF ENLIGHTENMENT

It is now time for you to enjoy and appreciate all of the different things that you have learned in classrooms, in life, and in your walk with the Lord. Perhaps you were enlightened by professors in college. You may not have enjoyed each class that you took because you were pressured to get a certain grade point average; however, now you can go back and restudy each lesson and enjoy and appreciate what the professors and instructors were trying to teach you.

Maybe you have taken an entire career to learn and to labor in a subject matter that you felt God has led you to. Before you retire, take time to reflect and enjoy the atmosphere, the people, and the lessons you have learned.

Ecclesiastes 3:13, *"And also that every man should eat and drink, and enjoy the good of all his labour, it is the gift of God."*

While you are taking the time to reflect and appreciate your life and all that you have learned, you may want to go somewhere where you can meditate and reflect on the goodness of God. You have learned a lot more in your life. You have learned in church and in the classroom. You have met people and learned about personalities. You have things that you have seen and possibly have souvenirs that you have picked up. You have learned from the places that you have traveled. Sometimes, through trials and tribulation, you may have wondered if God was in control. He has always been there for you.

Romans 8:28, *"And we know that all things work together for good to them that love God, to them who are the called according to his purpose."*

Genesis 50:20, *"But as for you, ye thought evil against me; but God meant it unto good, to bring to pass, as it is this day, to save much people alive."*

Take a few minutes and appreciate all the books that you read. Take a few minutes and think about all the teachers who have given much of their lives so that you could learn subjects that will help you through life. Pray for them by name and thank the Lord for them.

Next, take some time to remember the names of all of the people who have influenced you through your spiritual journey. Perhaps you are new to your knowledge of Jesus Christ. He wants to be with you through all of your trials. Maybe you have been in church all of your life. Either way, take some time and appreciate all the people who have taught you about the love of God. These people, maybe Sunday school teachers, deacons, pastors, and church staff, different members of the community, have given you wisdom and helped you to understand the Scriptures. Never get too busy to be thankful for those whom God has placed within your path. Appreciate the enlightenment!

How will this lesson help me?

Personal—As you take the time to appreciate all of the wisdom and knowledge that has been given to you, you will be better prepared to answer questions from your family, your church, and your community. You will be thankful and have joy that you have the words to say and the needed answers so that you can help others. You can provide words of cheer and encouragement at the right time.

Proverbs 15:23, *"A man hath joy by the answer of his mouth: and a word spoken in due season, how good is it!"*

Marriage and family—By appreciating what you have learned by creating the recipes that will help your family, you will be creating a more pleasant life for yourself. As you are enlightened by your spouse, you can create a much deeper, loving relationship with the understanding of what will bring peace and joy with spiritual closeness as you grow older. It is important that each person understands every ingredient that will be necessary so that the recipe is a success.

Proverbs 5:18, *"Let thy fountain be blessed: and rejoice with the wife of thy youth."*

If you are a teenager, you may want to watch and listen to other family members. This will help you to understand how you can help others. If you can be a blessing to your teachers and your friends in a positive manner, you may be able to create great mentorships that will last a lifetime.

Ecclesiastes 12:1, *"Remember now thy Creator in the days of thy youth, while the evil days come not, nor the years draw nigh, when thou shalt say, I have no pleasure in them."*

Church—When everybody in your church starts appreciating the wisdom that they received directly from the Bible as well as the teachings and lessons they learned from the pastor and school teachers, your church will gain knowledge and have a delightful spirit every time they learn something new. This will allow the Holy Spirit to work in each life. The Holy Spirit can then bring in new inspiration with more enlightenment to each individual.

First Corinthians 2:9–10, *"But as it is written, Eye hath not seen, nor ear heard, neither have entered into the heart of man, the things which God hath prepared for them that love him. But God hath revealed them unto us by his Spirit: for the Spirit searcheth all things, yea, the deep things of God."*

Community—Everybody appreciates knowledge and understanding. Many people check the facts and can appreciate meeting people who have seen and heard about great activities, read great books, and can show great things that have taken place. Your community will appreciate your involvement and your church's involvement in the community. This will help others because of the tremendous example that your church is setting. This may increase your attendance, as it creates an awareness of your activities.

Acts 4:20, *"For we cannot but speak the things which we have seen and heard."*

THIS PAGE HAS BEEN LEFT BLANK SO THAT YOU CAN MAKE NOTES ABOUT ENLIGHTENMENT

EMPOWERMENT
THE ANTICIPATION OF EMPOWERMENT

The "anticipation of empowerment" is an interesting concept for life, yet it mirrors what most people believe that it is what "success" entails. When you view the list of your desires that you created when you started this book, you will want to anticipate the (perceived) power that accompanies your dreams. Nearly every level of success has a level of power attached to it. We do not need to fear this power because we are of a sound mind with love for mankind.

Second Timothy 1:7, *"For God hath not given us the spirit of fear; but of power, and of love, and of a sound mind."*

The word "empowerment" can mean control, influence, or authority over yourself or others. Compare these two verses:

Matthew 28:18, *"And Jesus came and spake unto them, saying, All power is given unto me in heaven and in earth."*

Matthew 7:28–29, *"And it came to pass, when Jesus had ended these sayings, the people were astonished at his doctrine: For he taught them as one having authority, and not as the scribes."*

The Heavenly Father has given Jesus Christ all power. He can allow us the power needed in order to complete the tasks that He has set before us. This means that for some readers, empowerment is the ability and authority to usurp authority over another individual, such as a police officer, a parent over a child, a teacher with a student, a doctor with a patient, or a lawyer with a client. You may desire to be able to influence others as a pastor over a church or a Boy Scout leader. Look back at the desires that you originally wrote as you began to read this book. How many of those desires resulted in some level of empowerment?

You may think to yourself, *I don't want any power.* For some of us, the word "empowerment" simply means controlling one's own life, as in having a nice retirement. Freedom to choose your actions for the day is empowering! That is the essence of success. You may have grandchildren to whom you can leave an inheritance.

Proverbs 13:22, *"A good man leaveth an inheritance to his children's children: and the wealth of the sinner is laid up for the just."*

Proverbs 17:6, *"Children's children are the crown of old men; and the glory of children are their fathers."*

It is important to your future that you anticipate the amount of empowerment that will be handed to you as you achieve different levels of success. Perhaps you are like many people in your location or industry who have turned down a promotion. This has happened to me more than once. I was once offered "any title" I wanted at one large employer. I chose the option to take care of a loved one who was ill. Does that mean that I wasn't successful because I did not have the title of vice president yet? No, not at all. The success was the ability to have control of my own affairs. That is empowering. Your freedom of choice may be more empowering than any amount of money or any title.

Matthew 16:26, *"For what is a man profited, if he shall gain the whole world, and lose his own soul? or what shall a man give in exchange for his soul?"*

You may be offered some position of "success" and turn it down because it is offered at the wrong time in your life. I have watched this happen. I have spoken to some professionals who have had to make the choice of a "successful career position" in lieu of a "successful family life." Success is an element of either position. Some people who chose success lost a close connection with their family.

First Corinthians 2:9, *"But as it is written, Eye hath not seen, nor ear heard, neither have entered into the heart of man, the things which God hath prepared for them that love him."*

Remember, in any type of battle (even spiritual warfare), you will have the offense (such as power) and the defense. Sometimes, the best offense is a good defense.

Ecclesiastes 7:12, *"For wisdom is a defence, and money is a defence: but the excellency of knowledge is, that wisdom giveth life to them that have it."*

How will this lesson help me?

Personal—You can anticipate the power that you are about to receive. Be prepared for it. Plan for it! As you consider all of the dreams and desires that you have thought about while reading this book, it is important to remember that we only have the amount of power that was granted to us by God. When Jesus said, *"All power is given it to me in heaven and earth... Go ye, therefore..."* He reminded us that He is with us always as we go and do His work. That is empowering!

Hebrews 13:5–6, *"Let your conversation be without covetousness; and be content with such things as ye have: for he hath said, I will never leave thee, nor forsake thee. So that we may boldly say, The Lord is my helper, and I will not fear what man shall do unto me."*

Marriage and family—As many young couples prepare to get married, they often think of the empowerment of marriage. Some men think that they will have "control" over their wife and children. Some ladies get married so that they can become mothers and have some "control" over the lives of their children. Some children want to grow up and leave home so that they can have control over their own lives and their own destinies.

Marriage is not about control. Marriage provides a person with the authority and ability to prove your love to your spouse and your children. You have possibly heard somebody say the words "control your child," but that is a misnomer. You may restrain the physical body, but the spirit must be controlled by the child. You can pray for the child and ask the Holy Spirit to control the child.

Marriage does not give you power over others. Marriage allows you to have power over your own affairs so that you can show the love of God and His power.

Ephesians 5:28, *"So ought men to love their wives as their own bodies. He that loveth his wife loveth himself."*

Church—Your church has the power of influence. Your church has the power to change people's lives at every age and every economic status. As the people from your church meet people in the community, each person can be influenced by the power of the Holy Spirit. Your community will want to know how the Holy Spirit lives inside of the people in your church. This is an awesome power.

Acts 1:8, *"But ye shall receive power, after that the Holy Ghost is come upon you: and ye shall be witnesses unto me both in Jerusalem, and in all Judaea, and in Samaria, and unto the uttermost part of the earth."*

Community—Each of us should try to be used to bring peace on earth, good will toward men. As you anticipate your perceived power, think about how you can be used by the "Prince of Peace." The Holy Spirit has not asked us to riot or damage property. God has the power to destroy anything here on earth. That is not our place! By having the power of the Holy Spirit through prayer, we can change the hearts, minds, and spirits of kings, presidents, and rulers of this world.

Proverbs 21:1–2, *"The king's heart is in the hand of the LORD, as the rivers of water: he turneth it whithersoever he will. Every way of a man is right in his own eyes: but the LORD pondereth the hearts."*

Ephesians 6:11–13:

Put on the whole armour of God, that ye may be able to stand against the wiles of the devil. For we wrestle not against flesh and blood, but against principalities, against powers, against the rulers of the darkness of this world, against spiritual wickedness in high places. Wherefore take unto you the whole armour of God, that ye may be able to withstand in the evil day, and having done all, to stand.

Luke 2:14, *"Glory to God in the highest, and on earth peace, good will toward men."*

THE ACCEPTANCE OF EMPOWERMENT

Congratulations! You've made it to whatever you feel "success" is for you. You are accepting the perceived power that comes with it. It is important when you arrive that you respect the position and the people that made it possible. It is also important that you remain humble. Too many great leaders have failed to accept the parable that "pride goes before a fall." To be a respected leader, you will want to have great personal skills and be able to interact well with others. You will also need great personnel (human resources) skills.

Proverbs 16:18, *"Pride goeth before destruction, and an haughty spirit before a fall."*

Colossians 3:12–13, *"Put on therefore, as the elect of God, holy and beloved, bowels of mercies, kindness, humbleness of mind, meekness, longsuffering; Forbearing one another, and forgiving one another, if any man have a quarrel against any: even as Christ forgave you, so also do ye."*

Accepting empowerment with kindness and graciousness is important in every area of leadership. Let's look at some examples (in no particular order)…

Religion—I enjoy helping churches! The "acceptance of empowerment" for any religious leader should be taught in every religious college, university, and seminary around the world. There is a certain amount of power assumed by the person standing behind the pulpit or speaker's podium in every religious establishment. It is commonly understood that a religious leader has wisdom that was received from a higher power. When a religious leader usurps unwarranted authority as if he or she is God, then the follower can be misled.

Ecclesiastes 9:18, *"Wisdom is better than weapons of war: but one sinner destroyeth much good."*

Politics—If you are involved with politics in any manner, you will understand how important it is to be hospitable and cooperative with each area of the campaign. If you are collecting signatures in order to be on the ballot, your constituents will want to be sure that you listen to them. Therefore, the acceptance of empowerment will require you to be congenial in all of your actions.

We have all seen politicians who were interested more in defeating their competition than fulfilling the needs of their constituents. Accepting empowerment can, but does not necessarily, make you a great leader in society today. If politics is your aspiration, as you climb the ladder of success, be kind to everyone you meet because you will see them again when your political career ends. Accept empowerment with grace.

James 4:10–11:

Humble yourselves in the sight of the Lord, and he shall lift you up. Speak not evil one of another, brethren. He that speaketh evil of his brother, and judgeth his brother, speaketh evil of the law, and judgeth the law: but if thou judge the law, thou art not a doer of the law, but a judge.

Financial—If you are a fiduciary or have any type of control of another person's finances, it will be life-changing. This relationship may not change your life, but it will determine the financial destiny of your client. When you accept that amount of empowerment, you may want to refer back to our former lesson on "integrity" in this book. Accepting the empowerment to handle the finances of another individual may feel like a success, but it is also a great responsibility.

Psalm 112:3, *"Wealth and riches shall be in his house: and his righteousness endureth for ever."*

Proverbs 13:11, *"Wealth gotten by vanity shall be diminished: but he that gathereth by labour shall increase."*

Corporate—As a manager in the corporate world, you accept empowerment. You will soon understand that there are two ways to be in charge: you can "lead" each employee, or you can "drive" your employees. This can also be referred to as "the carrot or the stick." Great leaders empower their followers. Great leaders respect each other and their subordinates, thus building teamwork and camaraderie. If you hold the title of supervisor, manager, or vice president, you have succeeded. How you handle that success will determine your personal future. It will also affect the lives of your subordinates. You may want to follow Gideon's guidelines.

Judges 8:23, *"And Gideon said unto them, I will not rule over you, neither shall my son rule over you: the LORD shall rule over you."*

Education—Who is (or was) your favorite teacher? When you think of that name, it is quite likely that this same teacher had the "power" to change lives. This teacher was probably a great leader without being overpowering. This type of teacher encourages each student to work at the student's capacity because the teacher understands that each student comprehends differently. Some students are auditory and learn through listening. Other students are visual and must see the results. Many students are kinesthetic, and when they get the "feeling," then everything falls into place. If you are a teacher, then you are a success! You can help others by using the concepts in this book to determine how each student (and your fellow teachers) can achieve greater success.

Second Timothy 3:16, *"All scripture is given by inspiration of God, and is profitable for doctrine, for reproof, for correction, for instruction in righteousness."*

Proverbs 9:9, *"Give instruction to a wise man, and he will be yet wiser: teach a just man, and he will increase in learning."*

Here is a final thought on the "acceptance of empowerment"…

You have already achieved a certain level of success. You have proven that by reading this far into this book. This could be the fulcrum (pivotal point) that balances your success to gain momentum, or it is what will bring you to a plateau or a pinnacle where you cannot escalate your success. It is like the center of a "seesaw" or a "teeter-totter." It depends on the balance of life in each area of this book—"Desire," "Dedication," "Determination," "Decisions," etc.—and how much success you want to achieve. Accept your empowerment, but stay humble.

Micah 6:8, *"He hath shewed thee, O man, what is good; and what doth the* L*ORD* *require of thee, but to do justly, and to love mercy, and to walk humbly with thy God?"*

How will this lesson help me?

Personal—When you accept the amount of power that God has given you without overstepping it and without assuming more than was rightfully given, then you can use that power for all parties concerned.

Matthew 23:10–11, *"Neither be ye called masters: for one is your Master, even Christ. But he that is greatest among you shall be your servant."*

Marriage and family—The acceptance of empowerment in any marriage must be handled with great care and true love for the other individual as a friend and a spouse. The same is true with family. Have you ever thought that a family is much like education? If you have a close family relationship, then you have success. We often learn about life (good or bad) from our family. If you are in a happy, loving marriage, then you have success. You may not even realize how many people in your neighborhood and around the world would be thrilled to have your amount of success. If your marital relationship is not quite what you had expected, you may want to use this book and other books as a reference for a successful marriage.

Ephesians 5:25, *"Husbands, love your wives, even as Christ also loved the church, and gave himself for it."*

Colossians 3:19, *"Husbands, love your wives, and be not bitter against them."*

Church—Your church has a certain amount of power in your local area because they have the power to influence each person who attends your church. Think about that for a minute. If each person in your church has five close friends in the community, then your church has an influence five times greater than your attendance. I am not saying that they can change the minds of all of those people, but the insight of your people with the knowledge of the Bible can be an influence in empowerment for good for generations to come.

Proverbs 4:7, *"Wisdom is the principal thing; therefore get wisdom: and with all thy getting get understanding."*

Community—When each person in your community accepts their limited power and does not overstep their power on earth, each person will gain the respect of the persons with influence. There will be mutual respect established between politicians and constituents, police and citizens, military and civilians, and students will respect their teachers. In each of these areas, pastors and chaplains are needed. Let us all accept the power of influence with respect and humbleness.

Matthew 23:12, *"And whosoever shall exalt himself shall be abased; and he that shall humble himself shall be exalted."*

THE AUTHORING OF EMPOWERMENT

It is time once again to start writing. It is time to "author" your empowerment. This will be a key component to your success.

In my professional activities, I often work with instructors and teachers. When asked why someone would want to become an "instructor," quite often, it is a reason that relates to ego. This has to do with a person's self-image or self-esteem. (We will discuss these topics later in this book.)

As you author your ideas of empowerment, you will be able to understand that your original "desires," when you began to read this book, have a great deal to do with your ability to be empowered. Take some time now or in the near future to write (i.e., author) what type of power will be involved when you reach "success." Ask yourself these questions…

What will that empowerment look like in my life?

Will it result in a larger bank account? (This empowers a better retirement.)

Will it result in better cash flow? (This empowers a better daily life.)

Will it give me more fame? (This empowers recognition and opportunities.)

Will it provide me with a different "status" and different friends?

Why do I want this power?

Do I need this amount of empowerment for my self-image?

Will this empowerment "open doors" to greater opportunities?

Will this empowerment help me to leave a legacy for future generations?

Whose lives will be affected by the empowerment once I receive it? (This is vital.)

Would you want to be the parent of the next governor of your state?

Would your child want to be the heir (or heiress) of your company?

Perhaps you want to run a nonprofit to help others! That has great power!

Perhaps you may say that you want "no power" but to be left alone for a quiet retirement. *That* is the greatest of all powers! Whether you retire rich or "not so wealthy," if you have the "power of choice," then you have been empowered!

Take some time now and author (write down) why this empowerment is so important to you. This simple exercise may be the turning point in your success, and it can be life-changing. As I sometimes say:

"One day will change your life. One day your life will change."

These two sentences contain the exact same words. You get to decide which is right for you today! Is today your day for change?

How will this lesson help me?

Personal—When you start to see your thoughts in print regarding why you need the power of the decisions that you have made, you will be able to determine what God's purpose is for your life. Our Heavenly Father has all the power available on this earth. If He is your personal Savior, then whatever you ask in full faith, you may receive if it is in His will. Your Father loves you. He wants to be so close to you that your desires and His are the same. He wants to give you what you want. Please let Him do that. You may want to write a love letter to your Heavenly Father right now and put that letter where you can see it regularly. Thank Him for the power of choice and the power of influence! This could be life-changing! Enjoy it!

Marriage and family—In every area of life, the power to influence others might be the greatest power of all. If used properly, that power will allow you to help others. The power to make decisions that control your own life will be related to your relationship with God. Whether you are a husband, wife, or child, take some time to think about different types of leadership and empowerment. Write each aspect and how you can learn and teach leadership qualities to others in your family. Think about each member of your family and find ways to influence them to create a better society. Find ways to smile. Find ways to empower others to be better students and help others to have better family lives.

First Thessalonians 5:11, *"Wherefore comfort yourselves together, and edify one another, even as also ye do."*

Church—When your church starts writing down all of the reasons and ideas of how the power of influence through the Holy Spirit can change every area of your church and your community, then each person will be able to pray for the other person without any arrogancy and with pure humbleness of heart. Every person in your church can be an encouragement to every other person in your church at any age level or socioeconomic condition.

Ephesians 5:1–2, *"Be ye therefore followers of God, as dear children; And walk in love, as Christ also hath loved us, and hath given himself for us an offering and a sacrifice to God for a sweetsmelling savour."*

Community—In the community, certain rules and regulations must be written down and authored by legal experts. Some of these are called rules, regulations, laws, or statutes. Each one must be worded in such a way as to be interpreted by the courts as originally intended. It is important to understand the laws of your territory. Be sure to choose your advisors wisely in the areas of legal, financial, insurance, and other matters that are important to you.

Write down ideas that will help you to help those who are in power. How can you help your police, your mayor and other civic leaders? Should you be the leader?

Ephesians 5:14–16, *"Wherefore he saith, Awake thou that sleepest, and arise from the dead, and Christ shall give thee light. See then that ye walk circumspectly, not as fools, but as wise, Redeeming the time, because the days are evil."*

THE ACTIVATION OF EMPOWERMENT

When you completed the exercise on the authoring of empowerment, you began to think about how much power you truly want in your life. You also were able to visualize what "success" really means to you.

Do you realize that you have the power of influence? In each area of success that we discussed earlier in this chapter (finance, politics, marriage, family, etc.), there is an essence of the power of influence. This may be the true element of what success looks like for you. Influence is what happens in every negotiation. Every argument (as in a court case) has an element of the power of influence. That is the true "activation of empowerment."

Every marriage has an element of influence every day. That is what a marriage is. It is two individuals joining together and agreeing to influence one another for the good of the relationship. For instance, "What's for dinner?" Then there are harder questions like, "Who is doing the dishes?" And "Who will take out the trash?" How about, "Can we afford a new car (or motorcycle, boat, or airplane)?"

Sometimes the activation of empowerment comes with a question like, "Should I go back to college?" or "Should we save money for the kids to go to college?" The actions that you take in order for you to activate the power that has been given to you will determine how you visualize "success." It is important that you do not allow everyone else to determine your future. Use wisdom!

Proverbs 11:14, *"Where no counsel is, the people fall: but in the multitude of counsellors there is safety."*

It is important that you listen to others but choose your counselors carefully. For example, another great piece of advice is…

Ephesians 5:15, *"See then that ye walk circumspectly, not as fools, but as wise."*

What this means is "look around" before you take the next step.

As you review what you have written in your "authoring your empowerment" and you begin to activate your empowerment, take the time to be sure that success is what you had envisioned. Do not let your past life detour you; you are free to choose a new path!

Philippians 3:13–14, *"Brethren, I count not myself to have apprehended: but this one thing I do, forgetting those things which are behind, and reaching forth unto those things which are before, I press toward the mark for the prize of the high calling of God in Christ Jesus."*

How will this lesson help me?

Personal—As you activate your empowerment and use your power properly, you will start to understand the guidelines that you need to use in order to achieve your goal. All power has guidelines. When you get any type of authority or responsibility, there will be rules and regulations that will need to be followed for you to be as successful and influential as possible. Stay humble!

Proverbs 15:33, *"The fear of the LORD is the instruction of wisdom; and before honour is humility."*

Proverbs 18:12, *"Before destruction the heart of man is haughty, and before honour is humility."*

Marriage and family—As you activate the power of influence in your family, be sure that it is beneficial for all parties. Fathers have a great responsibility to show love in the same manner that their Heavenly Father shows love. The influence that a mother has on her children is amazing. She can help her children to be great leaders for the next generation.

If you are a teenager, you can influence and encourage every member of the family for good and build close relationships, which will benefit you as you build your family and your career in the future.

Ephesians 5:2, *"And walk in love, as Christ also hath loved us."*

Church—As your church begins to activate the power of influence with each other and in your community, you will want to remind each other that you walk by faith. When members of your church tell others about how they can have an entirely new life through Jesus Christ, the Holy Spirit can influence them to trust Him. As your pastor speaks to the congregation, he has the power to influence many lives. This is a great responsibility and should never be taken lightly!

Second Corinthians 5:7, *"For we walk by faith, not by sight."*

Community—Your community may have more power and influence than you can imagine. I am often amazed when somebody speaks to me about a small town and the impact that it has had on a person's life. A small-town church with a great pastor and a great congregation can influence an entire area for the cause of Christ and be beneficial to the entire area. If your church could give food to the hungry, shelter to the homeless, and comfort to the needy, God could be honored and lives could be changed.

You may want to try that idea in your church community sometime soon. Work with your local area and solve homelessness and hunger.

Matthew 22:36–40:

Master, which is the great commandment in the law? Jesus said unto him, Thou shalt love the Lord thy God with all thy heart, and with all thy soul, and with all thy mind. This is the first and great commandment. And the second is like unto it, Thou shalt love thy neighbour as thyself. On these two commandments hang all the law and the prophets.

James 1:27, *"Pure religion and undefiled before God and the Father is this, To visit the fatherless and widows in their affliction, and to keep himself unspotted from the world."*

THE APPRECIATION OF EMPOWERMENT

At any stage of our lives, it is valuable for each of us to look around and appreciate how much we have been empowered. Earlier in this section, you were asked to author and write down different ideas that have given you power. Some of these powers you currently have while other powers you had in your past. If you are a new believer in Jesus Christ, the Bible is as true for you as it is for believers of all ages.

Second Timothy 1:7, *"For God hath not given us the spirit of fear; but of power, and of love, and of a sound mind."*

Think about the power that the followers of Jesus must have felt when Jesus spoke these words in Matthew 28, *"All power is given unto me…Go… and, lo, I am with you always."* Since Jesus Christ never changes, then think of the power that exists today in your life.

Hebrews 13:8, *"Jesus Christ the same yesterday, and to day, and for ever."*

Take a minute and compare these two verses. Both of these are true and create a great perspective when you look at them at the same time.

John 1:1–2, *"In the beginning was the Word, and the Word was with God, and the Word was God. The same was in the beginning with God."*

First Corinthians 4:20, *"For the kingdom of God is not in word, but in power."*

One of the reasons that this book was written was so that you could understand the amount of power that you have. Take a look at the index of this book and think about how this book can change your life. You have the power of desire. That can never be taken away from you. You have the power of dedication where you can dedicate your life to some great purpose. You have the power to make decisions. You have the power to change your spirit and be inspired by different thoughts and actions. You have the power of imagination. You have been using that power throughout this book. You have the power to be motivated and to choose what motivates you. The power of choice can change your life. If you are unhappy with how your life is progressing, choose to make a change today. Reread this book and decide what you desire. Make that happen!

Here are some powers that you can use right now and in the future.

Power of choice—You can choose what will influence you in the future. You can choose heavenly things or earthly things. You can choose fame and fortune, but unfortunately, you can't take them with you when you leave this world.

Matthew 6:19, *"Lay not up for yourselves treasures upon earth, where moth and rust doth corrupt, and where thieves break through and steal."*

Power to believe—You have the choice to believe anything that is told to you. Be careful that you don't believe lies.

Matthew 24:11, *"And many false prophets shall rise, and shall deceive many.*

John 3:12, *"If I have told you earthly things, and ye believe not, how shall ye believe, if I tell you of heavenly things?"*

Power to accept Christ—You have the power to accept Jesus Christ as your personal Savior. You and I have done things that we knew were wrong. That wrong deed needs to go before a judge and be properly punished. Perhaps you have been to court, and the judge found you "guilty." Jesus Christ will judge those same deeds, but He can pardon those deeds. God did not send His Son into the world to condemn you. Ask Jesus Christ to forgive you.

John 5:22, *"For the Father judgeth no man, but hath committed all judgment unto the Son."*

Hebrews 9:27, *"And as it is appointed unto men once to die, but after this the judgment."*

Romans 10:13, *"For whosoever shall call upon the name of the Lord shall be saved."*

John 3:16, *"For God so loved the world, that he gave his only begotten Son, that whosoever believeth in him should not perish, but have everlasting life. For*

God sent not his Son into the world to condemn the world; but that the world through him might be saved."

Power of influence—It doesn't matter where you go or how long you live; you are going to have the power to influence others. You do not even realize how much power you have to influence people for good. Sometimes, all it takes is a smile or a wink to make somebody's day better. Sometimes, all it takes is a kind word or a pat on the back to give them hope that will change their life and change eternity. Always use the power of influence for the good of mankind. Try to smile more this week! In a true and humble manner, tell others how much God Almighty loves them.

First John 4:8, *"He that loveth not knoweth not God; for God is love."*

Micah 6:8, *"He hath shewed thee, O man, what is good; and what doth the LORD require of thee, but to do justly, and to love mercy, and to walk humbly with thy God?"*

How will this lesson help me?

Personal—This lesson was written to encourage you to use your power for the good of mankind. You are not powerless! You have never lost your power. You were created in the image of God. You were born on a particular day in a particular place for a reason. God has given you the power to influence those around you. Use that power for His glory.

Acts 6:8, *"And Stephen, full of faith and power, did great wonders and miracles among the people."*

Marriage and family—Realize that each family member has the power to influence one another. Each person also has the power of choice. You can choose to be honest with one another. You can choose to have a pleasant and loving atmosphere in your home. You can choose to have a great attitude and help to solve problems and issues that arise. Choose to build one another so that you can have great family reunions and great memories.

Ephesians 6:1–4:

Children, obey your parents in the Lord: for this is right. Honour thy father and mother; which is the first commandment with promise; That it may be well with thee, and thou mayest live long on the earth. And, ye fathers, provoke not your children to wrath: but bring them up in the nurture and admonition of the Lord.

Oh, and by the way, when your mom asks you to clean your room, she is not being mean! She is reminding you of a Bible verse that will help you…

First Corinthians 14:40, *"Let all things be done decently and in order."*

Matthew 23:11, *"But he that is greatest among you shall be your servant. And whosoever shall exalt himself shall be abased; and he that shall humble himself shall be exalted."*

Church—Do you realize how much power your church has to influence your members, your community, and other churches that are similar to yours across the country? You have the power right now to make choices about your church. It does not matter your age or your current leadership position. You can help your church to make an impact on the lives of others and their children. This will influence the generations to follow. Use this power wisely! We must use that power to edify and to build up. It should never be used for destruction!

Second Corinthians 13:10, *"Therefore I write these things being absent, lest being present I should use sharpness, according to the power which the Lord hath given me to edification, and not to destruction."*

First Corinthians 9:3–6:

Mine answer to them that do examine me is this, Have we not power to eat and to drink? Have we not power to lead about a sister, a wife, as well as other apostles, and as the brethren of the Lord, and Cephas? Or I only and Barnabas, have not we power to forbear working?

Community—You may not realize it yet, but you are a community leader. That choice is yours every day. You do not have to be an elected official to be a community leader. You have the power of choice and the power of influence that you can use starting today to build your community. When people around the country and around the world hear about your community, they should hear of wonderful things. Some of these ideas and activities can be put on the news so that people can emulate and copy what you're doing. You may help their cities and neighborhoods to be better also. Start today, use your power, and create a better tomorrow!

Ephesians 6:10–12:

Finally, my brethren, be strong in the Lord, and in the power of his might. Put on the whole armour of God, that ye may be able to stand against the wiles of the devil. For we wrestle not against flesh and blood, but against principalities, against powers, against the rulers of the darkness of this world, against spiritual wickedness in high places.

THIS PAGE HAS BEEN LEFT BLANK SO THAT YOU CAN MAKE NOTES ABOUT EMPOWERMENT

Anticipating and Appreciating Your Christian Life

ERRORS (YOUR BONUS "E")

On your way to success, you can count on the fact that there will be errors. It is how you react to those errors that will result in your level of success. Let's discuss some widely different situations so that you can relate.

If you are in school, you have made a number of errors. How is your grade point average (GPA) doing? This is determined by an "A" being worth four (4) points, a "B" being worth three (3) points, a "C" being worth two (2) points, and a "D" being worth one (1) point. It is very rare that a person will graduate from high school with a "4.0" GPA and score 100 percent on every test. That means that we have all made mistakes. Many of us would be happy to receive a "3.0" (a "B" average) or even a "2.0" (a "C" average). We all realize that nobody is perfect.

If you are an executive in a company, you have probably made a few mistakes. Typically, management will understand that certain mistakes can be overlooked and overcome. An ethical violation may cause an immediate dismissal at any level.

If you are licensed to drive a car, how is your driving record? Do you find yourself exceeding the speed limit? Do you watch other people speed or act recklessly?

Matthew 7:1–2, *"Judge not, that ye be not judged. For with what judgment ye judge, ye shall be judged: and with what measure ye mete, it shall be measured to you again."*

Maybe you have been saddened by the mistakes of a loved one, and they have asked you to forgive them. Do you hold a grudge, or do you try to understand and help and truly forgive that person?

Matthew 18:21–22, *"Then came Peter to him, and said, Lord, how oft shall my brother sin against me, and I forgive him? till seven times? Jesus saith unto him, I say not unto thee, Until seven times: but, Until seventy times seven."*

Maybe you know someone (possibly yourself) who has become like the "prodigal son" and they have left the ones who love them and forsaken others who might be able to help them. Maybe it is time to renew some old friendships or restore someone to the family or personal partnership. Think of this next story.

Luke 15:17–24:

And when he came to himself, he said, How many hired servants of my father's have bread enough and to spare, and I perish with hunger! I will arise and go to my father, and will say unto him, Father, I have sinned against heaven, and before thee, And am no more worthy to be called thy son: make me as one of thy hired servants. And he arose, and came to his father. But when he was yet a great way off, his father saw him, and had compassion, and ran, and fell on his neck, and kissed him. And the son said unto him, Father, I have sinned against heaven, and in thy sight, and am no more worthy to be called thy son. But the father said to his servants, Bring forth the best robe, and put it on him; and put a ring on his hand, and shoes on his feet: And bring hither the fatted calf, and kill it; and let us eat, and be merry: For this my son was dead, and is alive again; he was lost, and is found. And they began to be merry.

It is possible that many of your mistakes have been within your family. Perhaps there have been issues with you and your brothers and sisters. These same issues may cause problems at school or at work. Maybe you feel like you cannot forgive your family for what has occurred in the past. Perhaps your brother or sister is holding it against you.

Matthew 5:23–24, *"Therefore if thou bring thy gift to the altar, and there rememberest that thy brother hath ought against thee; Leave there thy gift before the altar, and go thy way; first be reconciled to thy brother, and then come and offer thy gift."*

Throughout this book, we have talked about your family and your marriage. Let your family know that you love them through good times and bad. Each person is different and will have different ideas and perspectives of relationships during our lifetime. Errors and mistakes will happen. Handle every relationship with care. Start today and rebuild the relationships that are important in life.

Philippians 3:13–14, *"Brethren, I count not myself to have apprehended: but this one thing I do, forgetting those things which are behind, and reaching forth unto those things which are before, I press toward the mark for the prize of the high calling of God in Christ Jesus."*

How is your relationship with God? Have you made mistakes? We all have!

How will this lesson help me?

Personal—This lesson was written to remind you that you are as human as the rest of us. You will fail at something. You will make mistakes. Do not be discouraged! You may be heartbroken! You may cry. Since all things work together for good to those who love God, it is up to each of us to learn from the lesson and move forward to accomplish the greater things in life that God has planned.

Isaiah 53:6, *"All we like sheep have gone astray; we have turned every one to his own way; and the LORD hath laid on him the iniquity of us all."*

Marriage and family—It is easy, in a marriage or a family, to blame the other person as if the mistake is never our own. As you anticipated getting married, you may not have anticipated that each of you would have different opinions. You will disagree in some manner. Learn from one another and discover why each person has a certain viewpoint. You were raised differently and had different events happen in life. This does not mean that an error has occurred. Each person may be right under different circumstances.

Proverbs 1:5, *"A wise man will hear, and will increase learning; and a man of understanding shall attain unto wise counsels."*

Whether you are a parent or a child, always keep this in mind…

Romans 3:10, *"As it is written, There is none righteous, no, not one."*

Church—Things will go wrong in every church. Because there are no perfect people, there are no perfect churches. When people start comparing one sin to another, it is important to remember what the Bible says about righteousness. Oftentimes, these errors in churches relate to either the spiritual, the financial, or physical issues.

Regarding the spiritual, I recommend reading:

John 5:39, *"Search the scriptures; for in them ye think ye have eternal life: and they are they which testify of me."*

Regarding the financial, I recommend reading:

Second Corinthians 8:21, *"Providing for honest things, not only in the sight of the Lord, but also in the sight of men."*

Regarding the physical, I recommend reading and comparing these two verses:

First Corinthians 7:1, *"Now concerning the things whereof ye wrote unto me: It is good for a man not to touch a woman."*

James 4:17, *"Therefore to him that knoweth to do good, and doeth it not, to him it is sin."*

Community—Will things go wrong in the community? Of course! That is why we have the county sheriff, the local police, and other law enforcement agencies. Will there be ethical violations? Of course! That is the reason why we have judges. They make decisions on properly handling matters using the current laws in your local area.

What if it's a personal violation against you? What does the Bible say you should do personally? How will this affect your testimony? How you react will affect your community.

Matthew 6:15, *"But if ye forgive not men their trespasses, neither will your Father forgive your trespasses."*

Matthew 18:21–22, *"Then came Peter to him, and said, Lord, how oft shall my brother sin against me, and I forgive him? till seven times? Jesus saith unto him, I say not unto thee, Until seven times: but, Until seventy times seven."*

Matthew 5:38–44:

Ye have heard that it hath been said, An eye for an eye, and a tooth for a tooth: But I say unto you, That ye resist not evil: but whosoever shall smite thee on thy right cheek, turn to him the other also. And if any man will sue thee at the law, and take away thy coat, let him have thy cloak also. And whosoever shall compel thee to go a mile, go with him twain. Give to him that asketh thee, and from him that would borrow of thee turn not thou away. Ye have heard that it hath been said, Thou shalt love thy neighbour, and hate thine enemy. But I say unto you, Love your enemies, bless them that curse you, do good to them that hate you, and pray for them which despitefully use you, and persecute you.

THIS PAGE HAS BEEN LEFT BLANK SO THAT YOU CAN MAKE NOTES ABOUT ERRORS

Anticipating and Appreciating Your Christian Life

SAFETY
THE ANTICIPATION OF SAFETY

This idea may be an important element that will help you to stay focused on your upcoming goal or success track. When you think about it, the anticipation of safety is a key element in every area of life! Every animal in the world runs toward safety. Many animals (even armies) will dig holes in order to have safety. Rabbits will hide under bushes to stay away from predators. People build storm cellars and bomb shelters. Great armies and military personnel will build forts for safety. Do you realize that every person who is in any unsafe condition has one primary focus? They each want safety!

If you play in high school sports, your coach's first responsibility is not to win the game. It is to keep you safe so that you can play your best game. If you are a parent, your thoughts are often centered around the safety of the family. Is your water safe? Is the food safe? Is the car safe? Is the house safe? There are advisors for each of these situations.

Proverbs 11:14, *"Where no counsel is, the people fall: but in the multitude of counsellors there is safety."*

Depending on what type of success you might want to achieve, you will need to remember that safety comes in many forms. Safety is protection from harm. You can visualize it this way. A safety belt can keep you safe if used properly. Don't get this confused with security. A security vehicle or "armored car" is more secure but may limit your freedom of movement and not allow you to reach your goal. If you are looking to have success in your career, you get to choose your level of safety. Job safety will possibly keep your physical body safe from harm.

Safety belts save lives. That has been proven. I highly recommend that you use the safety devices in every situation. If you are in a car, please stay safe and use your safety belt as appropriate. However, you will need to exercise more caution if you ride your bicycle. Your bicycle does not have a safety belt, yet we teach our toddlers to ride bicycles. By doing so, they learn caution and safety techniques like wearing a helmet. You may allow your family to ride horses. The saddle does not come with a safety belt.

Proverbs 21:31, *"The horse is prepared against the day of battle: but safety is of the LORD."*

As you achieve success, you should be able to anticipate and look forward to having a certain amount of safety.

Take a few minutes and think about the amount and types of safety you desire for your future, your family, and your success. The primary goal for some readers will be success in a long-term goal, such as a career in a certain field of interest. We all should have a desire to have a great marriage. It is interesting that all of these goals have a similar connection by having the elements of safety. Each company, each sports team, each corporation, and every marriage has the need for cooperation in order to achieve the correct balance of safety.

How will this lesson help me?

Personal—As you consider your safety for the years to come, you will want to have a group of counselors whom you trust that you can call on when needed. These may be your pastor, your accountant, your lawyer, your doctor, and your brother or a trusted friend. By having this group of individuals who each have different expertise, you will be able to have some level of safety throughout your life for yourself and for your family.

Deuteronomy 12:10, *"But when ye go over Jordan, and dwell in the land which the LORD your God giveth you to inherit, and when he giveth you rest from all your enemies round about, so that ye dwell in safety."*

Marriage and family—Your family desires (and deserves) safety. When your family goes to sleep at night, they want to know that they can rest comfortably knowing that they are safe from harm throughout the night. When you kneel by the bed and pray with your child, they should know that you and God are there for their safety. Your spouse must trust you that when each family member comes home, they should feel that it is a safe place to dwell together.

Proverbs 31:11, *"The heart of her husband doth safely trust in her, so that he shall have no need of spoil."*

Church—It is important for your church to understand that safety comes from the Lord. Do not be afraid that the Lord is returning; just be prepared. Remind your church to trust in the Lord and every situation.

Proverbs 29:25, *"The fear of man bringeth a snare: but whoso putteth his trust in the LORD shall be safe."*

Sometimes in church, you may see a person who has not been to church in a few years. Maybe they have been living in a different city or just been away from church due to their lifestyle. Be sure to welcome them back as if they had never left. Do what Jesus did and be a blessing to them. Go out to eat with them. Compare these two scriptures and follow the example of what Jesus did with the publicans, heathens, and sinners.

Matthew 18:15–17:

Moreover if thy brother shall trespass against thee, go and tell him his fault between thee and him alone: if he shall hear thee, thou hast gained thy brother. But if he will not hear thee, then take with thee one or two more, that in the mouth of two or three witnesses every word may be established. And if he shall neglect to hear them, tell it unto the church: but if he neglect to hear the church, let him be unto thee as an heathen man and a publican.

Matthew 9:11–12, *"And when the Pharisees saw it, they said unto his disciples, Why eateth your Master with publicans and sinners? But when Jesus heard that, he said unto them, They that be whole need not a physician, but they that are sick."*

Each of us should strive to use the wisdom of Jesus Christ! Visitors and members (at every level) should find that your church is a safe place to renew their fellowship with the Lord. Since they can be close to the Lord at your church, take them out to eat (like Jesus did) and see how you can help them to be closer to the Lord!

Community—If your community knows that you are concerned about the safety of your buildings, that is an important quality in the eyes of the fire marshal, the police, and those in government. If your community knows that your church is safe from criticism from those who are not regular attendees, they will feel more welcome and likely to return. Each church should be a haven of rest where the community can come for spiritual guidance from teenagers, adults, and pastoral staff.

Isaiah 53:6, *"All we like sheep have gone astray; we have turned every one to his own way; and the LORD hath laid on him the iniquity of us all."*

Leviticus 25:18–19, *"Wherefore ye shall do my statutes, and keep my judgments, and do them; and ye shall dwell in the land in safety. And the land shall yield her fruit, and ye shall eat your fill, and dwell therein in safety."*

THE ACCEPTANCE OF SAFETY

As you accept the ideas of safety related to your vision of success, you will begin to see "the big picture" and the proverbial "light at the end of the tunnel" as success unfolds for you. In our previous segment on the "anticipation of safety," you began to look at ideas that will help you to have both short-term and long-term success in your profession, your school, your church, and your family. Now, it is your time to "accept" what levels you have chosen. What does safety mean to you? How are you going to accept that safety? Will this keep you secure?

This stage of your success is similar to the "two-step verification" that is used in computer programs. I am sure that you have used these procedures many times. First, you put your information into the computer program; then, you hit the "accept" button. What happens next? The computer asks you to "confirm your choice." What it is asking is, "Are you sure?" This is extremely important due to safety concerns.

Are you sure that this is the correct idea of success for you? Have you chosen the correct amount of safety that you will agree to work with and live with until "success" has been achieved? Your success will be like a long trip. Is your success vehicle ready? Are you financially prepared? Are you emotionally prepared? Are you spiritually prepared? How much safety have you included in your idea of success?

If your goal is to build a great organization, such as a church or other non-profit, safety will be important and will help you make decisions. The same is true in a family and a marriage. The safety of each person during the day requires the use of safety belts in the car and knowing where each person can be found. Then, for security, at the end of the day, you will lock the doors and be sure the home is secure.

Since this section of the book is about safety and your ultimate goal is to build a long-term relationship or a great marriage, you get to decide the balance that you want to accept for your situation for safety and/or security in the spiritual and emotional aspects of life. Is your loved one secure in the relationship? Does your loved one feel safe? Do you feel safe? Do you feel secure that this marriage will last? If you are trying to build a new company, do you trust each partner to make the best decisions? To whom will you go for advice? Whether you are building a church, a marriage, or a company, be sure every participant feels safe and secure.

Regarding safety, sometimes this type of discussion takes a board of deacons or a corporate board of directors some amount of time to decide what works best for their situation. What is the balancing point for your leadership to decide between safety and security? These two elements are so closely interrelated. The wealth of the company or the financial statement of the church may be wrapped up in security (and securities); however, the real wealth of the company is in the safety of each member or each person employed or associated with the organization.

Here is a good visual illustration. If you are getting ready to complete a triathlon or a marathon, you will need to wear certain safety gear during practice and during the competition. There will likely be security personnel to watch you along the route.

First Corinthians 9:23–24, *"And this I do for the gospel's sake, that I might be partaker thereof with you. Know ye not that they which run in a race run all, but one receiveth the prize? So run, that ye may obtain."*

When all members of the family and your church or organization feel safe and secure around one another, then you have already reached a special level of success. Be sure that your visitors and guests feel likewise. Keep up the good work!

How will this lesson help me?

Personal—As you look at your life right now, how safe do you feel? Think about what makes you feel safe and secure. Is it more money in the bank? Is it a larger income? Is it being surrounded by people whom you love and trust? You have the choice to decide. Think about your past. Think about your future. Do you want to feel the same level of safety and security in the future that you had in the past? How does your vision for the future compare to the past? Think of each area of your life and decide if they should remain the same or if a decision should be made to change so that you will have a better future. Sometimes, searching the Scriptures will give you all the answers that you need. At other times, you may need to check with your advisors and counselors for a quick solution. If there is an issue, ask the Lord to deliver you.

Psalm 40:13, *"Be pleased, O Lord, to deliver me: O Lord, make haste to help me."*

Marriage and family—Safety and security are what bond any long-term relationship. Whether as an employee with a company or a husband with his wife, each person should feel safe when they arrive home and when they are in the community. Many marriages start with love and understanding. Safety and security are part of that understanding. As you prepare to get married, have a discussion that covers topics such as physical safety and financial security. Be sure your ideas are consistent enough with one another so that problems may be averted later.

Parents and children should all feel safe when they go to bed at night. Be sure your children know of physical safety, such as having a fire escape route. Be sure that every family member has eternal security, knowing that they can go to heaven when their spirit leaves this world.

Church—Your church needs to feel safe to worship God. As you anticipated the amount of safety that will be needed in your church, did you consider all aspects of safety? Did you consider the physical issues regarding the building codes? Did you consider the spiritual aspects and the feeling of anticipation and excitement in your church so that everybody feels safe to worship God together? Your church should be like a haven of rest for the weary. Think about what you can do to make that a reality.

Psalm 107:29–31, *"He maketh the storm a calm, so that the waves thereof are still. Then are they glad because they be quiet; so he bringeth them unto their desired haven. Oh that men would praise the LORD for his goodness, and for his wonderful works to the children of men!"*

Community—Maybe you are a community leader, or maybe your church has activities in the community. Safety in the community is so important. Do you accept the amount of safety that you feel while walking down the street and while your church is having activities in the community? What can you do to help the police, your community leaders, and your political leaders to increase safety in your neighborhood and throughout your area? Could you build a rescue mission? Could you get involved in some other way that will make a lasting impression and help the generations that follow? Think about what you can do.

Stay safe!

THE AUTHORING OF SAFETY

This will be an important exercise for many of us. This one may take you some time. As you "author" (write down) the amount of (and elements of) safety that you want in each facet of your success for your career, your marriage, and your life, you will want to take a broad look at your success. This is often called the "10,000-foot view" or "the big picture." Take some time and consider all of the aspects of safety. Write them down. Many of these elements in every situation include words such as legal, insurance, and finance. In church and home, you will want to add categories such as spiritual and fellowship.

Note: this book is not meant to provide financial or legal advice!

Legal

If you are working on family issues, you may want to ask about a family trust document or a will. Each of these may have a slightly different outcome depending on which state, province, or territory in which you live. Be sure to have access to an attorney for quick questions. Be sure to write down your questions. Some services will allow you to have access to an attorney for a small monthly fee. Get your questions answered when you need help! Attorneys and counselors are prepared to answer legal questions in your jurisdiction. Write down what is important to you and your family for the future.

Proverbs 11:14, *"Where no counsel is, the people fall: but in the multitude of counsellors there is safety."*

If you are the coach of a team or even the director of a company or a non-profit organization, what is the possibility of a legal issue that might affect the entity or you personally? Do you have "in-house" counsel or an attorney on retainer? For instance, if your church has a legal issue on a corporate level, is your board insured or protected? If this is important, write down different aspects and bring them up at your next meeting.

Insurance

Whether you coach an athletic team, run a company, or have a family, be sure to have regular insurance reviews. There are many types of insurance that will be beneficial to you and your organization. There are many aspects to life insurance, health insurance, and automobile insurance. You may want to have different agents (possibly with the same company) as your advisors. Write down different questions that you would like to have answered. Your professional insurance agent will be pleased that you took the initiative to ask and they will be sure to find the answers needed.

Financial

Everything in life revolves around finances. If you have income, then you have the ability to plan for the future. Who is your financial advisor? If you are in charge of a family, a church, a business, or just yourself, you may need to know the difference between a "liability" and an "asset." Each of these will determine (and be determined by) your cash flow. Please be aware that "income" and "employment" are not necessarily the same thing. A job may not be necessary if you own an income-producing asset (like a business or an apartment building).

Luke 12:16–23:

And he spake a parable unto them, saying, The ground of a certain rich man brought forth plentifully: And he thought within himself, saying, What shall I do, because I have no room where to bestow my fruits? And he said, This will I do: I will pull down my barns, and build greater; and there will I bestow all my fruits and my goods. And I will say to my soul, Soul, thou hast much goods laid up for many years; take thine ease, eat, drink, and be merry. But God said unto him, Thou fool, this night thy soul shall be required of thee: then whose shall those things be, which thou hast provided? So is he that layeth up treasure for himself, and is not rich toward God. And he said unto his disciples, Therefore I say unto you, Take no thought for your life, what ye shall eat; neither for the body, what ye shall put on. The life is more than meat, and the body is more than raiment.

Physical Safety

There are many aspects to safety. You and I may ride horses, bicycles, and motorcycles. Is that safe? You and I may have jumped out of airplanes a number of times. Is that safe? (At least you learned how to pray!) Many of us are involved in different sports and athletic activities. Each sport has a different aspect of safety. If you oversee a company or a family, there is an element of safety needed. While you are at home, keep your family physically safe from harm. Be kind to one another. Protect each family member from harm, internally and externally! Write down your safety ideas for your home. You may have rules like, "Don't play ball in the house!" and "Don't jump on the bed." Write down the safety guideline, the reasoning, and the (possible) consequences for each.

Spiritual

As I mentioned before, there are many aspects to the word "spiritual." If you are involved in a church, there is a different (but similar) type of spirituality needed for the normal operation of the institution. If you want to have a successful family life, you will want the spirit in your home to be that of safety, security, and love. Does each family member enjoy coming home?

Take some time and write down ("author") all the aspects that will keep you and your family life, spiritual life, and success track safe and secure.

How will this lesson help me?

Personal—As you begin to write down the elements of safety you feel that you need personally in your life, you will be more prepared when somebody asks you to do something contrary to what you have written. These notes that you write as you "author" throughout this book are so important that you personally have made that decision so that you can determine the safety elements that you want as you move forward.

Use each category that we have mentioned and write notes under each so that you know how to react and know the answers needed for you to have a successful life.

Marriage and family—If you are not yet married, the ideas that you are writing down will help you determine choices in the future. If you're already married, these choices will help you prepare for the future. Your family should feel safe and secure in those choices.

Psalm 4:8, *"I will both lay me down in peace, and sleep: for thou, LORD, only makest me dwell in safety."*

Church—Is your church safe? Be sure to write down any elements of concern. Do your church members feel safe as they enter and leave the buildings? You may want to have a "suggestion box" or other location where concerns can be addressed. Is your church safe from physical harm so that when people walk through the building, there is no danger?

When your people look at the financial statement of the church, do they feel like your church is safe from a financial setback? Will your church still be active in twenty years and be available for weddings and funerals of your members and their children? I have seen a number of churches that had poor financial management. This will sometimes cause the loss of a high credit rating or even a foreclosure. Be sure to seek advice before issues arrive.

Community—I am sure that your governmental officials have authored or written down guidelines for every business and every church regarding safety. Fire marshals have certain guidelines. Police have certain guidelines. Even trash collectors have certain guidelines. These are all for your safety. The better you comply with these safety guidelines, the more you will build your reputation, personally and as a group. Also, the more favorable you will be appreciated as a neighbor.

Hebrews 13:17, *"Obey them that have the rule over you, and submit yourselves: for they watch for your souls, as they that must give account, that they may do it with joy, and not with grief: for that is unprofitable for you."*

THE ACTIVATION OF SAFETY

As you activate your safety, your entire success picture may start to come together. This is where you will do some great brainstorming and meditation. This will help you to understand what you feel will provide safety for you. It is like an idea that you think about as you wake up in the morning. You may think about it before you go to bed. The idea may wake you up as you dream about it. Sometimes you will ask yourself, *What if this happens? What will you do then?* Let's look at a few different aspects that will help you as you activate your safety.

Meditation

Meditation is a deep, continual thought pattern as you contemplate a certain number of related ideas on a particular matter. Take your time! Do not rush this process! You are different from every other person in this world. Your thoughts are different from any other person in your family. That is fine! You are unique! As you activate and make preparations for the safety of your success, you will start the activities that will provide safety and security for you, your church, your company, and your family.

Brainstorming

Brainstorming is different because it involves a group of individuals. There are some instances where this group will be referred to as the "think tank." Each member of the group should have the opportunity and the time to meditate on a particular topic. Every person's opinion should have some consideration.

If you are running a high school club, be sure to acknowledge and respect the opinion of each person. If you are leading a church deacon board, the opinion of the deacon will be important as each person has a different perspective of the community and their family.

If you are looking for success in a family, then each person might have a different opinion or idea that might affect the safety or the outcome. For instance, would it be wise for the family to go on a five-mile hike in the mountains? If you consider the safety aspect, do you have the right footwear and the gear needed? However, if you are considering the security, are there dangerous animals in the area?

Prayerful brainstorming in a church is important so that the leadership can have the mind of Christ and ask Him for wisdom.

First Corinthians 2:14–16:

But the natural man receiveth not the things of the Spirit of God: for they are foolishness unto him: neither can he know them, because they are spiritually discerned. But he that is spiritual judgeth all things, yet he himself is judged of no man. For who hath known the mind of the Lord, that he may instruct him? but we have the mind of Christ.

Brainstorming in a company is vital for the board of directors. The board may spend hours or days just brainstorming about one (seemingly insignificant) situation. A great brainstorming session may make the difference between levels of success.

If you are running an athletic program and want to activate the success of your program, use brainstorming to its fullest potential. What that means is that the team feels safe (and secure) as one complete unit. When they arrive at the playing area, they are one unit. Are they one solid and safe unit who are ready to win the event?

Networking

Activating the safety of your success may involve a great deal of networking. I know of many professionals who enjoy going to networking clubs. This is a great way to meet like-minded individuals. You may want to start a networking club. Find other people who like an idea that you are trying to promote. If you are concentrating on the safety of your company, you might go to a "trade show." Some pastors play golf in order to know what is happening in the world regarding business and politics. Others use golf in order to get ideas on how to present their ministry and be able to communicate well with business professionals and politicians.

Luke 2:46–47, *"And it came to pass, that after three days they found him in the temple, sitting in the midst of the doctors, both hearing them, and asking them questions. And all that heard him were astonished at his understanding and answers."*

Camaraderie

I have had the privilege of working on projects with many great individuals throughout my lifetime. I have watched groups of individuals create a spirit of camaraderie, which creates friendship, trust, and fellowship that can last a lifetime. When your organization begins to build camaraderie, you will have a desire to help build the safety of your comrades. Here are a few groups with which I have had the opportunity to be involved. You get to choose how their types of experiences can be relevant to your current and future success.

Pilots—I have been a pilot for most of my life. As an instructor, I have watched younger (and older) pilots build bonds of friendships that go beyond their aviation activities. Are you a pilot yet? Think about the camaraderie, but also understand the safety factors.

Military—It has been my privilege to assist many military veteran committees, parades, and activities. I am always impressed when I hear a veteran say, "I've got your six o'clock," which means that person will be sure that there is safety behind you. I have watched old veterans meet and reminisce. Camaraderie lasts forever!

First responders—I have had the privilege to be involved with first responders. Every member of the team is there to accomplish the mission with safety. I have met people who I had not seen for many years, but the friendship and memories last a lifetime.

Music—Each music group has a different level of camaraderie. Some of us sing in choirs. Some of us have played in bands or orchestras. There is an energy that is created by musical harmony. This is easily recognized in every style and size of musical group. If you want great camaraderie, add music. As you begin to activate the safety and security of your success, be sure that you have a certain amount of camaraderie. Remember "great minds think alike!"

Acts 2:46, *"And they, continuing daily with one accord in the temple, and breaking bread from house to house, did eat their meat with gladness and singleness of heart."*

How will this lesson help me?

Personal—As you activate your personal safety, you will want to have a checklist of the things that keep you safe in every area of life. These include your physical, your spiritual, your financial, and your social life. You will want to keep a list of parameters or guidelines that you will not cross. For your safety, you will want to have a list of substances that you will not allow in your body. You may need to make a list of places you will not go. Use the list that you've written while reading this book.

Marriage and family—Activating the safety of your family is important every day. Be sure that your children and your spouse feel safe in every activity. This includes your playtime, your family time, and your church activities.

Philippians 2:2–3, *"Fulfil ye my joy, that ye be likeminded, having the same love, being of one accord, of one mind. Let nothing be done through strife or vainglory; but in lowliness of mind let each esteem other better than themselves."*

Church—Safety in your church may deal with building safety. It will also deal with personal, emotional and spiritual safety. In any church, there will be some very private matters related to prayer and family issues. Be sure that you keep everything on a confidential basis. That is part of the safety of the church and the family in order to keep close fellowship and trust with one another for many years to come.

James 5:16, *"Confess your faults one to another, and pray one for another, that ye may be healed. The effectual fervent prayer of a righteous man availeth much."*

Community—As you activate the safety of your church, you will find that your people feel safe around each other in the community as they cross paths at the grocery store or while shopping. They will be able to greet each other and be happy to see one another. Other people will notice that, and they may want to start a conversation to receive the same type of greeting and fellowship. Having safety in the church does not mean just having safety at the church because the church is a fellowship of believers. It does not matter where we meet.

Acts 2:46–47:

And they, continuing daily with one accord in the temple, and breaking bread from house to house, did eat their meat with gladness and singleness of heart, Praising God, and having favour with all the people. And the Lord added to the church daily such as should be saved.

THE APPRECIATION OF SAFETY

There are many different types of safety that affect you every day. Take some time now and appreciate the men and women who keep you safe from physical harm and spiritual harm. Maybe write a note to the friends and family who have given you emotional support when you were (or are) having a rough day.

As I speak with many older people at different levels of success, we often discuss the "hard times" from our past, which were caused by our own decisions. Many successful executives have suffered through bankruptcy. Many have endured the death of a great mentor. (This has happened to me twice.) Sometimes, this involves a personal illness or handicap. Yet, through it all, each person has survived with the support of many others who have helped and been an encouragement along the way.

This lesson will be a little different than normal for this book. As you look back at your experiences in life, no matter what age you are, you will appreciate the safety you have enjoyed. As you move toward your "success," take some time and appreciate all of the ways the Lord has kept you safe. Who is there to protect you and keep you safe? Be sure to thank these sometime soon!

Jesus Christ

We often say that we love our Lord. Have you taken the opportunity recently to let Him know how much you appreciate Him?

Hebrews 13:5, *"Let your conversation be without covetousness; and be content with such things as ye have: for he hath said, I will never leave thee, nor forsake thee."*

Matthew 11:4–6:

Jesus answered and said unto them, Go and shew John again those things which ye do hear and see: The blind receive their sight, and the lame walk, the lepers are cleansed, and the deaf hear, the dead are raised up, and the poor have the gospel preached to them. And blessed is he, whosoever shall not be offended in me.

Pastor

Sometimes, your pastors may feel very unappreciated and overlooked. Take a minute this week and let them know how much you appreciate their leadership. They try to keep you safe from spiritual harm and physical harm.

Jeremiah 3:15, *"And I will give you pastors according to mine heart, which shall feed you with knowledge and understanding."*

Parent or Guardian

Parents work hard to be sure that their family has what is needed to survive daily. They also hope that you have what you need in order to live a safe, happy, and prosperous life. Be sure they know that you love and appreciate them.

Exodus 20:12, *"Honour thy father and thy mother: that thy days may be long upon the land which the LORD thy God giveth thee."*

Teacher

In my first book, *Overqualified/Underqualified*, I mentioned teachers as being underpaid but happy. Your teachers often care more about the students than they care about their own salaries. Let them know how much you appreciate them. They try to teach you how to have a safe and happy future.

Ephesians 4:11–12, *"And he gave some, apostles; and some, prophets; and some, evangelists; and some, pastors and teachers; For the perfecting of the saints, for the work of the ministry, for the edifying of the body of Christ."*

Police

Have you noticed recently that police officers are "real people" who care about their communities and want to keep your physical body and your property safe from harm and abuse? Find out what you can do to help your police officers to have a better day today and a better life. Make that happen. Show your appreciation.

Hebrews 13:17, *"Obey them that have the rule over you, and submit yourselves: for they watch for your souls, as they that must give account, that they may do it with joy, and not with grief: for that is unprofitable for you."*

Military

This is another group that is provided for your safety, yet they are underpaid but happy. Many military personnel feel unappreciated. Check with your local military recruiter or military installation to see what you can do to help them know that you care.

Luke 3:14, *"And the soldiers likewise demanded of him, saying, And what shall we do? And he said unto them, Do violence to no man, neither accuse any falsely; and be content with your wages."*

Builder Planning and Government

The men and women who work in this department are sometimes criticized for being so strict because they want to keep your church building safe and secure. Be kind to them. Maybe sit down and have lunch with them.

Matthew 9:11–12, *"And when the Pharisees saw it, they said unto his disciples, Why eateth your Master with publicans and sinners? But when Jesus heard that, he said unto them, They that be whole need not a physician, but they that are sick."*

Luke 14:28–30:

For which of you, intending to build a tower, sitteth not down first, and counteth the cost, whether he have sufficient to finish it? Lest haply, after he hath laid the foundation, and is not able to finish it, all that behold it begin to mock him, Saying, This man began to build, and was not able to finish.

How will this lesson help me?

Personal—Being thankful for all of the people who keep you safe can help you to make it through the day. You may be having a rough day, but if you think of all the people who are helping you right now to live your life, they can help you improve your situation. Be sure to whisper a prayer for them. Let them know how thankful you are that they are in your life. If you have a decision to make, look around before you take the next step.

Ephesians 5:15, *"See then that ye walk circumspectly, not as fools, but as wise."*

Marriage and family—Sometimes safety can be found in the words that you use. Using wisdom can keep you away from arguments or away from physical fights. Sometimes, safety is found in silence by not speaking. Nobody feels safe around a "family feud" (prolonged argument). Sometimes, this can be internal within your own family. At other times, it may be against a different family.

Romans 12:18, *"If it be possible, as much as lieth in you, live peaceably with all men."*

Matthew 15:11, *"Not that which goeth into the mouth defileth a man; but that which cometh out of the mouth, this defileth a man."*

Church—Be sure that your church is thankful for the people in the church who keep them safe. Also, be thankful for the people in the community that keep them safe. Inside the church, the pastoral staff and church leadership will help to protect them from spiritual harm. Perhaps your church has a security force or person in charge of safety. Be sure to send a thank you note to that person. Your church probably has a maintenance person who keeps the building safe. Be sure to think of that person because they are often overlooked. They will really appreciate it!

Community—Your community leaders often feel unappreciated. We often talk about the police and the firemen. Be sure to thank them on a regular basis. Possibly do fundraisers or activities with them. Be sure to thank the garbage collector. They work hard. Possibly find some way in your community to recognize them, especially during the holidays and other special occasions.

First Thessalonians 5:16–18, *"Rejoice evermore. Pray without ceasing. In every thing give thanks: for this is the will of God in Christ Jesus concerning you."*

THIS PAGE HAS BEEN LEFT BLANK SO THAT YOU CAN MAKE NOTES ABOUT SAFETY

SEPARATION
THE ANTICIPATION OF SEPARATION

On your journey to success, there are two vital opposites that you must anticipate; the first one is separation (those with whom you will not spend the same amount of time or energy) and synergy (those new alliances that will take up your time and help advance your success). Each of these will have their advantages and disadvantages. Yet, because you are traveling the road to success, your journey will be enhanced by both. Let's discuss the idea of separating yourself from your past and the anticipation of separation.

Philippians 3:13–14, *"Brethren, I count not myself to have apprehended: but this one thing I do, forgetting those things which are behind, and reaching forth unto those things which are before, I press toward the mark for the prize of the high calling of God in Christ Jesus."*

As you visualize your journey of success, who do you want to take with you? Who are you willing to leave behind? You may live in a small town and be successful without ever leaving your local area; however, in order to achieve your success, you may have to spend more time with some associates than you do with your family. If you move away from your hometown, you will be leaving family and friends. With modern technology and social media, you can still see your friends, but you will not be able to hug them until you visit them again in person.

What about your relatives? Are you sure you want to move away from your parents, grandparents, aunts, and uncles? Will you be able to come back home for the holidays? What will happen when you get married and have to choose which relatives to visit? Would you be happy to journey to a different country, like a missionary or political advisor, and not be near your family?

How do you feel about your current environment? If you grew up in the mountains, can you anticipate separating yourself from that beautiful environment and thinking about what life would be like if you moved to the plains? If you grew up in a small town, then the allure of living in a "big city" (whatever that is) may excite you for a season, but would you want to stay there forever?

Genesis 13:10–11:

And Lot lifted up his eyes, and beheld all the plain of Jordan, that it was well watered every where, before the LORD destroyed Sodom and Gomorrah, even as the garden of the LORD, like the land of Egypt, as thou comest unto Zoar. Then Lot chose him all the plain of Jordan; and Lot journeyed east: and they separated themselves the one from the other.

You may have friends who love you. How loyal are those friends? Would your friends want to go with you? Will you go to college alone or with friends?

John 6:66–67, *"From that time many of his disciples went back, and walked no more with him. Then said Jesus unto the twelve, Will ye also go away?"*

As you anticipate your journey toward success, when you envision leaving your friends, will this be an exciting event, or will you always feel a sense of loss? In some careers, you will always anticipate some degree of separation. Consider these lifestyles and the people that you may know:

Missionaries—These individuals and families have decided that their work for the Lord is more important than any earthly location. Their lives will revolve around helping a different location here on earth to be closer to their heavenly calling with our Lord. Some people might say that you are too young and in-experienced for the Lord's work.

First Timothy 4:12, *"Let no man despise thy youth; but be thou an example of the believers, in word, in conversation, in charity, in spirit, in faith, in purity."*

Military—When an individual signs up to serve with any branch of the military, they understand that they might be in different locations that same day. Many people like that opportunity because it adds variety and excitement to life. However, this might be hard on a family life. Can you anticipate this type of separation?

Philippians 4:6–7, *"Be careful for nothing; but in every thing by prayer and supplication with thanksgiving let your requests be made known unto God. And the peace of God, which passeth all understanding, shall keep your hearts and minds through Christ Jesus."*

College—Many of us will leave home to go to college. On your journey, you may relocate a few different times. This means that the things you see today (if you live near the oceans and lakes) will no longer be a short distance. Perhaps you live on a farm where you can see many miles from your front porch. You may have "culture shock" if you move to the big city. Enjoy your studies because when you graduate, you may relocate again. Always be ready to anticipate your separation.

How will this lesson help me?

Personal—Separation is emotional. Whether you are separating from a location, family, friends, or lifestyle, you will carry with you both good memories and different types of memories. Be sure that you are mentally prepared for all aspects of life as you anticipate the separation. There is a lot to think about. Life will be different because of the sights and different smells. Even walking down the street or walking next to the beach will be different. Be prepared for change.

Marriage and family—Whether you anticipate separation in your family life as you go away to college, to the military, or to a new job, be prepared to help your family understand that separation is sometimes beneficial. However, if you have a spouse and children, be extra cautious and take extra time to prepare as you will be changing churches, doctors, and lifestyles. As you prepare for the separation, be sure that the Lord is leading you.

Ephesians 6:4, *"And, ye fathers, provoke not your children to wrath: but bring them up in the nurture and admonition of the Lord."*

Proverbs 22:6, *"Train up a child in the way he should go: and when he is old, he will not depart from it."*

Church—Maybe you are thinking about working in the church ministry. This means that you will possibly be moving from one church to another. It is exciting if the Lord is drawing you to a new church where you can be helpful to new people; however, this means you will be moving from other people who you love and care about. Are you prepared for such a separation?

Perhaps you are well-established in your community, but your church has changed. You feel led by the Lord to move to a different church. As you think about separation and leaving certain people, be sure that no one is harmed in the process. God's love will surround you at any location. Be prayerful in all aspects.

Romans 8:38–39, *"For I am persuaded, that neither death, nor life, nor angels, nor principalities, nor powers, nor things present, nor things to come, Nor height, nor depth, nor any other creature, shall be able to separate us from the love of God, which is in Christ Jesus our Lord."*

Community—As you separate from one community, your presence may be missed without you even thinking about it. People from your church are going to miss you. People from the community are going to miss you. You will miss certain aspects of the community. Be sure that you keep in touch with old friends as you change your location. You will be glad you did!

Psalm 121:1–8:

I will lift up mine eyes unto the hills, from whence cometh my help. My help cometh from the Lord, which made heaven and earth. He will not suffer thy foot to be moved: he that keepeth thee will not slumber. Behold, he that keepeth Israel shall neither slumber nor sleep. The Lord is thy keeper: the Lord is thy shade upon thy right hand. The sun shall not smite thee by day, nor the moon by night. The Lord shall preserve thee from all evil: he shall preserve thy soul. The Lord shall preserve thy going out and thy coming in from this time forth, and even for evermore.

THE ACCEPTANCE OF SEPARATION

Are you sure you want to leave? Have you really thought about all the different aspects of leaving? Now you have anticipated and thought about all the separation that would take place between you and your family, your friends, and the location, it is time to accept that decision. This will be an emotional decision, sometimes for the good, which will give you smiles and happiness, but sometimes you might need to be prepared to be "homesick."

This happens to many of us at one time or another in our lifetime. You accept the fact that you want to move or need to move, but accepting the fact and internalizing it as being part of your new life will remind you that you only have so many years of life left. You may be going off to college or going to the military and you are excited for your future. This is an exciting time because you hope to have many years of happiness in front of you. You may feel like a pioneer or a pilgrim with great aspirations.

In some cases, you may be just about ready to retire and leave the friends whom you have worked with for many years. Even though it's an exciting time, it will still be an emotional time as you accept the reality of the years passed and the years to come, as you will have a different lifestyle. Is this what you want? If you retire and stay in the same location, you may get to spend time with many of the same people. Perhaps you will go to the same church and will fellowship together. On the other hand, you may want to retire and move to a different location. Often, people move to a better climate or a more hospitable living condition.

As you accept the idea of separation, you will envision your life to be a success. Then, there is a comfort level of approval within you. You have trusted that the Lord has led you this far and will continue to lead you throughout life. He will lead you home as you prepare for heaven as He prepares a place for you.

Remember leaders make decisions! If you think of "second-guessing" yourself, go back and realize why you have agreed, within yourself or with others, to make this move. If you're going to college, is this the right college? If you are becoming a missionary, are you sure that you are going to the right country or right area? If you are taking a new job, are you sure that is the job that will be most beneficial to you and to the Lord for many years to come? In every decision, there will be a "point of no return" where you will need to continue to move forward. Accept your decisions with confidence that the Lord will always be with you!

How will this lesson help me?

Personal—As you accept your idea of moving or simply separating yourself from certain people, the Lord will walk with you and guide you. Accept the fact that He will always be with you! You may try to run from God, but God is faster than you and will be with you when you get to your destination. You may think you are running to God. But remember the story of the "prodigal son":

Luke 15:20, *"And he arose, and came to his father. But when he was yet a great way off, his father saw him, and had compassion, and ran, and fell on his neck, and kissed him."*

Deuteronomy 31:8, *"And the LORD, he it is that doth go before thee; he will be with thee, he will not fail thee, neither forsake thee: fear not, neither be dismayed."*

Marriage and family—When your family decides to move, this will be an emotional time for the husband, the wife, the children, and even the grandparents and relatives. Make this an extra-loving time and a prayerful time as you make new friends and visit new churches. Be sure to keep your marriage close. Keep the Lord at the center of all decisions.

Ephesians 5:25–28:

Husbands, love your wives, even as Christ also loved the church, and gave himself for it; That he might sanctify and cleanse it with the washing of water by the word, That he might present it to himself a glorious church, not having spot, or wrinkle, or any such thing; but that it should be holy and without blemish. So ought men to love their wives as their own bodies. He that loveth his wife loveth himself.

Church—Sometimes, we leave a church because we have a new job elsewhere. At other times, it is because a loved one has passed away. A church is like a family. The great part of finding a new church where you can fellowship is that you can be accepted into the family or "brotherhood." Sometimes you will find comfort by meeting an old friend whom you have not seen for years who is close to the Lord.

John 14:16, *"And I will pray the Father, and he shall give you another Comforter, that he may abide with you for ever."*

Community—As you accept your separation from one community, you also accept joining another community. I sometimes go back to my hometown and look at the things that have changed and the things that have stayed the same. You will do the same either physically or mentally. You will see an old picture and say, "That's how it used to be." At the same time, you will look around at your current location and see how things are. Understand that the change was beneficial for your new community as well as your old community because God has led you every step of the way.

Proverbs 16:4, *"The Lord hath made all things for himself: yea, even the wicked for the day of evil."*

THE AUTHORING OF SEPARATION

This will be an interesting exercise as you prepare for any separation. You must prepare for the rest of your life because of the separation. There are so many things to think about that you will want to write down regarding how this move is going to change your life.

You may be a young child in elementary school or high school and your family is getting ready to move. You may want to write down the names of all of your friends who you will want to be sure that you know how to reach them in years to come. You will also want to bring along some small items that will bring great memories. For instance, if you live on the ocean, you may want to pick up a couple of seashells. If you live in the mountains, you may want to pick up a couple of small stones from a special location. You may want to take pictures of different sites you may not see again.

If you are going off to college, you will want to write down things that are important to you to remember about home. You also want to write down things that you will want to look up when you get to college. For instance, where would you like to go to eat? This is important because often you will meet people at the location where you eat. What about transportation? How will you get around? If you have a car, where will you get the oil changed?

In every type of situation where separation is concerned, be sure to consider your spiritual needs. Where will you go to church? With whom will you fellowship inside of the church? Where will you fellowship outside of the church with other believers with whom you can pray or possibly sing together? You may want to write about the different parts of your life and make lists that are important for each aspect of life. These may include church, exercise, study time, transportation, doctors, and time specifically designed to meet new friends or talk with old friends.

If you are moving because of a new job, think about where you are choosing to live in the neighborhood because that will have a direct effect on many different other parts of your life. It will impact the comfort of your family. Writing all of this down is an important step, as it will give you time to think about all the possibilities that may exist. You may want to brainstorm with some individuals who can provide you with leadership as you write these items. Be sure to pray as you write so that God can direct your thoughts.

How will this lesson help me?

Personal—Writing your ideas of separation will be beneficial to you now and in many years to come. The reason is that in a year or two (or more), you will be able to look back and remember. You can realize what you are thinking as you make these important decisions. These notes may be kept in a journal, in a diary, or just notes in a special location. In any situation, these notes will have valuable significance for many years to come and will become treasured memories.

Proverbs 3:3–4, *"Let not mercy and truth forsake thee: bind them about thy neck; write them upon the table of thine heart: So shalt thou find favour and good understanding in the sight of God and man."*

Marriage and family—This exercise is really important for your family and your marriage so that you can remember the decisions you made. You can look back and stay focused on the reason you are moving or separating yourself at this time. These notes that you are writing might keep your family together in close harmony because you discussed this action and remembered why it was important for your family to take this action. This may help your family to stay loving and close as you find your new church in your new friends. This may also determine future marriages, which may not have happened if you had not moved.

Mark 10:9, *"What therefore God hath joined together, let not man put asunder."*

Anticipating and Appreciating Your Christian Life

Church—You may be part of a new church or Bible study. You are looking for a brand-new home or building where you can grow and do God's work. This is an exciting time. You will be moving from your current location and moving to a new location. Typically, during such a move, some people will need to separate because the new location is farther away. However, the same people want to be close to their friends in the church. As you write down the amount of separation, be sure that you don't separate from the fellowship of those you love. You may want to treat this as a missionary journey.

Acts 15:40–41, *"And Paul chose Silas, and departed, being recommended by the brethren unto the grace of God. And he went through Syria and Cilicia, confirming the churches."*

Community—As you write down the separation from your community, be sure to write down the good things that will happen because you are separated. Perhaps you are leaving the community to go off to college so that you can return to the community and be more beneficial to your friends and family. Perhaps you were leaving the community to go off to the military so you could return and be the military recruiter in your hometown. Write down the benefits of leaving one community and the reasons for going to the new community. Don't "burn your bridges," as you may want to go back. Words like "home" and "hometown" may have a different meaning to you in years to come.

Mark 6:4–6:

But Jesus, said unto them, A prophet is not without honour, but in his own country, and among his own kin, and in his own house. And he could there do no mighty work, save that he laid his hands upon a few sick folk, and healed them. And he marvelled because of their unbelief. And he went round about the villages, teaching.

THE ACTIVATION OF SEPARATION

Activating your separation means that today is the day to start packing for a moving day. You may be moving today or sometime soon. The separation is about to occur. If you are moving, then our last exercise about writing the elements of separation should have provided you with a list of items that need to be accomplished quickly. Moving day can be very tiresome. You may be exhausted. You may have just packed up everything in the kitchen, and now you're hungry. Where can you go to eat? You may have just packed your bedroom, and now you're tired. Where can you rest?

Perhaps you are going on a plane ride. Were you able to stuff everything that you wanted inside of your luggage, or did you have to leave something behind? This will allow you to decide and determine what is most precious to you that you need to keep handy. The most important items you will want to keep with you will revolve around food and water, lodging and shelter, communication, and transportation. Always keep your Bible handy. You may need it for yourself or a fellow traveler who might be grieving.

If you are moving an entire household or family, it may take two to three days to load the moving van and all of your possessions. If you are moving just yourself and you have very few items, you may be able to move all of your possessions in a few hours and put them in a duffel bag or a large suitcase.

No matter what type of separation is occurring, you will always have memories. Good memories and other memories will always be with you. No matter what happens in your life always write down the good memories and enjoy your new ventures. Life is exciting! You only live it once. May the Lord be with you as you travel!

How will this lesson help me?

Personal—Moving day is exciting, but it is also exhausting. Because you are totally prepared to separate yourself and move forward with life with the help of God, your life can be more meaningful for you and for those you left behind. You are leaving behind friends and family, but you are also leaving behind great memories. Be sure to take some great memories with you as you go.

John 14:1, *"Let not your heart be troubled: ye believe in God, believe also in me."*

John 14:18, *"I will not leave you comfortless: I will come to you."*

Marriage and family—Moving day for a family can be an exciting time if everybody is in agreement and if everybody will benefit from the move. Be sure to keep a healthy family relationship as you move forward. Sometimes, separation from family will help a family to stay close because of fond memories. You are also creating new relationships. Enjoy saying goodbye with a kind heart. Remember the last hug, handshake, or kiss from your relatives. You may only see them again at weddings and funerals.

First Peter 5:7, *"Casting all your care upon him; for he careth for you."*

Church—Separating from a church can be an exciting time if you leave for college, the military, or a new job. Sometimes, you separate from the church so that you can be beneficial to the work of the Lord in a different way in the same community. You can have separation and still have unity.

Sometimes in our churches, separation is caused by the death of a loved one. Our loved ones are no longer with us in the body. We will meet them again in just a few years as we fellowship in heaven together.

Second Corinthians 5:8, *"We are confident, I say, and willing rather to be absent from the body, and to be present with the Lord."*

Community—As you actively separate yourself from your community and you drive away in the car, the moving truck, or the airplane, you will carry with you a sense of nostalgia. Your community will be different because you left. Sometimes, this is good for you and for the local residents. Be sure to take some time and, if possible, meet face to face with people who have meant something special to you, such as your pastor, your good friends, and your distant relatives. Communities change as people migrate from one location to another. Be a blessing to everybody as you leave so that when you return to visit, your fellowship will be sweet.

John 14:16, *"And I will pray the Father, and he shall give you another Comforter, that he may abide with you for ever."*

THE APPRECIATION OF SEPARATION

At this stage of your journey to a successful life, you are already gone. You are now at (or traveling to) a new location. You have made your journey, and you can appreciate all of the good and the "not-so-good" of your past.

On your journey to success, there may have been many times when separation has been beneficial. That leads to a good future. Sometimes, you have been separated due to misfortunes beyond your control. At other times, you have been separated because of opportunities that were in your control, and you had good judgment at that time.

Sometimes, you will appreciate the separation because of other ideas that were addressed in this book, such as anticipating your desires and then your desires changed. You may have appreciated your separation because of a lack of inspiration or lack of motivation. There are many reasons to appreciate separation.

There will be many times in your life that you appreciate separation because it will make the memories special. I probably would not have appreciated the small town where I grew up as much as I do now if I had never left there. I have lived in five states in my life, and each time I travel and remember those years, they bring back special memories. Sometimes, I will cross the path of an old friend, and we will share stories or memories. Those are special times!

You may have been separated permanently because of death. But you can appreciate the good times that were created during your lifetime. You can appreciate the mentorship and the friendship. You can appreciate the lessons learned that you can give to others before you pass away. Separation is not always a bad thing, as the Lord will be there to comfort you.

John 14:18, *"I will not leave you comfortless: I will come to you."*

There are times that you will appreciate separation because of an unfortunate incident. Do not let the spirit of animosity and sadness have a greater effect on you than the Holy Spirit. God has never left you.

Hebrews 13:5, *"Let your conversation be without covetousness; and be content with such things as ye have: for he hath said, I will never leave thee, nor forsake thee."*

How will this lesson help me?

Personal—In every life, separation will occur because you move away or someone else moves. At other times, separation will be caused by death. In either situation, memories will occur. Your goal should always be to keep precious memories. As the hymn by John Wright in 1925 mentions, *"Precious memories, How they linger; How they ever flood my soul."* That may be your desire. Make it your legacy!

Philippians 1:3–4, *"I thank my God upon every remembrance of you, Always in every prayer of mine for you all making request with joy."*

Marriage and family—As you separate from your family and go off to college or a job or the military, you will want to be able to look back on the precious memories of your childhood and your friends and appreciate the fact that you can move on and enjoy the journey.

If you are married or the head of your household, do what you can to keep a good family life and enjoy your loved ones. Be sure to hug them every day. Let each person know they are loved. By doing this, whether you leave them on a short-term basis or in death, there will be precious memories.

Psalm 1:1–3:

Blessed is the man that walketh not in the counsel of the ungodly, nor standeth in the way of sinners, nor sitteth in the seat of the scornful. But his delight is in the law of the LORD; and in his law doth he meditate day and night. And he shall be like a tree planted by the rivers of water, that bringeth forth his fruit in his season; his leaf also shall not wither; and whatsoever he doeth shall prosper.

Church—I enjoy going back to churches that I have attended in years past and seeing that the church is still growing strong and the people fellowship together, sing together, and pray together. As I have separated myself and moved to new locations, I can look back and appreciate the friendships and the wonderful times together. Those memories are precious and can bring smiles to each person involved.

Psalm 133:1, *"Behold, how good and how pleasant it is for brethren to dwell together in unity!"*

Community—Now you have left your home community, take some time to appreciate the people with whom you have had the chance to grow and mature. Appreciate the lessons learned. Appreciate the times you had the opportunity to speak with and fellowship with other believers on your way to heaven. It will not be long before you are all in heaven together. Keep precious memories alive and make precious memories wherever you go.

Colossians 1:9, *"For this cause we also, since the day we heard it, do not cease to pray for you, and to desire that ye might be filled with the knowledge of his will in all wisdom and spiritual understanding."*

First Samuel 12:23, *"Moreover as for me, God forbid that I should sin against the Lord in ceasing to pray for you: but I will teach you the good and the right way."*

THIS PAGE HAS BEEN LEFT BLANK SO THAT YOU CAN MAKE
NOTES ABOUT SEPARATION

SYNERGY
THE ANTICIPATION OF SYNERGY

As you prepare to conclude your reading of this book, this can be an exciting lesson that you can use for the rest of your life. There are many aspects and definitions of the word "synergy," but the easiest to understand is, "The sum of the parts is greater than the whole." What that means is that if a number of great minds work together, then they can accomplish more than each mind working separately.

First Corinthians 2:16, *"For who hath known the mind of the Lord, that he may instruct him? but we have the mind of Christ."*

As you journey toward your idea of a successful career and a family life, you will be able to network with great minds. Think about what you can do for a great future if you are serving the Lord in your job or your ministry and praying with other believers. You can have great synergy as it relates to your secular work and your work for the Lord.

Think about some of the ideas you could produce together if you have like-minded professionals who believe like you do but have a different perspective or viewpoint. As you view the idea of synergy at a high level, you can picture yourself sitting with the top professionals in your field of expertise. If you aspire to this high ideal and keep this focused in your mind, then you will accept these opportunities as they arise.

If you are a professional in your industry and you view yourself as an executive with greater knowledge, then you will be asked to sit on governing boards and panel discussions because people want to learn from you. If you can continue to study and learn more about how to grow your industry and what causes the industry to remain stagnant, you will probably get promoted. Be sure to network with people outside of your company to become well-known and possibly hired by other companies.

If you are an aspiring politician and you begin to run as a candidate for mayor or state representative when you are eighteen years old, you will immediately put yourself in a new category because you will have learned how to run a campaign. Even if you do not win your first election, you will now have knowledge and understanding given to you by men and women who know more than you. These great minds will soon be your colleagues as soon as you win an election. Think about this! If you win your second or third election at the age of nineteen or twenty years old, you will be sitting next to people twice your age who wish they would have started when you did. You will be part of a great network of synergy with great minds that will soon help you in your political career.

If you are a missionary and you feel alone, you may want to reach out to other missionaries or your mission board to learn more. You may want to go to a conference with other missionaries so that a few people can help to solve the problems of the organization. You may become the leader that they have been waiting for. You may be the answer to prayer and not even realize it.

Matthew 18:20, *"For where two or three are gathered together in my name, there am I in the midst of them."*

Maybe you are only twelve years of age. Now would be a good time to learn how to listen. Now is a good age to learn how to ask great questions. Now is the perfect time to learn about synergy! Think with me for a minute about the Lord Jesus Christ when he was twelve years of age.

Luke 2:42, *"And when he was twelve years old, they went up to Jerusalem after the custom of the feast."*

Luke 2:46–47, *"And it came to pass, that after three days they found him in the temple, sitting in the midst of the doctors, both hearing them, and asking them questions. And all that heard him were astonished at his understanding and answers."*

(I am not suggesting that you be away from your parents for three days!)

Later, when Jesus was around thirty years of age, Jesus chose twelve different personalities with which to fellowship. Each of these twelve spoke with the others on a regular basis. Jesus did not need their wisdom or their knowledge. These men needed each other.

I am always amazed as I read Matthew 26 and verse 50 when Jesus (as He was betrayed) addressed Judas with the title of "friend."

Matthew 26:47–50:

And while he yet spake, lo, Judas, one of the twelve, came, and with him a great multitude with swords and staves, from the chief priests and elders of the people. Now he that betrayed him gave them a sign, saying, Whomsoever I shall kiss, that same is he: hold him fast. And forthwith he came to Jesus, and said, Hail, master; and kissed him. And Jesus said unto him, Friend, wherefore art thou come? Then came they, and laid hands on Jesus and took him.

Not everyone in your mastermind group, your networking group, or even your deacon board will agree with you in every aspect of life. One may betray you! However, that does not mean that he is not your friend. Remember:

Romans 8:28, *"And we know that all things work together for good to them that love God, to them who are the called according to his purpose."*

How will this lesson help me?

Personal—As you aspire to success as a professional, you will come across the leaders in your industry who admire your understanding and wisdom. In every industry, you will find leaders. If that is your aspiration, you will be surrounded by other leaders. Stay humble. Stay kind to people at all levels of your industry and profession.

Micah 6:8, *"He hath shewed thee, O man, what is good; and what doth the LORD require of thee, but to do justly, and to love mercy, and to walk humbly with thy God?"*

Marriage and family—Sometimes, the greatest synergy that you will come across will come from those of your own household. Husbands, love your wives and respect their wisdom and knowledge. They will be your greatest asset! If you are a child, ask your parents for advice and wisdom. If you are a father, ask your children for advice and understanding and compare their words with the Bible.

Matthew 19:14, *"But Jesus said, Suffer little children, and forbid them not, to come unto me: for of such is the kingdom of heaven."*

Wives and mothers, you have my deepest respect! You may have the hardest job in the world. Read your Bible to your children! They will gain understanding that will be beneficial to you in years to come. Share this wisdom with your husband and pray for your husband.

Ecclesiastes 4:9–12:

Two are better than one; because they have a good reward for their labour. For if they fall, the one will lift up his fellow: but woe to him that is alone when he falleth; for he hath not another to help him up. Again, if two lie together, then they have heat: but how can one be warm alone? And if one prevail against him, two shall withstand him; and a threefold cord is not quickly broken.

Church—Synergy in a church will occur internally and externally. Internally, in most churches, your deacon board meets regularly to pray and ask the Lord for wisdom to lead your church in the near future. They make plans for years to come. You may also have regular teachers' meetings and staff meetings to plan events.

Externally, you might meet with other churches of like faith. Many times, you will have pastors' conferences or professional meetings where leaders can get together and discuss church matters, professional matters, and matters of the world as related to war and politics. Be careful not to use the church for political matters, but enjoy the synergy that it allows.

Matthew 22:18–22:

But Jesus perceived their wickedness, and said, Why tempt ye me, ye hypocrites? Shew me the tribute money. And they brought unto him a penny. And he saith unto them, Whose is this image and superscription? They say unto him, Caesar's. Then saith he unto them, Render therefore unto Caesar the things which are Caesar's; and unto God the things that are God's. When they had heard these words, they marvelled, and left him, and went their way.

Community—It is quite possible that many of the people in your church will also be professionals in the community. This is a great opportunity for synergy in your community. The people in your church at any age can use the wisdom from the Bible and help the leadership in their community. Can you imagine if every organization in your community, such as the hospital, the bank, the political committees, and others, all had a member of your church sitting on the governing board? They need great minds with the knowledge and wisdom of your church members on their board. You may want to make that the goal for your church!

Proverbs 2:5–6, *"Then shalt thou understand the fear of the LORD, and find the knowledge of God. For the LORD giveth wisdom: out of his mouth cometh knowledge and understanding."*

THE ACCEPTANCE OF SYNERGY

The acceptance of synergy will be a life-changing experience. When you think about being around people with wisdom and understanding, you may want to think of all of the different opportunities that there are to sit with great minds.

Proverbs 13:20, *"He that walketh with wise men shall be wise: but a companion of fools shall be destroyed."*

If you are interested in understanding how the legal system works, you may want to visit your county courthouse. Oftentimes, while the court is in session, you are permitted to sit in the courtroom (very politely and quietly in proper attire) and listen to the words of the attorneys and the judge. You may learn more by observation than what you could learn in a classroom because you are hearing the words that are spoken and the lives that are changed.

If your goal is to learn more about the military and you are in high school, you may want to learn more about the opportunities there are available in the military auxiliary units. Accepting synergy will allow you to sit with great minds and with current and former leaders who are willing to give you wisdom and understanding.

When you accept the synergy that is available to you and you speak with great minds who are professionals in your industry, then you will be amazed at some of the ideas that your colleagues have. You may be able to use these ideas personally and professionally to help you achieve what the Lord has for you. This understanding and knowledge can also be used in your church and by your congregation as you transfer that knowledge and wisdom to others.

Synergy can be added through networking groups, both professionally and in the community. There are many types of "brainstorming" clubs that are available where you can use your wisdom and gain understanding.

Romans 15:5, *"Now the God of patience and consolation grant you to be likeminded one toward another according to Christ Jesus."*

Philippians 2:2, *"Fulfil ye my joy, that ye be likeminded, having the same love, being of one accord, of one mind."*

If somebody asks you to join a networking group, you can decide if that would be the most beneficial use of your time. However, if somebody asks you to be on their board of directors or participate in a panel discussion, be honored that you were asked and express your appreciation. Use wisdom and decide if it is best for you to participate.

If somebody views your opinion as valuable, they may ask you to speak at their graduation or a banquet. You may also be asked to be the keynote speaker at their convention because you have the knowledge and wisdom that will be beneficial to their industry. You and God can decide what is best!

How will I this lesson help me?

Personal—When you accept the idea of synergy and are permitted to talk with great minds and exchange great wisdom and great ideas, your life will change. You will gain understanding, and you will be able to impart wisdom and knowledge to your family, your friends, and your church. The new people whom you meet will be amazed at your understanding and wisdom. Never stop learning!

Marriage and family—Every family member appreciates wisdom when it is portrayed in a loving manner. When you express wisdom and knowledge, be sure that you are able to substantiate and document the truth. Every family member should be able to have a loving conversation with each other because they want the best for one another. If one family member has a great idea, think of how it can be used within the family and in the world. Each family member will get new ideas on a regular basis from their teachers and other professionals. You can create great conversation at the dinner table and in the evenings by just talking and enjoying one another's company.

Church—As you accept synergy in your church, you will want to read through the Bible and understand what the Bible says about any particular subject. There are many times when disagreements happen because of interpretations. By using the wisdom and the synergy that is provided by the Bible and with great minds working together in a professional and ethical manner, your church may be beneficial to one another and to people in the community.

Be sure to read the words of the Bible and accept those words as truth. If you alter the words, then you alter the meaning.

Romans 15:5, *"Now the God of patience and consolation grant you to be likeminded one toward another according to Christ Jesus."*

Community—Every community revolves around the synergy of the city council, a board of directors, politicians, and public officials. We elect the best candidates who are willing to step forward and use their synergy and their ideas to build what is best for the community for many years to come. The same great minds may be elected to Congress so that they can represent us on a national level. We all need to pray together that synergy occurs on a national level using the wisdom from the Bible as God leads. If this synergy does not occur, then it may be you who is needed in public office so that you can help solve the world's problems in a biblical and ethical manner. Allow God to lead you as He sees appropriate!

Accept the synergy! Become the leader!

Philippians 2:20, *"For I have no man likeminded, who will naturally care for your state."*

THE AUTHORING OF SYNERGY

As you author and write down your ideas of synergy, you will want to think *big*!

Proverbs 22:29, *"Seest thou a man diligent in his business? he shall stand before kings; he shall not stand before mean men."*

Is that where you can picture yourself? Can you picture yourself standing with kings, presidents, and ambassadors? Imagine that for a few minutes! You may want to be successful in business. You may want to be successful in the ministry. You want to have a successful family life and a great marriage. Nobody can succeed on their own.

Ecclesiastes 4:9–10, *"Two are better than one; because they have a good reward for their labour. For if they fall, the one will lift up his fellow: but woe to him that is alone when he falleth; for he hath not another to help him up."*

Throughout your life, you will meet men and women in various levels of authority who respect your decisions and admire your capabilities. Be aware of the presence of these individuals in your life. We spoke earlier in this book about mentors. These professionals are willing to help you to succeed in business, in your ministry, and in your family.

If you are in high school and you are asked to run as a class president or other similar office, consider it an honor to have been asked. Consider your circumstances to be sure that is the direction that you should go. The fact that you were asked means that other people feel that your abilities, combined with the synergy of others, will create great leadership. Write down a few ideas where you can be a leader and helpful to your school and community.

Someone may randomly ask you to be a leader in politics, business, religion, or community activities, as they have been watching you and feel you have leadership abilities. You never know who is watching you. You can never tell who has the authority to offer you an elevated position, such as liaison, representative, or ambassador. Be prepared for it. As you discuss some of the ideas that are written in this book and you portray those ideas to people in leadership, others will take notice of your ideas. Enjoy the synergy. Enjoy the conversations with others in leadership.

Learn everything you can about how to speak and enjoy conversation with people in leadership positions. Especially learn how to enjoy great conversations with your spouse and your family so that when you arrive at home, you will be greeted with smiles and wonderful ideas. When you go to the grocery store or are seen in the community and you pass the mayor, the university president, or the judge from your local courthouse, be sure that they know your name in a good way.

If you are thinking about going into a profession and somebody asks you to be in charge or to accept a position such as a manager, foreman, or supervisor, do not say "no" immediately. Some people (possibly you) may think to themselves, *I'm not qualified* or *I could never do that!* However, you may be the greatest leader that many people have ever seen who would be able to accept the position immediately for the benefit of your company and your family. Take some time to pray about it!

Job 32:9, *"Great men are not always wise: neither do the aged understand judgment."*

If you are trying to build a great ministry for the Lord, many believers will be praying for you. Many leaders will be looking to you for advice. Many will want you to succeed in every area of your life so that you can be an example to others within your community and within your country. As you build your church and help your community you will be able to meet with other pastors and authorities in every walk of life. If you are in a small town, get to know your sheriff and county leadership. If there is a meeting where your presence could be beneficial, you may want to offer to assist the community in some manner. Could you be a chaplain for your sheriff, police, or fire department? Write down some ideas.

If you are thinking about dating or getting married, be sure that this person is someone with whom you could have wonderful conversations on a regular basis. If it becomes a serious relationship, you will want to make sure that you are able to understand why the person has that opinion. You may not always agree on every subject with the person whom you admire. None of us were raised exactly the same. We all have different opinions. Learn to enjoy conversations with your fiancé on a number of different topics before you get married.

Proverbs 9:12, *"If thou be wise, thou shalt be wise for thyself: but if thou scornest, thou alone shalt bear it."*

How will this lesson help me?

Personal—Take some time to write down different types of individuals and careers with which you would like to be associated at different times of your life. Each of us has a different type of hobby or activity where we spend time relaxing and enjoying life. As you make your list, you can decide if these activities will produce money, such as buying stocks, real estate, or businesses. Other people will have activities such as art, music, or social activities that will bring pleasure throughout their lives. Whatever you like to do, there are other people who like the same thing. Be sure that whatever you do is honest and beneficial to mankind.

Proverbs 18:16, *"A man's gift maketh room for him, and bringeth him before great men."*

Marriage and family—In most marriage ceremonies, you will be asked to recite marriage vows. I have never heard wedding vows mention synergy or conversation because these should be handled before you accept the proposal and considered throughout your engagement. However, the vows will typically have the words "as long as you both shall live" or "'til death do you part." That would make life hard if you do not admire, cherish, and build up one another.

Proverbs 5:18, *"Let thy fountain be blessed: and rejoice with the wife of thy youth."*

Numbers 30:1–4:

This is the thing which the LORD hath commanded. If a man vow a vow unto the LORD, or swear an oath to bind his soul with a bond; he shall not break his word, he shall do according to all that proceedeth out of his mouth. If a woman also vow a vow unto the LORD, and bind herself by a bond, being in her father's house in her youth; And her father hear her vow, and her bond wherewith she hath bound her soul, and her father shall hold his peace at her; then all her vows shall stand, and every bond wherewith she hath bound her soul shall stand.

Church—Your church at every grade level and at every age level can benefit from synergy inside and outside of your church. If each person in your church is able to create great ideas that will benefit each member of the church, then every member will be able to pray and enjoy life at a higher level. As your members work with people of the community outside of the church, then every member may be able to benefit as a friend who can give credibility in your high school and in the community. Encourage one another to be better each day. Write down ideas and ways to help each member to excel in the community.

Community—As you are involved in different levels of the community, you will become familiar with various dignitaries, allowing you opportunities to have casual conversations with leadership. When was the last time that you asked if you could be helpful to the president of your local Parent-Teacher Association (PTA) or other type of association in your community that will benefit the local school? Maybe your local area is putting on a parade that will involve schools, churches, local organizations, marching bands, and first responders. This may be a great place for you to be involved.

Proverbs 16:13, *"Righteous lips are the delight of kings; and they love him that speaketh right."*

Opportunities for synergy surround you! Take a few minutes right now and write down a number of ways that you can get involved.

THE ACTIVATION OF SYNERGY

As you begin to activate your synergy, you will encounter many wonderful people who will amaze you and want you to benefit from their expertise and influence. They are ready, willing, and able to help you far beyond your wildest dreams. It could be that God has put them in your path so that God can do for you "above all that we ask or think."

Ephesians 3:19–21:

And to know the love of Christ, which passeth knowledge, that ye might be filled with all the fulness of God. Now unto him that is able to do exceeding abundantly above all that we ask or think, according to the power that worketh in us, Unto him be glory in the church by Christ Jesus throughout all ages, world without end. Amen.

You may not believe it at this moment, but you may be in line to be the next defender of your people and speak with the King about a cause that may be hurting your great nation. Are you the next David who must defeat Goliath? That is the true activation of synergy.

First Samuel 17:29, *"And David said, What have I now done? Is there not a cause?"*

First Samuel 17:37, *"David said moreover, The LORD that delivered me out of the paw of the lion, and out of the paw of the bear, he will deliver me out of the hand of this Philistine. And Saul said unto David, Go, and the LORD be with thee."*

Earlier in this book, we talked about imagination. Now it is time to use the imagination and think of all the different avenues where your brilliance can be used with the synergy of great men and women who surround you or who will be surrounding you in the near future. God wants to use you more than you could ask or think. Since we know that all things work together for good, you will want to look everybody in the eye. You can smile knowing that you and God can work together and solve any problem that this world has placed in front of you.

You may want to learn to enjoy walking with God and the fellowship that He will provide you with great men and women. Because you walk with God and God wants to walk with those in leadership, God may be using you to be the liaison and His ambassador to your local area or to the world. Begin to activate that synergy today!

Proverbs 21:1, *"The king's heart is in the hand of the LORD, as the rivers of water: he turneth it whithersoever he will."*

How will this lesson help me?

Personal—You are about to cross the path of some great individuals! You may meet the principal of your local high school. You may think that the meeting will not be beneficial because of some incident; however, the exchange of ideas with this person in leadership may allow you to become a leader far beyond your expectations.

Genesis 50:19–20, *"And Joseph said unto them, Fear not: for am I in the place of God? But as for you, ye thought evil against me; but God meant it unto good, to bring to pass, as it is this day, to save much people alive."*

Marriage and family—You and your spouse together may be meeting some wonderful people who want to have you in a position of leadership because they see the quality of your relationship with others and how your wisdom and understanding can be beneficial inside your church and inside of your community. Other couples are watching you. People in leadership are watching you. Your spouse is watching you. Your children are watching you. All of these relationships can be beneficial to the Lord's work. It is up to you to activate that synergy.

Church—Can you imagine the power and the influence that your church can have on the members of your church as we build each other for the cause of Christ? If every person in your church only speaks good of every person in your church and talks about how wonderful your church is in the community, not in a boastful fashion but just in an honorable and appreciative manner, then your church can benefit people at all levels.

Community—Through a group effort, the hungry in your community may be fed. The homeless in your community can find shelter and warmth. Through the love from the people of your church and the people of your community working together, you will be recognized as an authority with your state government and even with your federal government because of your understanding that life is lived at the local level.

THE APPRECIATION OF SYNERGY

You will really appreciate this lesson because you will enjoy the imagination of being surrounded by greatness. Great men and women may surround you and ask you for advice, wisdom, and leadership in many aspects of life, which you might not have thought of if this had not been brought to your attention.

First Thessalonians 5:18, *"In every thing give thanks: for this is the will of God in Christ Jesus concerning you."*

Synergy is great minds working together. When you go to church, you may be in the leadership of your church. When you go to your work, you may be in a position of leadership. When you go home, you may be in a position of leadership. You may still be a teenager, and all of these may be true.

Proverbs 1:1–4:

The proverbs of Solomon the son of David, king of Israel; To know wisdom and instruction; to perceive the words of understanding; To receive the instruction of wisdom, justice, and judgment, and equity; To give subtilty to the simple, to the young man knowledge and discretion.

If you are an adult and you are in a position of leadership in any manner, look around at the other individuals who help you to be in leadership. Thank God for them! Your leadership position involves the lives of others whom you influence. By working with leadership positions in your family, in your church, in your community, and in your nation, you have the ability to change lives for the generations that follow.

If your pastor knows your name, consider it an honor because that means he can pray for you by name. If your mayor knows your name because you have helped your community in some manner, you may want to consider how you might be able to represent him at the state level and reciprocate that synergy by becoming a state representative or a state senator. In many states, you can do this at the age of eighteen. That's right! Be sure to check your state regulations. You might be able to be elected as a state representative and be of service to your local community because you understand how they need to be represented.

Synergy is an amazing concept. By working together with other great minds as you walk with God, God can use you to fulfill that which he needs to be done because you have become a servant.

Matthew 23:10–12, *"Neither be ye called masters: for one is your Master, even Christ. But he that is greatest among you shall be your servant. And whosoever shall exalt himself shall be abased; and he that shall humble himself shall be exalted."*

How will this lesson help me?

Personal—As you appreciate the synergy of all the great minds with whom you have been contacted, you may be sitting in the middle of a deacon board of the church or at a governing board meeting of a large corporation or a city council or you may soon be sitting in Congress. Do you love synergy? Realize that God can put you in the presence of whatever position God can use you in. Allow God to use you every day for the rest of your life. Allow God to put great men and women in your path to work with you and not just cross your path as you go in different directions. Allow yourself to walk with God and walk with great men and women. You may be able to introduce these great men and women to your God.

Marriage and family—When you realize that your family has some great minds, you will be amazed at what you can do together. I am sure some people will think, *Not my family*, and yet, in ten or twenty years, you may look back and realize how great the members of your family have become. You will appreciate the fact that you kept a relationship with each member of your family so that you can work on projects together for many years to come. Keep a close relationship with your spouse. Enjoy the relationship and the company of your children and your parents. They may be some of your greatest allies when troubles arise.

Church—Whether you are a teenager in church or a senior citizen, the next time you sit and watch others in your church who have prayed with you or for you, thank God for allowing you to be in their presence. If you are on the pastoral staff or in any leadership position, remember to keep every group in your church in your prayers. These people want the best for you. They look to you for leadership because they know that you walk with God, and by working together with you and God, God will be able to use them as you ask God for the wisdom of leadership. Learn to appreciate every person who attends your church, both visitor and member.

Community—As you finish any project in your city, you will appreciate the help that each individual has provided. These individuals may be government officials or community leaders from your local school or civic organization. Leadership comes in many different forms. You never know what a young person or a senior citizen knows about an individual who can help you by introducing you to other people and leadership. Use wisdom as you gain your leadership position so that you can help others throughout your community. They will appreciate you more than you can imagine!

First Thessalonians 1:2–3, *"We give thanks to God always for you all, making mention of you in our prayers; Remembering without ceasing your work of faith, and labour of love, and patience of hope in our Lord Jesus Christ, in the sight of God and our Father."*

THIS PAGE HAS BEEN LEFT BLANK SO THAT YOU CAN MAKE
NOTES ABOUT SYNERGY

Anticipating and Appreciating Your Christian Life

SELF (YOUR BONUS "S")

Self—That is what this book is all about. This book was written to be of help to you so that you could help yourself analyze each part of your life and reach your potential. By doing this, you can succeed better in each aspect of your life. Whatever you envision for your life, go back through this book and let it help to guide you through that missing element or weak point to your success. It has often been said that a chain is only as strong as its weakest link. There are many different lessons in this book; any of these could be the link that you have missed as you strive to be a success in your family, your church, or your community.

In the next few pages, you can examine your "self" and decide which of those behaviors and ideas will be beneficial to you in your future. These behaviors and ideas make you who you are as a distinct individual. Your mind thinks differently than any other mind on the planet. God has placed you in this world for a reason. God can use you in a way He has never used any person in this world before. Nobody else is in your location with your knowledge and your abilities at this time. You are unique! Let's look at some of the aspects of who you are.

Self-Image

An image is a reflection of who you are. Many people say, "I can see myself in the mirror." That is not actually true because what you are only seeing is an image of your physical body. That image or reflection looks like you. The real question is, "How do you look at yourself?" How do you envision yourself? What is in your mind and spirit? You may be able to tell more about yourself because of the words that you have been using to describe yourself.

Matthew 15:11, *"Not that which goeth into the mouth defileth a man; but that which cometh out of the mouth, this defileth a man."*

What do you think of yourself? How do you see yourself? You may have heard people say (and maybe you have said it to yourself) such phrases as, "I'm not good enough!" or "I'm not worthy!" or even, "God can't use me!" If that has been your self-image up to this point, then take the time right now to take another look at yourself. You are better than that!

Gensis 1:27, *"So God created man in his own image, in the image of God created he him; male and female created he them."*

First John 3:2, *"Beloved, now are we the sons of God, and it doth not yet appear what we shall be: but we know that, when he shall appear, we shall be like him; for we shall see him as he is."*

First John 3:20, *"For if our heart condemn us, God is greater than our heart, and knoweth all things."*

Self-Respect

Now that you have a different image of yourself, you can show more respect for yourself. You are the one who is loved by God. Maybe you come from a culture where respect is rarely shown to others. What actions can you take, starting today, that would show some self-respect?

1. When you see your image in the mirror every morning, look yourself in the eyes, take a few seconds, and smile at yourself. Do that a few times throughout the day. Practice so you can smile at others.
2. Say kind words to yourself that you wish others would say to you. Listen when somebody else is speaking, as these kind words may be directed to you in the near future.
3. When some person says a kind word to you, acknowledge it. (Stay humble!)
4. If you have a meeting at a specific time, be on time or early.
5. Be kind and polite to yourself.
6. Do your best in every activity. Take pride in giving your best effort.
7. Be clean physically, mentally, and spiritually.
8. Stay close to God. He wants you to be His child. He is a loving Father!
9. Show respect to others so that they can show you more respect.

Self-Worth

There are some temples on earth that are worth billions of dollars. These same buildings may survive for centuries, yet only mortal beings will ever live in such a temple. The inhabitants may never meet the maker of the structure. Let's compare that to what you (yourself) are worth. Your body is the temple of the Holy Spirit. You were bought at a price. You can meet your Maker and live with Him where the streets are made of gold. You have great value. How do you perceive yourself?

First Corinthians 6:19–20, *"What? know ye not that your body is the temple of the Holy Ghost which is in you, which ye have of God, and ye are not your own? For ye are bought with a price: therefore glorify God in your body, and in your spirit, which are God's."*

If you were given a nice house, would that make you happy? Would you feel a little better? Would people look at you a little differently because your future home has been "paid in full"? That would change your entire life!

John 14:1–3:

Let not your heart be troubled: ye believe in God, believe also in me. In my Father's house are many mansions: if it were not so, I would have told you. I go to prepare a place for you. And if I go and prepare a place for you, I will come again, and receive you unto myself; that where I am, there ye may be also.

How much do you value yourself? This may help you to look at yourself and feel more valuable. As you read this entire book, it is important that you determine what your desires are and what will give you the most fulfilled life. Be sure to stay humble and be thankful for every opportunity.

Micah 6:8, *"He hath shewed thee, O man, what is good; and what doth the LORD require of thee, but to do justly, and to love mercy, and to walk humbly with thy God?"*

Self-Forgiveness

This may be the hardest lesson for many of us on our way to success. Whether you want a successful marriage, a successful career, or a successful life, you may need to forgive yourself for actions from your past.

It is important to remember that as you forgive yourself, you will also want to be sure to forgive others for whatever action may have occurred in the past. Take a few minutes and compare these three verses, and you will notice the theme of forgiveness. You will also notice that God knows the past. God created you for a purpose. Be sure to forgive yourself and forgive others.

Matthew 5:23–24, *"Therefore if thou bring thy gift to the altar, and there rememberest that thy brother hath ought against thee; Leave there thy gift before the altar, and go thy way; first be reconciled to thy brother, and then come and offer thy gift."*

Matthew 6:12, *"And forgive us our debts, as we forgive our debtors."*

Romans 8:28, *"And we know that all things work together for good to them that love God, to them who are the called according to his purpose."*

Self-Acceptance

Forgiving yourself is sometimes hard. Accepting yourself as being imperfect but being loved by a perfect God can be overwhelming. Sometimes, we simply just don't know which way to turn! Have you ever felt that way?

Isaiah 53:6, *"All we like sheep have gone astray; we have turned every one to his own way; and the Lord hath laid on him the iniquity of us all."*

Sometimes, you do not live up to your own expectations. Do not be alarmed! Accept the fact that every person who has ever lived has been imperfect except for Jesus Christ. You will make mistakes just like the rest of us have made mistakes. Please do not do any harm to the temple of the Holy Spirit.

Romans 7:21–25:

I find then a law, that, when I would do good, evil is present with me. For I delight in the law of God after the inward man: But I see another law in my members, warring against the law of my mind, and bringing me into captivity to the law of sin which is in my members. O wretched man that I am! who shall deliver me from the body of this death? I thank God through Jesus Christ our Lord. So then with the mind I myself serve the law of God; but with the flesh the law of sin.

Instead, turn to the Creator of the universe.

Matthew 11:28–30, "*Come unto me, all ye that labour and are heavy laden, and I will give you rest. Take my yoke upon you, and learn of me; for I am meek and lowly in heart: and ye shall find rest unto your souls. For my yoke is easy, and my burden is light.*"

Accept yourself and be led by the Spirit of God. Become a son of God!

Romans 8:14, "*For as many as are led by the Spirit of God, they are the sons of God.*"

Philippians 2:15, "*That ye may be blameless and harmless, the sons of God, without rebuke, in the midst of a crooked and perverse nation, among whom ye shine as lights in the world.*"

Yourself—as God Sees You

In the past, you may have looked at yourself as unacceptable, poor, or worthless. Maybe as a person who nobody could love. If that is your case, take a few minutes and think about what Jesus said to the thief who died next to Him on the cross.

Luke 23:40–43:

But the other answering rebuked him, saying, Dost not thou fear God, seeing thou art in the same condemnation? And we indeed justly; for we receive the due reward of our deeds: but this man hath done nothing amiss. And he said unto Jesus, Lord, remember me when thou comest into thy kingdom. And Jesus said unto him, Verily I say unto thee, Today shalt thou be with me in paradise.

Perhaps you have been going through some hard times and you feel like God doesn't love you. You may be a little perplexed when you think about how much God loves you. The entire world feels that way. How can perfection love imperfection? We are all imperfect people. Sometimes, we wonder how we can love ourselves. That tells you how great our God is. God can accept you as you are, where you are, and it doesn't matter who you are. That is true love!

John 14:1–6:

Let not your heart be troubled: ye believe in God, believe also in me. In my Father's house are many mansions: if it were not so, I would have told you. I go to prepare a place for you. And if I go and prepare a place for you, I will come again, and receive you unto myself; that where I am, there ye may be also. And whither I go ye know, and the way ye know. Thomas saith unto him, Lord, we know not whither thou goest; and how can we know the way? Jesus saith unto him, I am the way, the truth, and the life: no man cometh unto the Father, but by me.

In this book, we have talked a great deal about God. So who is He?

God Is

John 4:24:

"God is a Spirit: and they that worship him must worship him in spirit and in truth."

Numbers 23:19:

"God is not a man, that he should lie; neither the son of man, that he should repent."

Second Samuel 22:33:

"God is my strength and power: and he maketh my way perfect."

Psalm 46:1:

"God is our refuge and strength, a very present help in trouble."

Psalm 59:9:

"Because of his strength will I wait upon thee: for God is my defence."

Psalm 94:22:

"But the LORD is my defence; and my God is the rock of my refuge."

Psalm 99:9:

"Exalt the LORD our God, and worship at his holy hill; for the LORD our God is holy."

Psalm 116:5:

"Gracious is the LORD, and righteous; yea, our God is merciful."

First Corinthians 1:9:

"God is faithful, by whom ye were called unto the fellowship of his Son Jesus Christ our Lord."

So what does God expect from us?

Matthew 22:36–40:

Master, which is the great commandment in the law? Jesus said unto him, Thou shalt love the Lord thy God with all thy heart, and with all thy soul, and with all thy mind. This is the first and great commandment. And the second is like unto it, Thou shalt love thy neighbour as thyself. On these two commandments hang all the law and the prophets.

Matthew 12:50, *"For whosoever shall do the will of my Father which is in heaven, the same is my brother, and sister, and mother."*

John 3:16, *"For God so loved the world, that he gave his only begotten Son, that whosoever believeth in him should not perish, but have everlasting life."*

First Thessalonians 4:17, *"Then we which are alive and remain shall be caught up together with them in the clouds, to meet the Lord in the air: and so shall we ever be with the Lord."*

THIS PAGE HAS BEEN LEFT BLANK SO THAT YOU CAN MAKE
NOTES ABOUT SELF

Anticipating and Appreciating Your Christian Life

CONCLUSION

This book was conceived to make an easy-to-follow method to know where you are in relation to your intended goal or idea of success. This method could be used individually or in your book club or classroom.

How Will These Lessons Help You?

Personal—Use this book to help you reach your personal goals!

Marriage and family—These ideas are meant to build strong marriages!

Church—With inspiration, motivation, and enthusiasm, your church may thrive!

Community—Your community may be a better place by using these ideas!

Where are you today? Do you have everything you need for a fulfilled life?

Some people will live their entire lives and not have a strong enough "D" (desire) to move forward.

Some people will have the D and the I (inspiration). Then, they ("DI") die. That is fine for them, as they lived an inspired life. That is good! Stay inspired!

Some people will have the D, I, and M (motivation); however, without "E" (enthusiasm), their life will seem DIM.

Some people will have the D, I, M, and E. They will have more safety and synergy.

Question: What do we call it when we convert a dollar to ten dimes?

Making change! I have now reminded you how to make change.

Only you can take the action to make it happen in your life.

Try this… Take a dollar and go ask a teller to give you ten dimes. Place three dimes on your dresser. Place three dimes in your kitchen where you will see them. Place three dimes where you will see them throughout the day. Keep a visual illustration of "3 DIMES" with you until you reach your goal.

Get a vision, focus, succeed!

I will enjoy hearing about your success!

POSTSCRIPT

Never Stop Anticipating

Enjoy life! We all have desires and aspirations at every age in life, from grade school to senior citizen. You will have hopes and ambitions where you have the ability to make a difference. Don't stop short of all that God will allow you to do on your journey to heaven! Many people will stop short of their dreams and goals. When I wrote my first book, *Overqualified/Underqualified*, I realized that only twenty-five to forty percent of students who start college will complete a degree. This book should help to improve those results. Decide to "de-terminate" and not stop short of your dreams.

At the end of each lesson, you were given a little guidance on how this book will help you with your personal life, marriage and family, church, and in your community. Whatever you desire, use the graph of the outline of this book and decide what area of your life needs attention. Maybe it is the "acceptance of desire" because you have not decided what you really want. Maybe your area of concern is the "activation of determination," and you keep defaulting on your New Year's resolutions. Many activities cease because of the "appreciation of momentum" and how fast events happen. It could be that you need help to "activate your enthusiasm" and really enjoy life again! You get to decide!

In your personal ambitions, please use this book to "know thyself" and understand why you perform the way you do. If you need further help, seek the proper guidance and sources where a "multitude of counselors" can be found. A solution can be mapped out for you. Reread the notes that you have "authored" throughout this book. *Walk circumspectly* and look around before you take the next step.

Use the lessons in this book to improve your marriage and family life. Throughout your life, find a way to have open and truthful discussions with your spouse, parents, siblings, and mentors. Create strong family bonds that will help build friendships and great memories.

Many churches will be able to use this book in their group sessions and Sunday school classes. Study this book with your friends while you are in high school. Your dreams will become more clear and real to you. You may also grow the influence of your church at your school. Show the love of the Lord with your community. Share this book and these ideas with community leaders.

This book was written in such a manner that these ideas will outlive each of us. These ideas can be used at every age and can be used with our friends and, later, handed down to our children and grandchildren. These ideas can be used in every language and culture. Be sure to keep these positive ideas alive for the generations to come!

I look forward to hearing about your success!

ABOUT THE AUTHOR

Wesley "Wes" Waddle grew up in the small city of Marion, Ohio (the home-town of President Warren G. Harding). He was the youngest of six children in a very poor family. After graduating from high school, he went to college in Indiana, where he earned his bachelor of science degree in secondary education with teaching fields in English and music. He was later asked to serve on governing board of the college, where he served for twelve years.

After graduating from college, Wes entered the banking business, working for a large bank in the mortgage division. Having a desire to excel in every area of life, he earned the title of Certified Mortgage Banker (CMB), which is the highest designation through the Mortgage Bankers Association.

Wes earned his private pilot certificate at the age of twenty-three. Wanting to be of service to his country but having a slight medical deficiency for an active-duty assignment, Wes became an officer with the United States Air Force Auxiliary, where he earned the rank of lieutenant colonel and squadron commander. He was also awarded the privilege of serving as a legislative liaison. Later, Wes earned his certified flight instructor (CFI) in aviation and is still an active instructor.

Wes has always been intrigued by real estate acquisition and has owned rental properties. He moved to Arizona, where he became an approved instructor through the Arizona Department of Real Estate. He has written courses and is permitted to instruct in the areas of contract law, real estate legal issues, and general real estate, including the National Code of Ethics. Wes still holds an active real estate license and will be working with multifamily real estate teams.

Having completed postgraduate studies in theology and religion, Wes has written courses and has taught about church leadership, working with the deacon board, and church real estate management.

At the time of writing this book, Wes is still a real estate instructor, mortgage banking instructor, and certified flight instructor. Using the concepts in this book, Wes will sometimes "coach the coaches."

Wes is married to a high school teacher. Together, they have three children.

Printed in the USA
CPSIA information can be obtained
at www.ICGtesting.com
CBHW081934090724
11357CB00009B/163